GENDER ESSENTIALISM
AND ORTHODOXY

ORTHODOX CHRISTIANITY AND CONTEMPORARY THOUGHT

SERIES EDITORS
Ashley M. Purpura and Aristotle Papanikolaou

This series consists of books that seek to bring Orthodox Christianity into an engagement with contemporary forms of thought. Its goal is to promote (1) historical studies in Orthodox Christianity that are interdisciplinary, employ a variety of methods, and speak to contemporary issues; and (2) constructive theological arguments in conversation with patristic sources and that focus on contemporary questions ranging from the traditional theological and philosophical themes of God and human identity to cultural, political, economic, and ethical concerns. The books in the series explore both the relevancy of Orthodox Christianity to contemporary challenges and the impact of contemporary modes of thought on Orthodox self-understandings.

GENDER ESSENTIALISM AND ORTHODOXY

Beyond Male and Female

BRYCE E. RICH

FORDHAM UNIVERSITY PRESS
New York • 2023

Fordham University Press has no responsibility for the persistence or accuracy of URLs for external or third-party Internet websites referred to in this publication and does not guarantee that any content on such websites is, or will remain, accurate or appropriate.

Fordham University Press also publishes its books in a variety of electronic formats. Some content that appears in print may not be available in electronic books.

Visit us online at www.fordhampress.com.

Library of Congress Cataloging-in-Publication Data available online at https://catalog.loc.gov.

Printed in the United States of America

25 24 23 5 4 3 2 1

First edition

CONTENTS

ABBREVIATIONS

Ad. haer.	*Adversus haereses,* Irenaeus of Lyons
Ad. Herm.	*Adversus Hermogenum,* Tertullian
Ad. op.	*Adversus oppugnatores vitae monasticae,* John Chrysostom
Agr.	*De agricultura,* Philo of Alexandria
Amb.	*Ambigua,* Maximus Confessor
Anima	*De anima,* Tertullian
An. et res.	*De anima et resurrectione,* Gregory of Nyssa
Antirrhetici	*Antirrhetici adversus iconomachos,* Theodore the Studite
Autolycum	*Ad Autolycum,* Theophilus of Antioch
Bon. conj.	*De bono conjugali,* Augustine of Hippo
C. Eun.	*Contra Eunomium,* Gregory of Nyssa
C. Faust. man.	*Contra Faustum manichaeum,* Augustine of Hippo
CD	*Church Dogmatics,* Karl Barth
Cap. phil.	*Capita philosophica,* John of Damascus
Car. Nis.	*Carmina Nisibena,* Ephrem the Syrian
Civ. Dei	*De civitate Dei contra paganos,* Augustine of Hippo
Collatio	*Collatio legum mosaicarum et romanarum,* Theodosius the Great

Com. Eph.	*Commentarium in Epistolam ad Ephesios,* Jerome
Com. Gen.	*Commentarium in Genesim,* Ephrem the Syrian
Confes.	*Confessiones,* Augustine of Hippo
Coni. ad.	*De coniugiis adulterinis,* Augustine of Hippo
Const. hom.	*Sermones in constitutionem hominis secundum imaginem Dei,* Anastasius of Sinai
Dial. Tryph.	*Dialogus cum Tryphone,* Justin Martyr
Did. apost.	*Didascalia apostolorum*
Doctrina	*De doctrina christiana,* Augustine of Hippo
Ep.	*Epistulae,* various authors as noted
Ep. Greg.	*Epistula ad Gregorium,* Gregory of Nyssa
Ep. Leo.	*Epistula canonica ad Leotium,* Gregory of Nyssa
Ep. Smyrn.	*Epistula ad Smyrnaeos,* Ignatius of Antioch
Exposit.	*Expositio fidei,* John of Damascus
Gen. ad lit.	*De Genesi ad litteram,* Augustine of Hippo
Gen. c. Man.	*De Genesi contra Manichaeos,* Augustine of Hippo
Hist. an.	*Historia animalium,* Aristotle
Herm. pas.	*Hermae pastor*
Hom. in Eph.	*Homiliae in Epistolam ad Ephesios,* John Chrysostom
Hom. in Gen.	*Homiliae in Genesim,* Origen of Alexandria / Augustine of Hippo
Hom. in Joan.	*Homiliae in Joannem,* John Chrysostom
Hom. in Rom.	*Homiliae in Epistolam ad Romanos,* John Chrysostom
Hom. mart. Jul.	*Homilia in martyrem Julittam,* Basil of Caesarea
Hom. op.	*De hominis opificio,* Gregory of Nyssa
Hom. Pel. II	*Homilia II in S. Pelagiam,* John Chrysostom
Hymn. eccl.	*Hymni de ecclesia,* Ephrem the Syrian
Hymn. par.	*Hymni de paradiso,* Ephrem the Syrian
Incarnatione	*De incarnatione Verbi de Dei,* Athanasius of Alexandria
Leg. allegor.	*Legum allegoriarum,* Philo of Alexandria

Lib. arb.	*De libero arbitrio*, Augustine of Hippo
Lib. c. Eut.	*Liber de persona et duabus naturis contra Eutychen et Nestorium*, Boethius
Mal. cog.	*De malignis cogitationibus*, Evagrius of Pontus
Migratione	*De migratione Abrahami*, Philo of Alexandria
Nat. hom.	*De natura hominis*, Nemesius of Emesa
Opif.	*De opificio mundi*, Philo of Alexandria
Paed.	*Paedogogus*, Clement of Alexandria
Paradiso	*De paradiso*, Ambrose of Milan
Periphys.	*Periphyseon*, John Scottus Eriugena
Pas. SS. Serg.	*Passio SS. Sergii et Bacchi*
Pas. SS. Perp.	*Passio SS. Perpetuae et Felicitatis*
PG	*Patrologia Graeca*, Migne
PL	*Patrologia Latina*, Migne
Praescrip.	*De praescriptione haereticorum*, Tertullian
Princip.	*De principiis*, Origen of Alexandria
Refutatio	*Refutatio omnium haeresium*, Hippolytus of Rome
S. Dros.	*De S. Droside martyre*, John Chrysostom
SS. Bern. et Pros.	*De SS. Bernice et Prosdoce*, John Chrysostom
Sol.	*Soliloquia*, Augustine of Hippo
Spir.	*De Spiritu sancto*, Basil of Caesarea
Strom.	*Stromata*, Clement of Alexandria
Symp.	*Symposium*, Plato
Symp. dec. virg.	*Symposium sive convivium decem virginum*, Methodius of Olympus
Tim.	*Timaeus*, Plato
Trin.	*De trinitate*, Augustine of Hippo / Richard of St. Victor, as indicated
Usu part.	*De usu partium*, Galen
Virg.	*De virginitate*, John Chrysostom
Vit. contempl.	*De vita contemplativa*, Philo of Alexandria

Vit. Eph.	*De vita S. Patris Ephraem Syri,* Gregory of Nyssa
Vit. Mac.	*De vita Macrinae,* Gregory of Nyssa
Vit. Moy.	*De vita Moysis,* Gregory of Nyssa
Vit. sua	*De vita sua,* Gregory of Nazianzus

καὶ ἐποίησεν ὁ θεὸς τὸν ἄνθρωπον κατ᾽ εἰκόνα θεοῦ ἐποίησεν αὐτόν
ἄρσεν καὶ θῆλυ ἐποίησεν αὐτούς
—Gn 1:27 (LXX)

οὐκ ἔνι Ἰουδαῖος οὐδὲ Ἕλλην, οὐκ ἔνι δοῦλος οὐδὲ ἐλεύθερος,
οὐκ ἔνι ἄρσεν καὶ θῆλυ· πάντες γὰρ ὑμεῖς εἷς ἐστε ἐν Χριστῷ Ἰησοῦ
—Gal 3:28

PART I

1

SETTING THE STAGE

What is the main task of Orthodox theology at the outset of the new millennium? My own answer is that what is required more than anything else is a fuller understanding of the human person. . . . What does it mean to be a human being according to the image and likeness of God? In what does the uniqueness of our personhood lie? . . . More particularly, how are we to understand the distinction within humanity between male and female? Connected with this is a wide range of questions concerning gender and sexuality, with which we as Orthodox have scarcely begun to grapple.

—KALLISTOS WARE[1]

Introduction

Within contemporary Eastern Orthodoxy, debates over sex and gender have become increasingly polemical over the past generation. Arguments began with questions about women and the priesthood but have expanded to include a full raft of subjects: feminism, sexual orientation, the sacrament of marriage, definitions of family, the adoption of children, and the care of transgender individuals whose medically assigned sex does not match their gender identity. The initial responses in each of these cases reflect a presupposition of *gender essentialism*, defined here as the view that men and women fall into two groups that are ontologically and fixedly different from each other. Gender essentialism is commonly coupled with a dimorphic sexual binary and a presumption of heteronormativity, meaning that assigned biological sex (male/female), gender identity (man/woman), gender roles (masculine/feminine), and a heterosexual orientation are assumed to naturally sort human beings into two complementary groups whose members pair off as husband and wife and form families.[2]

In this book I will examine the set of beliefs and practices within Orthodoxy clustered around issues of gender and biological sex that give rise to the essentialist paradigm. I will argue that when applied universally, these beliefs and practices fail to consider the uniqueness of individual human persons. As a result, those who insist on the universal adherence to these beliefs and practices place a stumbling block—first to particular persons and subsequently to the Church as the Body of Christ—in the path to theosis.

An Immanent Critique

I conceive this book as an immanent critique. By this I mean a critique internal to contemporary Orthodoxy itself, evaluating shared communal practices by the lights of the tradition's own commitments. Such a critique highlights discrepancies between professed beliefs and the communal practices that attempt to embody them. It then suggests alternatives that more fully move toward the shared vision of the community.

The ultimate goal of the Orthodox faith is *theosis* (sometimes translated as "deification" or "divinization") or divine-human communion that transforms humanity and the created order through participation in the divine life. To this end, Orthodox Christians over time have developed and passed along a rich tradition of ascetical, sacramental, and social practices conceived to prepare practitioners for divine-human communion.[3] These practices sometimes include sex-specific roles and gender expectations. For example, the roles of presbyter and bishop are performed solely by men, as is the role of deacon in almost all modern Orthodox communities. Likewise, the sacrament of marriage is limited by heteronormative sexual distinctions, as are further notions of the roles of fatherhood and motherhood.

For each of the questions arising from contemporary culture mentioned above, the initial Orthodox reaction has been an appeal to tradition. Priests have always been male. Marriage has always been between a man and a woman. Sexual activity outside of marriage has always been deemed sinful. A child is best cared for by a mother and a father. Amid these responses, we may observe two issues. First, while the responses are often couched in terms of an unchanging religious tradition, it is sometimes the case that the tradition reflects the values of a larger culture more than spiritual truths. However, more importantly, challenges to the practices in question, while often characterized as alien to Orthodoxy, are more and more frequently raised by Orthodox Christians themselves. The questions are connected not only with changes in our larger society, but with genuine struggles of Orthodox Christians and their journey toward theosis.

But what does it mean to make an argument from tradition? And to what tradition are we appealing? Orthodoxy contains many streams. To maximize both its credibility and utility, an immanent critique is best set within a specific context. To that end, my argument operates within the commitments of the so-called "Paris School," a shorthand for the Russian intelligentsia in exile that regrouped in France after the 1917 Bolshevik Revolution. The Paris School itself contains multiple streams of theological reflection, associated with particular figures.[4] From among those streams, I will engage with three: the patristic revival begun by Russian émigré priest and theologian Georges Florovsky; the Russian religious and philosophical renaissance which includes Sergius Bulgakov and Nikolay Berdyaev; and a third strand of apophatic theology inflected by French philosophical personalism, popularized in the works of Vladimir Lossky. My argument will move beyond an engagement with the works of these Paris School thinkers to include reflections by theologians they inspired and to ask questions that the Paris School theologians did not themselves ask.[5]

I have chosen the Paris School and its heirs as conversation partners for several reasons. First, the Orthodoxy embodied in their works gives rise to many of the expressions of Orthodoxy in Western Europe, North America, and Australia today. But more importantly, I wish to focus on three of their central values as arbiters in my own work: the distinction between Tradition and traditions, their appeal to a limited collection of inviolable dogmas, and their engagement with patristic theology. These commitments prioritize the vast array of traditions associated with Orthodox theology, offering criteria that assist in constructive theological reflection. I will briefly elaborate on these three elements in turn.

Tradition and Traditions

Orthodox regularly appeal to "tradition" (often with a capital T) as the final arbiter of theological conflicts.[6] But what might such an appeal mean? For Paris School theologians, Tradition is not simply an encyclopedic catalog of every text and custom to be produced in the history of the Church. Rather, as Vladimir Lossky writes, *Tradition* is the encounter with the Holy Spirit, a vertical movement in which the Spirit descends and intersects with the horizontal line of *traditions* handed on through time and space by successive generations of the Church. "Tradition in its primary notion," Lossky tells us, "is not the revealed content, but the unique mode of receiving revelation, a faculty owed to the Holy Spirit."[7] This is contrasted with traditions, or customs and teachings that have been passed along by generations of Orthodox practitioners. Like Jacob's marker at Peniel, traditions mark sites where Orthodox Christians have encountered the Divine.[8]

Not all customs and practices contribute to the ultimate goal of divine-human communion. Many are neutral, neither inherently good nor bad. What matters is their capacity for leading to communion with God. However, the mere repetition of traditions is no guarantee of continuing encounter with the Spirit. In fact, preserved among the traditions in our churches are mere human customs and values that not only may not facilitate continuing divine-human communion, but also may actively impede it.[9]

This conception of Tradition is important to my argument for two reasons. First, it provides the criterion by which I will evaluate various customs within the community: the encounter with the Holy Spirit that transforms humanity in divine-human communion. Second, with deification as the ultimate goal, one may ask which practices within the church are life-giving according to the Paris School's conception of Tradition and which have become dead ends.

Limited Inviolable Dogma

Based on a schematization originally proposed by Vasily Bolotov, the heirs to the Paris School commonly divide the tradition into several elements: the dogmatic pronouncements of the seven ecumenical councils, *theologoumena,* or the learned opinions of the fathers of the undivided Church, and the personal theological opinions of later theologians.[10] Of these, only the dogmatic declarations of the ecumenical councils are considered unchanging. These declarations (1) address Trinitarian and Christological issues of salvific importance; (2) find support by the evidence of Holy Scripture; and (3) enjoy the consensus of the entire Orthodox Church. Because of their central role in the Orthodox faith, dogmas are protected by decree from changes by further councils, even down to changes in word choices.[11] Without claiming to exhaust the fullness of theological reflection, the dogmatic pronouncements of the ecumenical councils mark the boundaries of the theological conversation of the Church. At the same time, theologians such as Lossky warn against standing on dogmas alone as a minimalist body of thought to reject constructive theological reflection that addresses new questions.[12]

This understanding of dogma, focusing on a minimal set of immutable theological formulations, is useful to my argument in two ways. First, by clearly identifying the essential elements of Orthodox theology, the Paris School historiographers open space to explore, question, and critique a variety of received theological formulations, including reflections on sex and gender. An immanent critique in consonance with the Paris School tradition cannot contradict the dogmatic statements of the ecumenical councils but is free to explore and question other received traditions. Second, as we will see in chapter 4, dogmas can prove useful in the production of a theological anthropology by offering guideposts and boundaries.

The "Return to the Fathers"

Beyond the dogmas of the Church, the Paris School places value on the *theologoumena,* or educated theological opinions, of the fathers. The centrality of the "return to the fathers" as a source for theological reflection is embodied in attempts at a *neopatristic synthesis,* an idea that takes its name from work by Georges Florovsky. This neopatristic synthesis has three major points.[13] First, the return to the fathers cannot be reduced to cherry-picked prooftexts used to support a theological argument, a far too common move even among authors and heirs of the Paris School tradition. A true synthesis requires extensive study of the patristic sources with due consideration of their historical background, the cultural and philosophical trends of the day, and the circumstances that occasioned the authors' work. Second, a synthesis would not simply be a compilation of views, but rather an attempt to identify a core message. Florovsky understood that the fathers do not speak on all topics in a monolithic or unified voice. At points, their views contradict one another or even their own writings. Finally, Florovsky understood the neopatristic synthesis as a living conversation partner in the reflection on issues that had not yet arisen in the patristic period. This final point opens the door to formulating new theological reflections that are consonant with the core message of the fathers.

Returning to the idea of immanent critique, I suggest that the ultimate goal of divine-human communion is shared by both patristic and contemporary Orthodox authors. As such, this common end goal should serve as arbiter in moments of disagreement. Like our own constructive theological endeavors, patristic claims must be measured against their ability to foster love of God and neighbor.

The return to the fathers provides the impetus for the reexamination of patristic texts in chapter 2. There I will argue that a common claim heard within Orthodox conversations—that the fathers are of one mind on issues of gender and biological sex—is simply not true.

Engagement with Culture

In any book addressing modern questions such as this one, the author must come to a decision concerning the role to be played by philosophy and science. The theologians of the Paris School and their heirs are ambivalent about the usefulness of these areas of knowledge in theological reflection. On the one hand, the thinkers of the Russian religious and philosophical renaissance undertook engagements with many Western European philosophical currents. The entire sophiological enterprise looks to German Idealism and Romanticism as conversation partners in articulating the relationship between God and creation. Nikolay Berdyaev often cited Freud, while his friend Paul Evdokimov looked to the archetypes of Bachofen and Jung for his own anthropological models. In the current generation, Kallistos Ware suggests that Orthodox theological anthropology has much to learn from philosophers, non-Orthodox theologians, social scientists, and psychologists. He calls for a "genuinely ecumenical" understanding of the human person as a fruit of dialogue.[14]

On the other hand, Orthodox thinkers are also critical of the adoption of extra-traditional sources for theological reflection. Georges Florovsky blamed the adoption of Roman Catholic theological categories and German Romanticism for what he saw as a twisting of authentic Orthodoxy. For his own part, Thomas Hopko claims that Orthodoxy takes scientific claims very seriously. However, he offers two caveats. First, the sciences are restricted to empirical observation. They may offer insights into physical nature and observable human behavior, but they are unable to address the spiritual, the metaphysical, or the divine. Second, both Orthodoxy and the broader Christian tradition teach that we live in a world that suffers from the fall. Thus, scientists study things as they currently exist, but they have no access to things as they were protologically created or as they will exist in the eschaton.[15]

Despite any reservations these authors may express, Orthodox Christians do not exist in a vacuum. Rather, in addition to membership within the Church, we are also citizens of various countries. We speak a variety of human languages and are formed within a variety of cultural contexts. And we are in good company. The fathers and mothers of the church found themselves in a variety of cultures. Some were classically educated and equipped with the tools of various philosophical schools. In response to the great Trinitarian and Christological controversies, they borrowed and adapted metaphysical terminology from various philosophical systems. They wrote not only treatises, but also sermons, poetry, and hymnody in popular styles to convey their teachings. The theologians and religious philosophers of the Paris School follow in these footsteps, taking inspiration from contemporary philosophical and religious thought and adapting it to their own ends. Like their patristic forebears, the Paris School theologians and their heirs use what the broader cultures they inhabit have to offer. Their best works preserve the primacy of dogmatic definitions while respectfully incorporating and critiquing various elements of patristic *theologoumena* and formulating their own new contributions to Orthodox theological reflection.

The fathers were not scientists in our modern sense. In service to the Church, they borrowed largely from Platonic principles.[16] This raises two moments of note. First, scientific thought about creation in the patristic period tends toward an understanding of a source and emanations. This thought develops, especially in the Greek tradition, with reference to the divine *Logos* in whom all other *logoi* (eternal, immutable principles thought of as God's intentions) for both ideas and objects have their grounding. The theory of *logoi* begins in the works of Philo and is subsequently adopted and altered in the works of Origen, Athanasius, the Cappadocians, and Evagrius of Pontus, coming to fullness in the work of Maximus Confessor.[17] For Maximus, contemplation of the *logoi* leads to communion with the *Logos* and a mystical union with God. This contemplation takes place in the *nous* or rational soul. When the *nous* has been properly purified through ascetic practice, it grasps the eternal *logoi* in a spiritual reality that is based neither in empirical sense perception nor in mental understanding. Rather, it transcends both to see things as they are in their ontological foundations. These roots go beyond the created world to the *Logos*. Such contemplation "from above" allows the person to see the world as it is spiritually rather than how it appears to us in our day-to-day encounters or our thoughts. This approach is very different from how we normally think of science today as an empirical inquiry into the world.[18]

The second moment of note is an effect of the first. The Platonic models that influence the fathers' worldview envision a created order of symmetry and mathematical regularity. Each concrete object inheres to a particular and clearly delineated *logos*. When the fathers talk about science in their theological reflections, their Platonic outlook focuses on the regularities of creation. Theirs is a theoretical vision of the cosmos, only loosely grounded in empirical observation.[19] As such it does not account for the complexity and disorder encountered in the world. This worldview still underlies some of the modern Orthodox thought that we will explore in chapter 3, where male and female are envisioned as distinct principles that produce two separate kinds of human beings—men and women—whose natures and functions are dictated by the principles themselves. In such a worldview, deviation from the theoretical principle can only be accounted for by the effects of sin. As we will see, especially in chapter 4, there is a great deal of complexity and variation within the various biological and psychosocial expressions of human individuals for which the Platonic worldview cannot adequately account.

In terms of immanent critique, I will here suggest (and further explore in later chapters) that the Platonic worldview, which values conformity over variation and alterity, must be weighed against the ultimate goal of divine-human communion. Though the spiritual disciplines promoted by the Church reflect the accrued wisdom of centuries of collective experience, a one-size-fits-all approach can be detrimental to the spiritual lives of unique human persons. Within pastoral practice this is commonly recognized in the concept of *oikonomia*, by which clergy make allowances for personal circumstances as they counsel individuals. The ultimate goal of divine-human communion is always held in sight; however, the ways of reaching the goal are different for each person, depending on their combination of strengths, weaknesses, gifts, and character.

The Role of Experience in Orthodox Tradition

As we saw above, Orthodox thinkers embrace scientific explanations with some hesitation. Because we live in a world that has been affected by sin, it is not enough to show empirically that things exist in a particular state.

Following Maximus Confessor, contemplation of the *logoi* of ideas and created things leads the purified *nous* back to the *Logos* and communion with God, allowing a person to see things not as they appear in the world or how they might be rationally conceptualized, but rather as they are spiritually. But here we must pause and ask: How is the *nous* purified? The fathers who embrace contributions from philosophy and the sciences also emphasize prayer, meditation on the scriptures, and participation in communion within the Church. These practices are again stressed by various thinkers within the Paris School tradition.

Florovsky, echoing the earlier teaching of Clement of Alexandria, argues that the coherence within the body of traditional teaching can be apprehended only within the context of faith, in communion with "the personal God." Only faith can bring formulas to life and make them convincing. Faith, in turn, only occurs because of communion with the living person of Christ, which occurs within the Church.[20] Lossky affirms that truth is revealed within the Church, through initiation of its members into the sacraments.[21] We must add to this the "principle of consonance," a phrase taken from Athanasius's *On the Incarnation of the Word of God*. Athanasius argues that to possess true knowledge (in his context, from the scriptures), one must have an honorable life, a pure soul, and the virtue of Christ.[22] It is not enough to simply engage the text. A person must also wash and cleanse their soul and address their manner of living. Imitation of the lives and works of the saints produces a shared frame of reference. Only then is it possible to grasp the truth that the saints convey.[23] Thus, right experience transforms the heart and mind to perceive spiritual truths that are unavailable to us outside the shared life of spiritual practices and sacraments of the Church.

But what happens when a person participates in the life of the Church through its sacraments, takes seriously the communal life of shared spiritual practices, and still does not come to the same conclusions regarding the spiritual nature of the created order? As described above, the model of the world promoted by Maximus and many other Orthodox thinkers is built on Platonic foundations that emphasize the symmetry and regularity of the created order. In contrast, the world we live in is filled with disorder and a lack of regularity in its infinite details. As I noted above, some Orthodox explain deviations from their espoused ideals by an appeal to the effects of sin. To return to Maximus's own language, the *logoi* of ideas and created things remain unchanged after the fall, but the *tropoi* or ways

in which they exist may be fundamentally at odds with the original intention within God's plan.[24] But here I suggest that we have a problem. While
we must certainly acknowledge the effects of sin in the world, we must be
very careful about suggesting that variations—both those that are infrequent by comparison with statistical norms, but also those that are at odds
with Platonic ideals—are automatically the results of sin or, as is sometimes claimed, are sinful in themselves. This does not mean that all variations are beneficial or acceptable. Nor is acknowledging this necessarily the
beginning of a slippery slope. In discerning a proper response, I see four
key moments. First, if members among the faithful share a minority report (and here, I would broaden this to include anyone who engages the
community in good faith), their observations should be taken seriously.
Second, the minority report (whether from an individual or a group) must
be subjected to communal discernment. Communal discernment is the tradition's way of separating misapprehension or delusion from experiential
evidence that requires modification of existing beliefs and practices. Third,
this communal discernment is not a matter of majority rule, but rather of
spiritual discernment. Finally, since the ultimate aim of the community's
beliefs and practices is fuller divine-human communion, the criterion for
discerning this communion is the manifestation of the fruits of the Spirit,
most fully revealed in a continually growing love of God with one's whole
being and a love of neighbor and self. Any minority report submitted
for communal discernment can be validated or rejected by the observable
presence of the spiritual fruits produced in the person and the cultivation
of love for God and one's neighbor.[25] As I return in Part II to the list of
gender- and sex-related questions with which this chapter began, I will
propose some modifications to current practices. My suggestions consider
the ultimate goal of divine-human communion, in light of the reports
of contemporary science, claims from gender and queer theory, and the
emerging voices of those within the Orthodox Church whose experience
runs counter to traditional claims, particularly around the ministerial priesthood and the sacramentality of spousal and familial relationships.

Sex, Gender, and Related Terminology

As I continue to set the stage for the following chapters, a word about the
vocabulary of sex, gender, and other associated concepts is in order. Until
the 1960s, the English words *gender* and *sex* were used interchangeably

as synonyms. This remains the case in conversational speech even today. However, early sexologist John Money vested the two words with separate meanings. In exploring the nature of intersex conditions, Money turned to philology, borrowing the word *gender* to signify "a person's personal, social, and legal status as male or female without reference to sex organs." He coined the term *gender role* to denote "the things a person says or does to reveal him- or herself as having the status of boy or man, girl or woman." Finally, Money coined the term *gender identity* to refer to the subjective experience of gender.[26] The word *sex* was then reoriented to refer only to the biological characteristics that separate male and female: hormones (and pubertal differentiation), chromosomes, gonads, internal reproductive structures, and external genital morphology. Second-wave feminists adopted this distinction between gender and sex to emphasize what is socially constructed and what is biologically bound or determined. Vested with this distinction, *sex* allowed for the idea of a group of humans called *women* who could contest the *gendered* conditions of their lives, especially areas of inequity and oppression, as things that can be changed rather than simply accepted as immutable or preordained.

In recent years, *sex* and *gender* have been used as synonyms with only sporadic differentiation between concepts.[27] For the purposes of this book, I will continue to distinguish between the two as a helpful tool in exploring patristic and modern Orthodox assumptions about bodies and cultural expectations. However, biological sex itself will become a subject for further exploration on two fronts in chapter 4. First, individual human bodies complicate the simple binary of male and female sexes. Second, some critical theorists have argued that scientific classifications of sex are also based in gender constructs. With the greater awareness of the complexities embodied by actual human beings, we face new questions about the adequacy of the labels we use to identify an individual as male or female.

One-Sex and Two-Sex Bodies

Key to correctly interpreting the materials presented in the following chapters is a conscious understanding of what Thomas Laqueur calls the *one-sex* (or *one-flesh*) and *two-sex* models of human physiology.[28] Spanning a period of two millennia, Laqueur uses medical and philosophical texts of the classical, antique, medieval, and early modern periods to present male and female bodies as material epiphenomena that reflect deeper ontological realities of gender.[29] In the primary one-flesh model offered by Galen, men and women are not separate, incommensurate sexes, but specimens of the same human anatomy on a scale from greater to lesser perfection. Men are those humans who achieve sufficient heat while gestating in the womb for all their limbs, including their genitalia, to fully articulate. In contrast, women do not reach an internal temperature warm enough to cause their sexual organs to be fully articulated externally.[30] In this model, the ovaries and uterus are analogous to the male testes and scrotum,[31] while the vaginal canal is an undescended penis, terminating in the labia, which Galen suggests is analogous to the male foreskin.

Laqueur argues that the one-sex body was the dominant paradigm of earlier times, but in our own world a two-sex model prevails. As the name implies, rather than gradations of perfection on an ascending scale, the two-sex model treats men's and women's bodies as two distinct human forms with differing anatomy, physiology, and diseases. If for the ancients the body served as an indicator of one's more fundamental gender, our own sensibilities indicate the opposite. Biological sex, male or female, is commonly considered the more foundational characteristic, which in turn dictates the epiphenomena of gender with corresponding roles and behaviors.

We can illustrate Laqueur's point with an example. On hearing someone is pregnant we often ask: "Is it a boy or a girl?" The answer sets in motion a series of expectations, from the color of clothing and gender-specific gifts showered on the expectant mother, to the descriptors we will use as we dote on the newborn ("What a handsome young man!" "She's beautiful!"), to the ways we engage in play. Such social cues continue throughout a child's development and into adult life, dictating norms for dress, behavior, and family roles. They also affect access to medical care, employment opportunities, compensation in the workforce, and the likelihood of becoming a target of violence.

Laqueur's model enjoys a great deal of popularity in a variety of fields, including literary and cultural studies. However, it has also come under strong criticism, based primarily on three factors. First, Laqueur's periodization is often drawn into question, especially the dating of the transition from a one- to a two-sex paradigm, which varies anywhere over a 150-year period from the late-seventeenth to the early-nineteenth century.[32] Second, his narrative depends on a selection of classical texts from the Hippocratic and Galenic corpuses that emphasize the one-sex model to the exclusion of references from the same period that support a two-sex model.[33] Finally,

Laqueur's descriptions tend to elide dissonances between Aristotle and Galen, though the theories of sexual reproduction offered by the two differ in important and incompatible details.[34]

I have adopted Laqueur's descriptors (e.g., one-sex/two-sex), while keeping in mind the criticisms of his claims of univocity among ancient authors and the period covered. While multiple models were indeed present in the ancient world, Galen's views enjoyed great popularity in the Greek-speaking world and are reflected in the works of patristic authors such as Gregory of Nyssa,[35] Basil of Ancyra,[36] and Nemesius of Emesa.[37] Galen's ideas regarding human sexual reproduction are also repeated in a text by Aetios of Amida, physician to Emperor Justinian,[38] and may also have influenced particular elements of Latin patristic theology.[39] Finally, the debates over the date for the invention of the two-sex model that dominates our own time are of little consequence to my argument. All the modern Orthodox thinkers surveyed in chapter 4 are on this side of the divide, regardless of the exact date of transition. Their reflections are marked by a binary distinction between male and female on which their proposed gender roles and expectations in turn depend.

Conclusion

In this chapter, I have set in place a methodology of immanent critique. I have identified theosis, defined as divine-human communion, as the ultimate aim within the Orthodox community in the tradition of the Paris School theologians. The community holds a collection of beliefs and observes a set of practices adopted in pursuit of this goal. Progress toward this aim can be discerned by the community by attentiveness to the presence of the fruits of the Spirit. Beliefs and traditions that act as stumbling blocks to participation in divine-human communion are subject to critique and change. A limited collection of beliefs has been given the status of dogma. These declarations respond to questions of salvific import and were accepted through broad consensus of both the hierarchy and the laity of the Church. Because these *dogmata* are formulated in the language and philosophical categories of the cultures that adopted them, it is important to engage with them through the broader exploration of the philosophical, linguistic, social, and cultural background of those who framed both the questions and the responses. These contexts, likewise, inform the broader corpus of patristic theological reflections. Both dogmatic definitions and the wider body of patristic writings make use of philosophical and scientific knowledge of their times. However, their use is selective rather than a wholesale adoption. Key to proper discernment is participation within the faith community, in personal and corporate worship and prayer, in the sacraments, and in engagement with the community's collective wisdom transmitted in scripture, hymnody, liturgy, hagiography, and ascetic practice.

With these elements in mind, let us move forward. In chapter 2, I will present what a variety of patristic authors have said about biological sex and gender. This survey will help the reader to discern trends in patristic thought that will aid in evaluating the arguments presented in chapter 3. They will also inform my own attempts to articulate an apophatic theological anthropology in chapter 4. Key to contextualizing both patristic and modern reflections on gender and biological sex is an awareness of the one- and two-sex body models. The patristic authors wrote in a period in which men and women were seen as individuals whose bodies exhibited varying degrees of perfection. Physical embodiment was a material epiphenomenon that revealed the underlying gender of the person, with men tending to be superior to women, but all bodies were essentially of one type. By way of contrast, our own time tends to view male and female as two incommensurate sexes whose physical bodies are the more fundamental reality from which gender roles and expectations develop. The two-sex model is often tied to a form of determinism in which the differences between male and female dictate not only biological concerns, but broader categories of charisms, vocations, interpersonal relationships, familial roles, and roles in the broader society. Contemporary Orthodox Christians have raised concerns about beliefs and practices within the Orthodox community related to these categories. Some have suggested that current beliefs and practices reinforced by essentialist arguments, may inhibit, or even prevent, progress toward the ultimate aim of divine-human communion. Thus, the community is called to listen, examine these beliefs and practices, and discern proper responses. Minority reports are to be evaluated with an eye to the ultimate aim of theosis. Growth in the fruits of the spirit is the criterion for evaluation.

As this book unfolds, I will argue that gender essentialist commitments impede the aim of divine-human communion. This claim will find support in conclusions drawn from the overview of the patristic tradition offered in chapter 2. Having examined a variety of patristic reflections, the reader will be in a better place to evaluate the claims rooted in essentialism presented in chapter 3. Contrary to what is often claimed, the essentialist model is not supported by the patristic tradition. Moreover, I will show that the sources of gender essentialism can be traced to extra-Orthodox sources. The provenance of these ideas is not grounds for dismissing them. However, this does place the essentialist model on an even footing with an alternative, personalist model that I will present in chapter 4. Again, both systems are conceived with an eye toward the ultimate goal of divine-human communion. However, I will argue that the personalist model has the potential to better facilitate this goal. Finally, in Part II, I will offer suggestions for modifying a set of gendered and sexed practices as they are currently conceived within the tradition. I am not interested in change for the sake of change, or to align Orthodox practices more closely with emerging norms in contemporary cultures. Rather, the changes I will propose are oriented to greater divine-human communion.

Let us now turn to an exploration of patristic theological reflections on gender and biological sex.

2

(NO) MALE AND FEMALE

RECAPITULATING PATRISTIC REFLECTIONS ON GENDER

[The] real reintegration of Christian tradition should be sought in a
neopatristic synthesis. The first step to be taken is that we should learn to
read and study the fathers not merely as historical documents, as links of
a "venerable" but obsolete "tradition," as pieces of antiquity, but as living
masters from whom we may receive the message of life and truth.

—GEORGES FLOROVSKY[1]

Introduction

For the past fifty years, Orthodoxy has largely operated under the
banner of a "return to the fathers," associated with Georges Florovsky's
proposal for a neopatristic synthesis. Florovsky suggested that when reflecting on matters of doctrine, we should look for the "mind of the fathers."
However, he was also completely aware that not all contemporary questions
are answered or even posed in the patristic corpus. Thus, he described the
task of constructive theology as moving forward with the fathers, adopting
their vision as we embrace new questions that arise both within the Church
and in dialogue with the broader world.

In this chapter I will attempt to apply Florovsky's model by conducting
a survey of patristic texts concerned with biological sex and gender. While
my examination is not exhaustive, I look at enough texts to get a feel for
the diversity of thought within the tradition, and points of convergence. My
approach is modeled on a Foucauldian genealogy.[2] I am not interested in

arguing for a straightforward transmission of unchanging texts across time. Rather, I will also examine discontinuities, creative reappropriations, and returns to earlier models. My goals for this chapter are three. First, I wish to challenge the idea that patristic conceptions of gender can be traced through an unbroken transmission of a univocal teaching. Second, I wish to show that rather than a single, pristine, originating source, there are many sources the patristic writers draw upon: biblical, philosophical, poetic, and situational. There is no single root that we can recover. Third, having dispelled the idea of a single source or an unbroken, univocal transmission of teaching, I will offer what seem to me to be candidate ideas for moving forward with the fathers to explore elements of a theological anthropology that takes into consideration both contemporary questions of sex and gender and the modern responses already formulated.

To meet these goals, the bulk of this chapter will examine patristic reflections with gendered components. These texts were not written in a vacuum. The period during which the examined authors write is one of great religious diversity in which many different groups vie for the name *Christian*, and competing ideas are being sorted into categories of orthodoxy and heterodoxy. The fathers (and mothers) of the Church are shaped by biblical and liturgical texts, but also by encounters with ideas originating outside of the Church. For both the Latin and Greek patristic traditions, the Greek philosophical schools are indispensable conversation partners, while a short look at the Syriac tradition shows the influence of the poetic thought world of Semitic culture. Each contribution responds to its own questions and uses conceptual frameworks available in unique historical, geographic, philosophical, and linguistic contexts. With these arguments in hand, my hope is that you, the reader, will be better equipped in the subsequent chapters to evaluate contemporary Orthodox arguments that attempt to legitimate their claims through appeals to patristic tradition, often vaguely characterized as the teaching of "the fathers."

Before turning to the patristic texts, it is useful to first examine several key textual sources and authors that shape the context in which our authors write and think. Patristic thinkers, informed by their own cultural contexts, incorporate many sources into their own theological reflections, including the Bible and the works of authors like Plato and Philo of Alexandria. In the four sections that follow, I will briefly lay out these "authorities," with which the fathers regularly interact as they reflect on biological sex and gender. My list is by no means exhaustive. I have focused on passages that appear frequently in the reflections and arguments that follow. I am not attempting to give readings of these passages in their original contexts. My primary interest is in exploring features important in the later appropriations by the fathers that we will explore in this chapter, as well as contemporary Orthodox thinkers we will explore in chapter 3. With these limitations in mind, let us proceed.

Plato

With the Hellenization of much of the ancient world, Greek myths and philosophical reflections spread throughout the Mediterranean.[3] Plato's writings, which predate the New Testament by several centuries, provide material for the various iterations of Platonism that inform both Hellenistic Judaism and early Christian thought.

Symposium

Plato introduces a comical account of love and sexual difference through the character of Aristophanes in the *Symposium*.[4] Here, human beings are originally possessed of two heads, four arms, and four legs. They come in three sexes: some are androgynes,[5] possessing both male and female genitalia, while others are double-males and double-females. When the humans launch a war against the gods, Zeus splits each in twain, "just as people cut up sorb-apples for preserving or slice eggs with a hair."[6] Aristophanes suggests that humans continue to wander about, searching for their other half in hopes of finding completion. When they find one another, they embrace with great longing to become one flesh again. Aristophanes concludes his tale with a poet's tribute to love (*erōs*), which seeks "to restore us to our original state by trying to make unity out of duality and to heal our human condition."[7] While the patristic authors had little use for the double-male and double-female creatures of Aristophanes's tale, the idea of an androgyne, split and then reunited, has significant resonance with their work, as we will see below.

Timaeus

Plato offers an extensive cosmogony in the *Timaeus*. In the title character's account, the Craftsman (*dēmiourgos*) fashions a material universe that matches the form of a cosmos that existed previously in the eternal model alone and fashions the heavenly creatures (both celestial bodies and gods of popular religion). He mixes the leftovers from the World Soul and creates individual souls, one for each star in the sky. Each soul is assigned to a star, which it rides like a chariot, taking in a view of the cosmos. During the flight, the Craftsman explains the nature of the universe and the rules that ordain its proper function. He then tasks his first creations, the gods, with the production of bodies for each soul. These bodies, made of corruptible matter, possess the faculty of sensation (*aisthēsis*) and allow humans to experience love (*erōs*). Each soul is endowed with equal advantage. Perhaps most interestingly, each soul receives a male body. But the mixing of elements in their corporeal forms causes each soul to move erratically. Those who attain balance through successfully mastering their passions during life are freed from their bodies at death to return to their star, while those who live lives of cowardice or injustice return to a second corporeal life as women! Successive failures result in reincarnations as lesser animal forms, while the successful mastery of one's passions eventually leads back to a disembodied and blissful life with one's star.[8]

While the narrative does not specify how the first women's bodies are formed, it does not take long before the gods introduce a biological mechanism for the continuous production of new human beings. The penis, once appended to the body, exists as an "ensouled living thing"[9] with its own passions and a resistance to reason. A similar animated substance introduced into the female body becomes the womb, possessing an independent desire for childbearing. The animated substances give rise to love (*erōs*) in the man and desire (*epithymia*) in the woman, which come together in sexual union to plant the seed. The woman provides nourishment for the living creatures, still small and unformed, until they mature to the point of birth.[10]

Several moments in this fantastic narrative are worthy of special attention. First, the idea of a procession and return, common to various stages of Platonic thought, is a powerful image for many of the theologians in our survey, particularly within the Greek tradition. Also note that in the beginning, all humans enjoy identical conditions in which to thrive. Only subsequently, with the appearance of reincarnated human beings, are male and female sexual characteristics introduced. Yet even without penises or wombs, the first and second iterations of human beings are characterized as men and women, respectively. It is also noteworthy that the appearance of women is the direct result of their failure as men to live a just life.[11] While our own modern sensibilities associate biological sex with reproductive organs, the author associates masculinity and femininity with moral traits, a sensibility that continues throughout the patristic sources examined below. Further, sexual desire is not a part of the male or female body or even the appetitive part of the soul, but rather of the generative organs that possess their own souls.[12] The theme of the unruly penis with a will of its own reappears in our survey as well. Finally, though the Greek physician Hippocrates had postulated the existence of male and female seed as early as the fifth century BCE, this account appears to understand human reproduction as analogous to the agricultural model of planting seed in the earth. "[Like] plucking the fruit from a tree," recounts Plato, "they sow the seed into the ploughed field of her womb. . . ."[13] This understanding is also common in biblical texts and some patristic texts, though it is replaced in the later patristic period by the Galenic model.[14]

Phaedrus *and the Chariot Metaphor*

The image of the chariot in the *Phaedrus*[15] also echoes in the works of several authors in our survey. Here, Plato's Socrates portrays Zeus as the prototypical charioteer, pulled through the skies by two winged horses. In contrast, two horses of different breeds and constitutions pull the human's chariot:

> [O]ne stands in the position of greater beauty (i.e., on the right), in form erect and well-jointed, high-necked, hooked nose, white to behold, black-eyed, a lover of honor with a sense of moderation and shame and a companion of true opinion, without need of the whip, ruled by command and word alone. But the other is crooked, bulky, poorly slung together, stiff-necked, thick-necked, snub-nosed, black-skinned, cloudy-eyed, hot-blooded, a companion of wantonness and insolences, shaggy about the ears, obtuse, and scarcely obedient to whip and goad.[16]

The human charioteer represents the intellect (*nous*), being pulled along by two moral impulses—the one his better nature, sometimes characterized as the irascible (*thymos*), which pursues what is noble and virtuous, while the other is bent toward concupiscence (*epithymia*), which follows after bodily appetites, desires, and lusts. As we will see below, many subsequent authors appropriate the chariot metaphor, introducing new gendered elements along the way.

Septuagint (LXX) Texts

While the Hebrew Scriptures antedate the Platonic corpus, for our purposes they enter the conversation with the Septuagint, the Greek translation prepared by the Jewish community at Alexandria in the third century BCE. These Hellenized Jews understood *Timaeus* and the creation narratives of Genesis to be descriptions of the same events. Two passages are key to the patristic conversation around gender.

"Male and Female" (Gn 1:27)

From the first creation account, written in response to the Babylonian Captivity, the opening creation narrative gives a cosmic overview of the six days of creation. On the final day, as the pinnacle of the created order, the author writes, "God created the human; in the image of God he created it; male and female he created them."[17] Here the author creates a *parallelismus membrorum,* or a poetic, grammatical parallel in which "the human" and "male and female" function as synonyms. Against the backdrop of the Babylonian creation narrative *Enuma Elish,* in which only the king is created in the image of the god Marduk, the Hebrew text offers a theological counter-narrative in which not only the ruler, but all of humanity, both male and female, bears the image of its Creator.[18]

"A Suitable Helper" (Gn 2:4b–25)

Immediately following the first creation account, the received text of Genesis contains a second, older creation narrative in which God creates the first human from the dust of the ground and breathes into it the breath of life.[19] Seeing that it is not good for the human to be alone, God causes a deep sleep to fall over Adam, removes one of Adam's ribs/sides (*pleura*), fills in the affected area opposite it with flesh, and then fashions from the extracted material a suitable helper (*boēthos homoios autōi*).

There are three moments of note in the Septuagint translation of this familiar text. First, the original human is referred to as *anthrōpos* (vv. 7–8, 15, 18) or *adam* ("Adam," a transliteration of the Hebrew *ʾādām* vv. 16, 19–22) until the gender binary appears in v. 23, when the human (*adam*) proclaims that she (*autē*) will be called woman (*gynē*) because she was taken from man (*anēr*). Adam's own postoperative gender is foregrounded only in opposition to the newly created helper.[20]

The second moment of interest is the word *pleura*, which is traditionally translated as "rib" in this narrative. Like its Hebrew counterpart *selaʿ*, the Greek *pleura* can also be translated as "side."[21] Taken together with the description of God filling with flesh the opening created in Adam, the image is one of an original creature divided into two halves. Whether the preoperative Adam was androgynous or sexless finds no unanimity within the patristic tradition, as we will see below.

Finally, the Greek translation for "helper" is *boēthos*, which is rendered as *ʿēzer* in the Masoretic Text. Through long conditioning, the word "helper" has come to connote in English a subordinate who provides additional support.[22] However, it should be noted that this word is based on the same Greek root used in the verb *boēthein*, meaning "to come to aid; to succor, assist, aid." It is used to describe the actions of allies in a military campaign, and is the same word used to describe God throughout the LXX in passages commonly rendered in English as "strength," "help," and "rock."[23] As an interesting linguistic note, *boēthos* is grammatically masculine. We will revisit the interplay of grammatical and culturally constructed genders, beginning with Philo.

Philo of Alexandria

Best known for his allegorical interpretation of Septuagint texts, Philo often makes use of Platonic themes.[24] Through the writings of Eusebius, Jerome, Epiphanius, and several others, Philo's reputation grew through several centuries to a near father of the Early Church.[25] No survey of the resources for theological reflection of the patristic period would be complete without an examination of his contributions. While allusions and quotations from the Platonic corpus appear throughout Philo's works, we will focus primarily on his *The Creation of the Cosmos*, in which he exegetes the creation narrative of Genesis. Philo utilizes the intellectual language of allegory inherited from Greek philosophy, such as images from Plato's *Timaeus* and the chariot metaphor from Plato's *Phaedrus*.[26]

De Opificio Mundi

Philo is the first biblical commentator to reflect on the double creation of humanity. Unlike many later exegetes, who will focus on the double creation of image and likeness in the two clauses of Gn 1:27, Philo's double creation is concerned with harmonizing the accounts given in Gn 1, in which God creates humanity as male and female, and the creation of Adam alone in Gn 2.[27] He concludes that in Gn 1:26–27, Moses refers to the genus of human being (*to genos anthrōpon eipōn*), separating its species into male and female (*arren te kai thēlu*). Echoing themes from *Timaeus*, Philo writes that there are no individuals at this point, but they are apparent to the one who gazes most intently as though into a mirror.[28] This first human (*anthrōpos*), created in the image of God, is "a kind of idea or genus or seal [that] is perceived by the intellect. [It is] incorporeal, neither male (*arren*) nor female (*thēly*), and is immortal by nature."[29] In contrast, the human created from the clay of the ground and inbreathed with the breath of life (Gn 2:7), is a "sense-perceptible object," which "consists of body and soul, is either man (*anēr*) or woman (*gynē*), and is by nature mortal."[30] While Adam and Eve are said to be male and female, Philo's prototypical human is presexual.

In the second creation, Philo writes that the first man resembles God and the cosmos in the relation between his mind and body. But with the appearance of the first woman, his lot changes. The man recognizes a kindred image in the woman and greets her. She in turn responds to his greeting, and love (*erōs*) springs up between the two. In a clear allusion to Aristophanes's anthropology in the *Symposium*, the two join as separate halves of a single living being.[31] But such an intense love leads to bodily pleasure, spiraling down into wickedness and unlawfulness and a loss of immortality and well-being.[32] Philo allegorically interprets the serpent that tempts Eve as sexual pleasure. Playing on the grammatical gender of a series of Greek words, he uses pleasure (*hēdonē*) as a metonym for the snake and sets the masculine intellect (*nous, logismos*) representative of Adam in opposition to the feminine perception (*aisthēsis*) that he sees standing for Eve. Perception/Eve is easily lured by Pleasure (*hēdonē*) as "she" offers up wiles (*goēteia*) and deceptions (*apatē*).[33] This allegorical reading will appear again in the survey of patristic texts.

The Chariot Metaphor Redeployed

Philo also alludes to the image of the Platonic chariot in several works. In his exegesis of Gn 1:26–27, he suggests that to be created "in the image and likeness of God" refers to "the director of the soul, the intellect."[34] The intellect rules over the human body in a manner analogous to the Great

Director (*ho megas hēgemōn*) and the created order, echoing the description of Zeus as the archetypical charioteer in Plato's *Phaedrus* myth.[35] The human intellect contemplates its surroundings and is lifted on high to explore the air and the world of intelligible things, echoing further the flight of the mind.[36] Many other philological points link Philo's use of the chariot metaphor in multiple texts to its Platonic predecessor, but the exegete also adapts and redeploys the imagery to his particular purposes.

Philo takes up Plato's chariot allegory once again in his *On Cultivation*, redeploying the image with his own embellishments: "Desire (*epithymia*) and spirit (*thymos*) are horses, the one male, the other female. For this reason, the one is proud, wishes to be unrestrained and free, and has a high neck, *just like a male*; but the other is mean, slavish, rejoicing in thievery, eating up house and home and destroying it, *for she is female*. The intellect (*nous*), who is single, is both rider and reinsman."[37] Philo also alludes to Plato's tripartite soul in his *Allegorical Interpretation of Genesis*, but without explicit reference to the charioteer or his horses.[38] However, in this instance he speaks not of the charioteer/*nous*, but of the reasoning faculty of the soul (*to logikon*), which governs the high-spirited (*to thymikon*) and lustful (*to epithymētikon*) parts. These names will reappear again in works of Evagrius of Pontus below. This same spirit/desire dichotomy is also referred to in *On the Migration of Abraham* as the masculine and feminine passions that guide the human soul that has rid itself of mind (*nous*) but does not seek to replace them with divine wisdom.[39] These gendered concepts can be traced further through the Alexandrian tradition.

Philo's early work of harmonizing Plato and the texts of his own Jewish tradition are essential to many of the authors in both the Latin and Greek patristic traditions. Not only do they accept his synthesis as though the two different cultural traditions are describing the same creation events, but they also follow his lead in exploring various allegorical interpretations beyond the literal meaning of the scripture.

The New Testament

During Philo's lifetime, the authors of the emerging Christian faith began writing texts that eventually formed the New Testament. The Early Church appropriated to itself the Hebrew scriptures. But while claiming a continuity with these earlier traditions, the writers of this new movement also reimagined the creation and the order of the world, fixing their thoughts in new scripture and liturgical formulations and continuing into patristic reflections. While our survey will refer to several examples, two scriptural allusions are practically universal among the patristic authors as they reflect on gender.

"No Male and Female" (Gal 3:27–28)

In his letter to the church at Galatia, Paul writes: "As many of you as were baptized into Christ have clothed yourselves with Christ. There is no longer Jew or Greek, there is no longer slave or free, there is no longer male and female; for all of you are one in Christ Jesus."[40] Modern scholars believe that the last words of this passage are a quote from an ancient baptismal formula used in the Early Church.[41] Baptism into Christ is a theological act that not only erases cultural identity markers, but heralds one's participation in a new creation. Immediately prior to this declaration, Paul announces that he has been crucified with Christ and that it is no longer he who lives, but Christ who lives in him.[42] For Paul, baptism marks this new life that Christians live in the flesh, a life that has been recapitulated by Christ in contrast to Adam and echoed as the second/last Adam.[43]

Marriage and the Resurrection
(Mk 12:18–25, Mt 22:23–33, and Lk 20:27–40)

A second passage from the synoptic gospels provides another vital theme for patristic reflection. In this account, the Sadducees approach Jesus with a riddle. According to Mosaic Law, if a man dies childless, his brother is to marry the deceased's wife to produce an heir. In the Sadducees' scenario, this process of levirate marriage continues through a family of seven brothers, each of whom marries the same woman and dies without producing an heir. The Sadducees ask Jesus, "In the resurrection, then, whose wife of the seven will she be?"[44] Jesus responds in part by saying, ". . . in the resurrection they neither marry nor are given in marriage but are like angels in heaven." The text of Luke goes on to say, "Indeed, they cannot die anymore, because they are like the angels and are children (*huioi*, literally "sons") of God, being children (*huioi*) of the resurrection."[45] The comparison between resurrected humans and angels (who are considered to be sexless) is often cited in patristic reflections, as well as the ongoing debates among Orthodox theologians that we will examine in chapter 3.

Patristic Reflections

Within the patristic sources, I group texts around five themes. The first group of texts uses traditionally masculine imagery and terms as a way of symbolizing women's movement toward spiritual perfection. The second series of texts uses Greek grammatical gender to ascribe positive and negative attributes to masculinity and femininity, respectively, often in relation to the divisions of the soul borrowed from Platonism. The third group of texts tends to convey a sense of equality between men and women, including common struggles and common rewards. A fourth group of Greek texts suggests either a full erasure of sexual difference or an annulment of its current purposes and consequences. However, a significant minority report in which bodies are sexed from the beginning and in the eschaton appears in both the Latin and, to a lesser extent, Syriac traditions. The final group of texts spans authors East and West to explore the origins of the human soul with particular emphasis on traducianism, or the idea that a human child receives not only body, but also soul from her parents, opening interesting avenues for the discussion of gender. Some readers may wish to skim these sections, returning to attentive reading at the section titled, "Forward with the Fathers."

Before proceeding, a word of caution is in order. In grouping these texts together under five major headings, I have sought to identify major recurring themes. However, the very act of grouping can lead to unintended effects. Unless noted below, I am not implying dependence between texts within a category. As we will see, patristic authors write in different geographic, linguistic, and cultural contexts, responding to different questions. As these writers enter dialogue with the broader philosophical tradition of their education, biblical texts, and commentaries on scripture, each offers both moments of continuity with the various received traditions as well as new directions. Keeping this in mind will help the reader to avoid oversimplifying what are a wide variety of contexts.

Masculine Spiritual Perfection

As noted above, the association of positive moral traits with men and negative traits with women has a long tradition in the ancient world, presented in our survey first in texts by Plato and Philo. This trend also appears in various biblical and early extra-canonical texts.[46] The turn of the first millennium was replete with such imagery, along with suggestions that women might become men through the embodiment of manly virtues. The Gospel of Thomas tells of Christ making Mary Magdalene into a man.[47] At the turn of the third century, Clement of Alexandria suggests that the "gnostic" woman (meaning here a Christian seeker of knowledge) is translated into a man when she becomes unfeminine, manly, and perfect.[48] Such imagery remains consistent across both Greek and Latin traditions for several centuries. In the diary she left at her death, the martyr Perpetua (d. 203 CE) recounts a dream. In preparation for the contest of the arena, she is stripped naked and becomes a man. Her entourage then rubs her down with oil (common practice for sports, but also symbolic of anointing) before she enters the arena to wrestle not against wild beasts, but against the Devil himself.[49] These passages are not to be taken literally, but rather as expressions of allegorical or spiritual states.

In the fourth century, Cappadocian theological writings are also replete with this sort of gender-bending imagery.[50] In his encomium on Julitta, Basil of Caesarea speaks of the martyr's "most manly (*andreiotatēn*) struggle."[51] Gregory Nazianzen writes of his mother and role model Nonna that she was "a woman in body, but in her way of life more than a man."[52] Gregory of Nyssa asserts that each of us can choose between a female birth into "the material and passionate disposition" or a male birth into "the austerity and intensity of virtue."[53] Such a life is available to all who will undertake the ascetic struggle, regardless of their bodily sex. In his biography of his sister Macrina, Nyssen deliberates the appropriateness of calling Macrina a woman, "naming her for her female nature when she came to be above nature."[54] In subsequent passages, Gregory describes Macrina lying upon her deathbed—a pair of planks covered in sackcloth—calmly facing her death.[55] In contrast Gregory describes himself, along with the young women of the convent, giving themselves over completely to crying, wailing, and lamentations at the moment of Macrina's death—actions that Gregory and the women know the stern Macrina would not have approved of were she still alive.[56] John Chrysostom also follows the well-established pattern of describing several women who in martyrdom acquired a manly spirit (*andreia*). He tells us that Pelagia is "Of course, a woman in gender and sex, but in heart a man,"[57] while Drosis and other women like her "are made manly" (*andrizōntai*) in martyrdom.[58] Domnina, together with her daughters Bernice and Prosdoce, Chrysostom writes, possessed "the spirits of men" in facing their martyrdom even though they were in the bodies of women.[59] In the Latin tradition, Augustine expresses a similar association of virtue with masculinity in his sermons commemorating Perpetua and Felicitas. He praises the "manly spirit" (virilis animus) that acted in the weaker sex.[60] Recalling the "neither male nor female" of Gal 3:28, he extols the virtue of Perpetua's mind "that conceals the sex of her flesh."[61]

However, the valuing of masculine imagery for the perfected human is not universal. The Syriac tradition, under the strong influence of encratism, holds that Adam and Eve were not sexual beings until after their expulsion from Eden. In the waters of baptism, Christians return to a state in which there is neither male nor female. Echoing the passage in Gal 3:28, along with bridal imagery found throughout the New Testament, Aphrahat writes: "There will be neither male nor female, servant or free, but all are children of the Most High, all are pure virgins betrothed to Christ, their lamps shining out there as they enter the bridal chamber together with the Bridegroom."[62] This imagery of virgins betrothed to Christ is common in Syriac texts, carrying forward into the many writings of Ephrem the Syrian.[63] Such descriptions of virgin souls in the eschaton are both a return to the original purity of Eden and an echo of the Jewish metaphor portraying Judah and Israel as the wives of God. This conjugal imagery carries into the New Testament portrayal of the Church as the Bride of Christ.

Allegorical Interpretations of Grammatical Gender

In the second grouping of texts that I am proposing, there is a very strong link in the tradition between the idea of grammatically gendered language and divisions within the individual human being. For example, the intellect (nous) is characterized as male, while the bodily portion that perceives through the senses (aisthēsis) is characterized as female. Likewise, within Philonic and patristic appropriations of Plato's chariot metaphor, the two halves of the soul (psychē) are often characterized in masculine and feminine terms. This distinction, abetted by the grammatical gender of the Greek nouns, is played upon by several of the authors within our survey.

While discussing the Gospel according to the Egyptians,[64] Clement tells us that the "male and female" of Gal 3:28 denote temper and desire, which are overcome by means of penitence and shame, uniting spirit (pneuma) and soul (psychē) in obedience to the Word.[65] Origen also presents an allegorical interpretation in Homilies on Genesis in which the inner man consists of a male spirit and female soul (ex spiritu et anima constat).[66] When the spirit and soul live in harmony, they produce sons (good inclinations) and over-come the flesh. But if the soul seeks after bodily pleasures and abandons the spirit, "she" will be condemned by God as a shameless harlot, and her sons will be led to the slaughter.[67] Origen's description of the lack of unity between the spirit and soul of the inner man echoes the Philonic appro-priation of Plato's chariot metaphor, with the higher-minded spirit and the soul whose ardor for God has cooled as analogous to the white and black horses, respectively.[68]

Among the Latin fathers, Ambrose echoes this same gendered schema in his *On Paradise*.[69] Introducing the Greek terms *aisthēsis* for sense perception and *nous* for intellect/mind,[70] the bishop of Milan refers to Philo by name as he writes, "The serpent is a type of the pleasures of the body. The woman stands for our senses and the man for our minds. Pleasure stirs the senses, which, in turn, have their effect on the mind."[71] While short-lived in the West, this allegorical schema of feminine weakness and masculine strength has a very long life in the Greek tradition, settling into a pattern of repeated references to the grammatically feminine *epithymia* (translated variously as "sexual desire," "desire," "concupiscence") and grammatically masculine *thymos* (translated as "anger," "temper," "spirit," "high-spirit," "irascibility") in the work of theologians for many successive generations. In many cases, the original allegorical link to Adam and Eve eventually drops from con-sciousness even as the grammatical and allegorical gendering continues.

In the Cappadocian tradition, the chariot metaphor is finally put to rest in Gregory of Nyssa's *On the Soul and the Resurrection* by the author's older sister, Macrina. In the dialogue, Gregory asks for clarification of the nature of desire and anger in the human being. Are they, along with the intellect, members among a multitude of souls in the human? In response to Greg-ory's question, Macrina declares that there are many opinions offered on this matter, but the burdens of the theologian place certain constraints on constructive theology:

> But although some could theorize freely concerning the soul as the consequence of their reasoning led them, we have no part in this free-dom (I mean the freedom to say whatever we want), since we always use the Holy Scripture as the canon and rule of all our doctrine. So, we must necessarily look towards this standard and accept only that which is congruent with the sense of the writings. Therefore, we shall abandon the Platonic chariot and the pair of horses yoked to it, which

pulled unequally, and the charioteer controlling these horses, through all of which Plato presents symbolically a philosophy concerning these faculties in relation to the soul.[72]

Here we find Macrina explicitly stating the principle of the primacy of scripture over philosophical constructs or experience as a guide for theological reflection. Macrina's insistence on the bible as the "canon and rule" reflects a Christian challenge to a cultural context steeped in Platonic metaphysics and allegorical imagery. In the shadow of Nicaea, the standards for orthodox dogma had begun to take shape, turning to the Bible as an authority over the appeal to Platonic philosophy, including texts hearkening back to preexistent, chariot-riding souls.

In her subsequent exposition, Macrina explains that desire and anger are impulses of the soul. They are neither good nor bad. When they are ruled by the intellect, they turn the human soul toward God. She closes by alluding to the images of the desire of Daniel and the anger of Phineas.[73] The latter echoes Origen's description of the scene in which the priest Phineas kills an Israelite man engaged in sex with a Midianite woman: "The earthly food of anger, therefore, becomes our food when we use it rationally for righteousness. . . . We must think likewise also about concupiscence and the individual affections of this kind. For when 'our soul longs for the living God and faints,' concupiscence is our food."[74]

Macrina's injunction that theologians abandon the chariot metaphor only goes so far. While the overt allusion disappears, Evagrius of Pontus takes up the allegorical division of the human soul into feminine concupiscible (*epithymia*) and masculine irascible (*thymos*) parts in his *On Thoughts*. For the desert monk these qualities are brought into submission through ascetic practice:

A human being cannot drive away impassioned memories unless he takes care for *his concupiscible part and his irascible part*, exhausting the former with fasts, vigils, and sleeping on the ground, and calming the latter with patience, freedom from resentment, and almsgiving. . . . In this way the new self is formed, renewed "according to the image of its Creator," in whom, on account of holy impassibility, "*there is no male and female*"; in whom, on account of the one faith and love, there is "neither Greek nor Jew, circumcision nor uncircumcision, barbarian nor Scythian, slave nor freeman, but Christ is all in all."[75]

Here again we find the juxtaposition between the Genesis creation narrative in the allusion to the image of the Creator and the new creation in Christ of Galatians in which the image contains no male and female. Echoing the explanation found in Clement's earlier work, an allegorical reading of the "male" and "female" of Gal 3:28 symbolizes the passions of irascibility and concupiscence, respectively.[76] This Evagrian allegorization of Gal 3:28 will come up again below when we turn to Maximus Confessor.

In the Latin tradition, Augustine advances his own allegorical reading of the sexes, similar to the dichotomy between masculine intellect (*nous*) and feminine sensation (*aisthēsis*) of the Greek tradition. In what is to become a life-long, evolving theme within his work, the future bishop of Hippo proposes that the mind of each human being is divided into two parts. In his *On Genesis: A Refutation of the Manicheans*, Augustine adopts the Philonic and Origenian division of masculine reason versus feminine desire or appetite of the soul.[77] Recalling Adam's declaration "this is bone of my bone, flesh of my flesh," Augustine moves beyond Philo's original allegory to suggest that the bone from which God fashions the woman represents fortitude, while the flesh represents temperance, both characteristics derived from Adam.[78]

A decade later, while reflecting again on the creation account of Genesis 1, Augustine offers a differently formulated male/female allegorical division in his *Confessions*.[79] As he wraps up his reflections in the final chapter, he writes that the human is created in the image of God. The human soul (*anima*) includes a mind (*mens*) that in turn includes two forces: a feminine rational action that is subject to the superiority of masculine intellect.[80]

Following his *Confessions*, Augustine returns once again to the creation narrative in *The Literal Meaning of Genesis*.[81] Here he again attributes a male/female division to the human mind. He tackles the suggestion that Gn 1:27 refers to the creation of the human spirit, while Gn 2:27 refers to the creation of the physical body.[82] Augustine points out that human beings are sexed as men and women in body only. However, he then shifts his focus, alluding to "the most subtle arguments," which suggest that an upper, directing part of the mind is tasked with "the contemplation of eternal truth," while a lower, conforming part is responsible for "the management of temporal affairs." These are, in turn, characterized as male and female. He further argues that only the upper mind, "which clings in contemplation to the unchangeable Truth," can be considered created in the image of God. The lower mind, having forsaken such contemplation in order to care for worldly concerns, is only included in the *imago dei* when taken *in toto* with the higher.[83] To justify his reading, Augustine appeals to 1 Cor 11:17, where Paul writes: "For a man ought not to have his head veiled, since he is the image (*eikōn*) and reflection[84] of God; but woman is the reflection of man." On the surface, this passage appears to claim that only man (*anēr*) is created in the image of God, while woman (*gynē*) is another step removed, created in the image of man. As Augustine returns to this theme later in the same text, he is not yet satisfied with the argument, which he now suggests without attribution as the idea of another author.[85]

Augustine offers his fullest exposition of the gendered hierarchy of the human rational mind in *On the Trinity*.[86] Broadening his argument beyond the original context of the creation narrative to focus on the effects of the fall, he suggests that the "outer man" is the corporeal body that humans possess in common with animals, while the "inner man" is the rational mind (*mens*). Again, he subdivides the rational mind into wisdom (*sapientia*) and knowledge (*scientia*). The former clings to "the intelligible and unchanging Truth," while the other is "deputed to the task of dealing with and controlling . . . lower matters." Using Gn 2:20 as an exegetical lens, Augustine argues that just as no helper was found for Adam among the animals, necessitating a helper be derived from his own body, so also his mind is divided so that his helper might handle the affairs of this world. As Genesis notes that "they shall be two in one flesh," so also shall these two parts be in one mind.[87] Once again he offers his reading of 1 Cor 11, introduced in *The Literal Meaning of Genesis*, to defend women as also being created in the image of God. Considering his somewhat convoluted reasoning, it is better to quote from his argument at length:

> Why is it then that "the man (*vir*) ought not to cover his head because he is the image and glory of God" (1 Cor 11:7), while the woman ought to because "she is the glory of the man," as though the woman were not being renewed in the spirit of her mind, which is "being renewed for the recognition of God according to the image of him who created him" (Col 3:10)? Well, it is only because she differs from the man in the sex of her body that her bodily covering could suitably be used to symbolize that part of the reason which is diverted to the management of temporal things, signifying that the mind of man does not remain the image of God except in the part which adheres to the eternal ideas to contemplate or consult them: and it is

clear that females have this as well as males. So, in their minds a common nature is to be acknowledged; but in their bodies the distribution of the one mind is symbolized.[88]

Augustine's argument boils down to an arbitrary distinction. The male-sexed body is considered unmarked (neutral, normative), while the female body, carved from Adam's flesh, is *not-man* (*vir*). Having established this symbolic pair, Augustine vests the man with pointing to the upper mind and the woman with pointing to the lower. However, there is no intrinsic reason for this distinction, as each human (*homo*) possesses both elements of the mind that he wishes to symbolize.

Concluding Book XIV, Augustine returns to his newly introduced reading of Gn 2:20 to explain his rejection of the allegorical mind/senses distinction that his mentor Ambrose had adopted from the Greek tradition. Because the senses (*aisthēsis/corporis sensa*) are common to both humans and animals, he cannot reconcile the female/sensation allegorical reading with the biblical declaration that no suitable helper for Adam could be found among the animals. His solution is to assign both male and female allegorically to the rational mind, the part of the human being created in the image of God, which the animals do not possess, to highlight the woman's unique qualification as helper. Thus, over a span of thirty years, Augustine fully develops his own argument whereby he (1) dispenses with Origenian allegory as a fitting mode of reading for the creation narrative, (2) defends women as also being created in the image of God as found in Gn 1:27, (3) allegorizes the seeming contradiction in Paul's argument in 1 Cor 11 to reaffirm that women share in the image of God, (4) affirms the regeneration of both women's and men's minds in the waters of baptism per Gal 3:26–28, and (5) offers an alternative to what he sees, in light of Gn 2:20, as a flawed allegorical reading embraced by Philo, Ambrose, and the many authors of the Greek patristic tradition.[89]

Equality of the Sexes in the Practice of Virtue

Turning to my third proposed grouping of gendered themes, we return to the second century. Clement of Alexandria develops the theme of equality among the sexes as both men and women move toward the same eschatological goal. He does so by building on the synoptic gospel teaching on marriage and the resurrection discussed above. In *The Instructor*, Clement

writes that men and women alike are under the Instructor's charge: they
have the same virtue, the same God and master, the same Church, the same
temperance and modesty, the same marriage yoke. For Clement, the only
difference between them is that the man marries while the woman is given
in marriage. "But in that age," he continues, "it is no longer so. There, the
rewards of this common and holy life, which is based on conjugal union,
are laid up, not for males and females, but for the human (*anthrōpos*); the
sexual desire (*epithymia*) which divides humanity is laid aside. Indeed,
the name 'human' (*anthrōpos*) is common to both men and women."[90]
For Clement, humanity is currently divided specifically based on sexual
desire between the sexes.[91] Unlike the encratists whom he wrote against,
Clement advocates for marriage and having children as the means for
spreading the Church. However, sexual union has a time and place. In his
Miscellanies, Clement describes the dispassionate state toward which the
"gnostic" man should strive once his children are born. He should think
of his wife as he would a sister. Once they put off their flesh, they become
as siblings with one Father. Souls, Clement tells us, are neither male nor
female. And, again, they no longer marry nor are they given in marriage
after this life.[92] Here there are echoes of Philo's first man, beyond the limitations of male and female, as well as allusions to Jesus's words to the
Sadducees concerning the affairs of the risen dead. But there is also a Stoic
influence in Clement's urbane sensibilities.[93] For Clement, the goal of the
elite, "gnostic" Christian, who pursues deeper spiritual learning, is to realize
the ungendered state of the soul through dedication to rigorous ascesis.
Those who accept this challenge live into an inaugurated eschatology, embodying spiritual truths that will be fully revealed in the resurrection. As we
have already seen, Clement believes that the Christian woman is called to
become like a man. However, both men and women are called to put aside
their (sexual) passions as they continue in their spiritual development.[94]

Reference to the angelic life would later become a staple of Christianity, as bishops of the Church argued for a cessation of the regular activities
of marriage and raising children. The virgins of the monasteries would live
consecrated lives within the inaugurated eschaton, examples of the angelic
life that is to come. Basil of Caesarea, who separated the men and women
of his monastic communities for the sake of chastity, nonetheless prescribed
the same spiritual practices for them all, regardless of bodily sex: "I wish
you to know that we rejoice to have assemblies of both men and women,
whose conversation is in heaven and who have crucified the flesh with the

affections and lusts thereof; they take no thought for food and raiment, but remain undisturbed beside their Lord, continuing night and day in prayer."[95] For Basil, the ascetic struggles of men and women alike bring the same bodily passions under submission, leading both monks and nuns into the same divine-human communion.

Yet there are subtle differences in the rhetoric employed by Clement and that of Basil and his contemporaries some two centuries later. Clement calls for all Christian husbands and wives to procreate (in opposition to his encratistic opponents), while also mastering their passions. Later, as Christianity becomes a licit religion and Genesis becomes the pattern for imperial society, the life of angels exemplified in the monastic communities of the Cappadocians entrusts only a few with the role of eschatological harbingers. Other subtle changes also occur. Virginia Burrus has noted that after Nicaea, which defined two persons of the Trinity without reference to any female deity as the Father and his only begotten Son, the parameters for what defines Christian manhood also change. In earlier Greco-Roman culture, masculinity was first conceived of as a public performance under constant evaluation. To be a man required being gendered as a male: a male body, but also male disposition, the superior in every relationship with non-men (women, slaves, children, and barbarians). A man controls his passions, appetites, and desires. And manliness is also equated with both courage and moral integrity.[96] But the language of manliness takes new directions with the advent of Nicaea. Burrus traces the separation of the language of begetting from the biological wombs of mothers. Along with God the Father who begets his only Son before all ages, new metaphors of begetting arise, separating orthodox Christians as "sons of Christ" from heretics like Arius and his sons, no longer known as Christians but as heretical Arians.[97] Among the Cappadocian fathers, new ideals of what it means to be a man also appear. While previous ideals focused on obligations to society and family, Basil of Caesarea paints a picture of manhood that withdraws from the public sphere, from obligations to society and family, and the renunciation of fame. Instead, Basil's portrait of manliness includes voluntary poverty and manual labor.[98] Likewise, Gregory of Nyssa can become more manly through the emulation of his sister Macrina, Nyssen's response to the dying Socrates of the *Phaedo*. Following Athanasius's imagery of an orthodoxy in which men beget legitimate sons through a succession of right belief, Gregory portrays himself as a spiritual son of his older brother, Basil. Burrus's exploration of Nyssen's *Against Eunomius* emphasizes Basil as a promiscuous giver of generosity (through his teachings), sowing in the wombs of unproven souls. Eunomius fails to bring forth proper spiritual fruit. In contrast, Burrus suggests that Gregory knows how to make himself just enough of a woman to receive Basil's word into the womb of his mind and to conceive and bring forth a proper theological word, thereby establishing his manhood.[99] With the incorporation of birth and submission to legitimate masculine authority (e.g., God the Father, the Christian mentor), the images used by the Cappadocians differ from earlier conceptions of virtue and manliness in ways that appropriate traditional feminine aspects. Matthew Kuefler suggests a similar shift in what it means to be a man within the Latin tradition. While Burrus's account tends toward an interior reconceptualization of masculinity, Kuefler considers the material realities of the decline of Roman military might in the shift to interior spiritual battles fought by soldiers of Christ and the recasting of lowliness as brides of Christ to signify virtue.[100]

Erasure or Annulment of the Physical Division of the Sexes

In my final proposed grouping of textual themes, the nonessential nature of sexual difference is picked up again in the works of Gregory of Nyssa. In his *On the Soul and the Resurrection*, he explores the motif of the "garments of skin" that God provides for Adam and Eve once they have discovered that they are naked.[101] In the text, Macrina teaches that the skins are an irrational addition to the human intellect: "These are the things which are received from the irrational skin: sexual intercourse, conception, childbearing, dirt, lactation, nourishment, evacuation, gradual growth to maturity, the prime of life, old age, disease, and death."[102] It is these irrational skins which the human sheds at death, returning to its pristine, original state. Gregory's interpretation differs from Clement's, in that he does not call for an earthly spiritual progression that leads to a cessation of sexual activity. In his own context, while celibacy is still a privileged state, the defense of conjugal relations within Christian marriage has become an issue. Rather, he points to a future, eschatological state in which human frailties will no longer exist.

Gregory returns to the division of the sexes in *On the Making of the Human Being*. Here, he puzzles over the idea that the human is created in the image of God and is also created both male and female. While Gregory appropriates portions of Plato's creation accounts, his redeployment of themes from *Symposium* reflect a highly Christianized understanding that rejects several key elements of the original story.[103] Concerning the latter statement, Gregory writes: "I presume that everyone knows that this is a departure from the Prototype: for 'in Christ Jesus,' as the apostle says, 'there is neither male nor female.'"[104] Gregory's commitment to the Galatian declaration of "no male or female in Christ"[105] appears to contradict the narrative in Gn 1:27b where God creates the human as male and female. In his attempt to reconcile these two passages, he appropriates the idea of a double creation. However, rather than strictly focusing on the two creation accounts of Gn 1–2, Gregory redeploys the idea to harmonize the two statements in Gn 1:27 with his own commitments to a strictly non-anthropomorphic doctrine of God. Gregory offers a theodicy to explain why human beings experience this life in corruptible, sexed bodies, even as scripture begins with the claim that humans are created in the image of God— a God that Christian tradition teaches is beyond the categories of male and female.

Gregory proposes that humanity in its current form inhabits a middle space between brute animals and the divine. Though in the Genesis narrative the human receives the intellect (in the image of God) prior to the animal nature, the latter is provided to humans for procreation in God's foreknowledge of humanity's coming fall.[106] Rejecting the Origenian allegorical reading of God's command to increase and multiply, Nyssen argues, ". . . He bestowed on man (*anthrōpos*) the power of increasing and multiplying; but when He divided it by sexual distinctions, then He said, 'Increase and multiply, and replenish the earth.' For this belongs not to the Divine, but to the irrational element, as the history indicates when it narrates that these words were first spoken by God in the case of the irrational creatures. . . ."[107]

Gregory goes on to suggest that once the foreordained complement (*plērōma*) of human souls is produced through sexual generation, this age will end. Citing 1 Cor 15:51–52, he asserts that the dead will be resurrected in glory, while those who are still alive when the last trumpet sounds will be changed in the twinkling of an eye, taking on the bodies promised with the Parousia.[108] The resurrection will be a restoration to humanity's prelapsarian state, which Gregory argues must resemble that of the angels, based on his reading of the synoptic gospel teaching on marriage and the afterlife.[109] The division of the sexes and marriage in Gregory's treatise are often interpreted as the Plan B of creation, fulfilling God's plan for the full complement of humanity without overriding free will or the sinful inclinations of the human heart. Two factors are involved in this reading. First, Gregory proposes that were it not for humanity's fall into sin, we could have reached our full complement in an ineffable manner like angels. For they, too, are a multitude, yet they neither have sexed bodies nor procreate in the manner of animals. Second, a synthetic reading that combines the "garments of skin" motif from *On the Soul and the Resurrection* with Nyssen's discussion of the animal nature in the current text creates the view that in our eschatological embodiment, a variety of changes will take place. Gregory's readers have interpreted those changes variously from a cessation of sexual activity to the erasure of sexedness altogether. While in the current text Nyssen suggests that humanity will be freed from the heaviness of the flesh and that we will no longer be dependent on physical food, Macrina's full list of human frailties from which resurrected humans will be freed is not discussed here.[110] John Behr argues that what Gregory suggests will end with the eschaton is marriage, which in the text stands in as a shorthand for procreation, driven by fear of death, through which one generation produces the next.[111] Other Orthodox theologians have understood Gregory to say that our resurrected bodies will no longer be sexed at all.[112] As none of us has yet to experience our resurrected bodies, the point remains purely speculative.

Elements of Gregory's treatise on human sexual differentiation reappear in the Greek tradition in the works of John Chrysostom, Maximus Confessor, and John of Damascus, and in the Latin tradition in John Scottus Eriugena. However, each theologian uses Gregory's original claims differently, pushing Nyssen's ideas in entirely new directions.

In his *On Virginity*, John Chrysostom echoes Gregory's ideas about the original lack of sexual intercourse among humans; however, in an interesting departure from his source material, Chrysostom assumes that male and female were a part of God's original plan, even before the need of sexual intercourse for human reproduction. Championing the contemporary push for virginity within the Church, Chrysostom suggests that even before the fall, Adam had need of a helper. Only after their expulsion from paradise did "desire for sexual intercourse, conception, labor, childbirth and every form of corruption" enter the world.[113] He follows Gregory's earlier conjecture that humanity could have reached its full complement without childbirth, suggesting the angelic model of multiplication to replace human reliance on sexual procreation.[114] On a final interesting note, Chrysostom claims that there are sufficient humans on the earth in his time to exclude the birth of new children as a reason for marriage, a moment we will return to in chapter 6 in our discussion of the sacrament of marriage.[115]

As previously noted, Gregory dispenses with the original double-man and double-woman of Plato's *Symposium*, while retaining the opposite-sexed couple, redeployed in God's plan for populating the postlapsarian world. The original Platonic motif becomes much clearer in Maximus Confessor's appropriation of Nyssen's work. In *Difficulties* 41, Maximus writes that the human is introduced into the world as the last of all created beings. It is tasked to serve as a kind of natural bond (*syndesmos tis physikos*) that mediates between the divisions of nature (Uncreated/Created, Intelligible/Sensible, Heaven/Earth, Paradise/Inhabited World, and Male/Female), uniting them into a whole while preserving the distinctiveness of the parts. In terms of the fifth division, the human is to eschew all natural distinctions between male and female by means of a "dispassionate disposition to divine virtue."[116] However, contrary to plan, humanity turns its desire toward created things rather than the uncreated God. Consequently, the human's bonding properties are compromised, resulting in a loss of cohesion between the various divisions of the created order. While the rejection of the gods in Aristophanes's account results in the punishment of human persons, Maximus's account of human rebellion has consequences for the entire created order. To correct the problem God "institutes the natures anew," becoming human to restore the corrupted bonds.[117] In his reinstituted human nature, Jesus Christ has no need of marriage (synonymous with procreation). By his birth from a virgin, he demonstrates a different and ineffable method of human increase that does not require sexual intercourse. "There was no necessity for these things to have lasted forever," he tells us. "*For in Christ Jesus,* says the divine Apostle, *there is neither male nor female.*"[118]

While Maximus uses Gal 3:28 as a biblical proof-text for his assertion that there is no longer male and female in Christ, a simultaneous, allegorical reading is also possible. Maximus is an heir to the Evagrian tradition of associating the grammatically feminine concupiscible and the grammatically masculine irascible parts of the soul with respective female and male gender characteristics, as well as the anthropology of Gregory's *On the Creation of the Human Being*. Thus, his allusion to Gal 3:28 can easily be read as an appropriation and synthetic redeployment of the Nyssen and Evagrian traditions in a single statement. Lars Thunberg suggests that what is truly at stake for Maximus in the declaration that there is no longer male and female in Christ is not sexedness *per se*, but the negative modes of activity (or to use Maximian terminology, the *tropoi*) of the irascible and concupiscent passions of the human being.[119] Such a reading is reminiscent of Macrina's claim in Gregory's *On the Soul and the Resurrection*, in which the two faculties are deemed good when they are used to turn the soul toward God. In similar fashion, Maximus sees the end of the ascetic struggle as realized in Christ when the passions are realigned to an ardor for God that binds the human to the Creator. However, unlike Macrina, who is concerned with the faculties of the soul, the inclusion of the Evagrian tradition would give Maximus a double meaning. It is clear enough when Maximus states, "There was no need for these things to have lasted forever," that he envisions an end to the division of the sexes.[120] But as an heir and reformer of the Evagrian tradition, could he not also be aware of the monk's novel allegorical reading as Thunberg suggests? Such a reading complicates the idea of a straightforward appropriation by Maximus of Gregory's original speculative theology regarding the origin of the sexes, assigning new meanings to the "male and female" of Gal 3:28 as they are repurposed to symbolize passions within the human soul. It further adds texture to our survey, highlighting another rupture in meaning between the various deployments of gendered tropes within the tradition. Some contemporary Orthodox theologians point to Nyssen's *On the Making of the Human Being* and its long reception in the Greek patristic tradition to suggest something akin to a *consensus patrum*.[121] However, as this genealogical trace indicates, Gregory's anthropology is received, understood, and redeployed by subsequent theologians in a variety of ways. When we briefly examine the Latin and Syriac traditions, we will also discover that when all three strands are taken together, the variety of teachings and images belies any sort of common teaching among the fathers that one might propose when highlighting only a particular Greek line of thought. These divergent interpretations are often smoothed over in contemporary Orthodox theology when clergy and scholars assert a uniformity that begins with "the fathers say" when, in fact, the fathers say many different and contradictory things.

In his *The Orthodox Faith*, John of Damascus synthesizes many of the thinkers who came before him. The Damascene first mentions the sexual differentiation of the human being in contradistinction to the Godhead: "Now, it is obvious that man (*ho anthrōpos*) begets in quite another manner, since he is subject to birth and death and flux and increase, and since he is clothed with a body and has the male and female in his (physical) nature—for the male has need of the female's help (*boētheias*, from the same root explored above)."[122] John appropriates Gregory's earlier theme of God's foreknowledge of the fall and providential plan for the fulfillment of the human race. Only this time, rather than couching Gregory's words as speculation, they take on the full force of doctrine. His new synthesis also carries echoes of the Creator/Craftsman (*ho dēmiourgos*) found as far back as Plato's *Timaeus* as well as the woman's role as helper. In an interesting departure from Nyssen, Chrysostom, and Maximus, the Damascene's explanation of the Orthodox faith explicitly claims that the Creator fashioned the first human (*anthrōpon*) as male (*arrena*), even before the fashioning of a female to provide his aid.[123] He differs from Nyssen and Chrysostom by stopping short of suggesting that an analog to angelic multiplication is the key.[124] But most interestingly, in contrast to Gregory, John claims that male and female are part of what it means to be human from the outset. Gregory's quandary regarding the two statements of Genesis in which the image of God is mentioned next to the creation of male and female appears to be of no concern for the Damascene.

The line of thought begun by Gregory of Nyssa and augmented by Maximus finds a home in the Latin tradition in the work of Johannes Scottus Eriugena.[125] In his *The Division of Nature*, the Irishman attempts to seriously think through the consequences of shedding the garments of skin in the resurrection, coming to a novel conception of what it would mean to be neither male nor female. Following Gregory, Eriugena writes that "the Divine History mentions but one Paradise and but one man created in it—though the one man includes both male and female, if the words of the Holy Fathers are to be followed."[126] Borrowing from Maximus, he conceives of a world comprising five divisions and the human being whose purpose was to hold them all together. But while Maximus sees the virgin birth of Christ as the moment at which the division between male and female is abrogated, Eriugena elaborates on Maximus's image of procession and return, identifying not the Nativity, but the Resurrection as the locus of overcoming the division between the sexes.[127] He writes, ". . . the Lord Jesus united in himself the division of (our) nature, that is, male and female. For it was not in the bodily sex but simply in man that He rose from the dead. For in Him there is neither male nor female, although it was in that masculine sex in which He was born of a Virgin and in which He suffered that *he appeared* to His disciples after His resurrection. . . . For otherwise they would not recognize Him if they did not see the shape that was known to them."[128]

In an essay exploring this distinctive elaboration in Eriugena's anthropology, Donald Duclow notes the discomfort experienced by many at the contemplation of a future world without sexual division.[129] Eriugena voices this apprehension through his Alumnus:

> For who is there who, hearing such things, would not be horrified and at once break out in these words: 'Then after the resurrection there will be no sexual division of male [and] female if each is to be totally removed from human nature? Or what form will appear in man if no one has either male or female form? Or what sort of recognition will there be if there is to be an extermination of both sexes and an amalgam of all men, whether spiritual and incorporeal or visible and corporeal (and) circumscribed by place and time, into a simple unification, not divided by *difference of forms?*'[130]

Here the Alumnus sums up not only the fears of those in Eriugena's day, but those of our own day as well when we attempt to challenge gendered norms and the sexual binary.

The Minority Reports: Sexed Bodies in Eden and Heaven

The idea of an originally sexless humanity that was later adapted in light of God's foreknowledge of the fall to produce the full complement of human persons—found in Philo and Gregory of Nyssa along with the subsequent line of Nyssen's interpreters—presents what I will label as the dominant view of sexed bodies within the Greek patristic tradition. Though not a perfect succession of authors, the teaching survives more or less intact from Philo to Gregory of Nyssa's initial suggestions in *On the Making of the Human Being*, to John Chrysostom's and Maximus Confessor's more certain usage, to the Damascene's *Expositio* as a confident confession within the Greek patristic tradition. It also appears later in Eriugena's *The Division of Nature* in the Latin West.[131] We might be tempted to stop here and declare *consensus patrum*. However, further examination of writings both East and West yields two more narratives, minority reports that diverge, each in their own ways, from Gregory's notion of an unsexed protological humanity. In the fourth-century Syriac tradition, we find a distinctive account of the differentiation of the sexes, while in the Latin West the arc of

Augustine of Hippo's theological writing moves from an allegorical reading in the spirit of Philo and Origen to a unique view of prelapsarian and eschatologically sexed bodies. The dialogical communities in which these two figures lived and wrote are separated by time, geography, language, and theological concerns. Yet they share a struggle against the heterodox beliefs of their day which, in both cases, leads to anthropological teachings different from those popular in the Hellenized Christian context.

Ephrem the Syrian (c. 306–373 CE) was born in Nisibis, a town on the eastern frontier of the Roman Empire, home also to a large Jewish community whom he engaged in polemical debate.[132] While the Greek and Latin fathers continued in the vein of Philo, translating the thought world of the Hebrew Scriptures into the vocabulary and conceptual frameworks of contemporary Greco-Roman philosophy, Ephrem's worldview shares much more in common with the images and concepts of rabbinic thought.[133] His biblical commentaries, teaching hymns, and verse homilies make extensive use of Semitic poetic imagery. In the final decade of his life, Ephrem relocated to Edessa, where he discovered that the group known as Christians were Marcionites and the Nicene adherents were known as Palutians (after their bishop). The city was also home to factions of Bardaisians (who espoused astrology along with a more Nicene Christianity), Arians, and Manicheans.[134] Many of Ephrem's works are written as corrections to the teachings of these groups. He adopted the popular musical form of the *madrāšê*—first used by Mani, Bardaisan, and his son Harmonius—for spreading his teachings.[135] Thus, the dialogical community within the Syriac church was enriched through the selective incorporation and redeployment of both theological motifs and mediums of transmission in its continuing interactions with other groups vying with Nicene Christianity.

Among the images of the rabbinic midrashim on Genesis that Ephrem and others borrowed is the trope of Adam as an androgyne.[136] Interpreting Gn 1:27 with Gn 2:21–25 in mind, he suggests that, when the text reads "male and female created he them," the author is signaling that Eve exists already within Adam. Ephraim asserts that Eve was in Adam's body, soul, and spirit, but not in his mind.[137] They share their various components in common yet are separate entities. In his subsequent commentary on Gn 2:21–22, Ephrem plays on the two meanings of Adam as humanity and individual. Adam "was both one and two" when God presented him with the finished Eve: "He was one in that he was Adam and he was two because he had been created male and female."[138] Moving from prose to song, Ephrem writes in one *madrāšâ* that "Before Eve, there was a complete body, without division."[139] In another hymn he portrays Eve as "the vine-shoot from Adam/man," who "grew from itself and through itself."[140] Ephrem's emphasis on Eve's physical, psychical, and spiritual presence as a part of the unitary being of the original Adam/human goes beyond Greek and Latin descriptions that focus only on the rib/side.[141] Finally, in an argument against the Arians, Ephrem suggests that Eve's title of "the mother of all the living" is symbolic, pointing to the three names of the Godhead, unity within a diversity of persons.[142] While the Greeks resort to categories of essence (*ousia*) and *hypostasis*, Ephrem uses biblical imagery to create an analogy between Eve, who contains within herself all other human persons, and the Godhead as the union of Trinitarian Persons.[143] We will revisit the images of vine-shoot and Eve as totality of the living below. For now, Ephrem provides a different story: an androgynous original human who is subsequently divided into male and female individuals with no reference to the fall.

Turning to the Latin West, we have already seen Augustine's allegorical interpretation of the gendered, rational mind. In terms of physically sexed bodies, Augustine also differs from Greek theologians. In his earliest work, Augustine's primary purpose was to refute Manicheism, which he had previously embraced. The Manicheans taught that through human procreation incorporeal souls are trapped in physical matter. In addition to their suspicion of physical bodies, they also criticized the stories of the Jewish scriptures, especially the mythological accounts that unfold in the beginning of Genesis. Following the earlier work of Philo and Origen, the Cappadocians had popularized allegorical readings of these scriptures that also became popular in Latin exegesis, particularly with Ambrose. Augustine's early commentary follows this allegorical interpretation in Gn 1:28.[144] But in short order, the tides began to turn.

At the dawn of the fifth century, a series of conflicts arose among Latin Christians resulting in the conflation of the rhetoric of pro-virginity asceticism with the anti-materialist teachings of Manicheism. These conflicts prompted Augustine to offer a series of mitigations that would soften his earlier stance. The bishop of Hippo presents his fullest exposition on human sexual difference in his *City of God*.[145] Revisiting the theme of Gn 2:21–23, Augustine rejects the idea that sexual reproduction is a result of the fall. He suggests instead that in the prelapsarian state, human sexual organs "would have been moved by the will rather than being excited by lust."[146]

Thus, in a way different from all other patristic sources we have examined, Augustine insists that the original human pair were sexed in their bodies from their inception and would have engaged in sexual intercourse for procreation.

When it comes to the eschaton, Augustine also differs from our other authors. In Book XII of *City of God,* Augustine acknowledges that there are those who teach that coming to "complete manhood"[147] and being conformed to "the image of the Son of God"[148] should be taken to mean that women will rise not as females, but as males.[149] Augustine responds that both sexes will be resurrected, without lust or the resultant unruliness of the genital organs. He further declares that physical faults will be removed from women's bodies. Their female organs will still be present, but they will no longer be used for childbirth, a reality that will elicit praise from those who witness both God's creation of women and his subsequent freeing of women from the bondage of corruption.[150] Returning to Mt 22:29–30, the passage on marriage and the resurrection so important to other authors of our survey, Augustine insists that "they shall not marry, nor shall they take wives, but they are like the angels of God in heaven"[151] does not imply a transformation into sexless beings, but rather "they will be equal to the angels in immortality and in felicity, not in flesh or in resurrection, of which the angels had no need since they could not die." He goes on to argue from silence: had Jesus meant that there would be no women in heaven, he could have "easily and quickly addressed the issue by denying the woman's sex."[152] Thus, Augustine argues, only the practice of marriage comes to an end in the eschaton. In response to the suggestion that coming into complete manhood would require women to become men, Augustine picks up the image of the Body of Christ, in which all the redeemed are members with Christ as the head.[153] In this regard, he claims, that woman is included in the naming of man, "taking 'man' (*virum*) to mean 'human being' (*homine*)."[154]

In the final years of his life, Augustine reviewed his extensive oeuvre, amending and clarifying his earlier thoughts. Thus, in his *Retractions,* in reference to his original allegorization of God's command to "increase and multiply," he declared that he could not support any interpretation of Gn 1:28 that would claim that Adam and Eve would not have had children unless they had sinned.[155] Likewise, returning to an earlier claim that human genitals are dishonorable "because they do not have the kind of beauty that those members which are located in full view" possess,[156] he amended his use of Paul's original language, locating the dishonor in their unruliness after the fall, echoing his later explanation from *City of God*.[157] Augustine's theology of sexed bodies both before the fall and in the resurrection offers a second report at variance from the dominant Greek view. Male and female are, for Augustine, neither a divine Plan B nor ephemeral states to be erased in the eschaton. Augustine's views are subsequently repeated through the Latin Christian tradition.

Traducianism

In this final section of our survey, I offer a series of texts in support of traducianism, or the idea that the soul of a child, like its physical body, is derived from its parents. While the dominant view in Roman Catholicism follows instead the doctrine of creationism in which God creates each human soul and unites it with the body, traducianism remains one acceptable *theologoumenon* among others in the Orthodox tradition. In both East and West, the formulations of traducianism and creationism are responses to arguments in Platonism and followed by Origen for the preexistence of souls.[158]

I include traducianism in this survey of theological reflections on biological sex and gender for reasons that will become clearer as my argument progresses in later chapters. For now, I note that traducianism muddies the distinction between two discrete male and female principles as portrayed by some gender essentialists. If both body and soul are passed to a baby as an inheritance from one's father (as the model often portrays), then the case of a father who begets a daughter complicates the idea of an ontological distinction between the male and female principles. A traducian model, comfortable in the one-sex body model that we explored in the previous chapter, instead hypothesizes a common inheritance of flesh and soul for all human beings, regardless of an individual's expression of biological sex.

Traducian texts appear across Christian traditions. In the previous discussion of Ephrem the Syrian, we saw the claim that Eve was originally contained in Adam—body, soul, and spirit. Further, as the "mother of all the living," Eve contained within herself the whole of the future generations of humanity. Ephrem's image follows an agricultural model in which Eve, the vine, arises from Adam and produces the fruit of future generations as a single plant.

In the Greek tradition, Gregory of Nyssa argues against both the preexistence of souls and the creation of bodies that will only later be ensouled.

In his model, a father provides not only what will develop into the human body with its fully articulated limbs, but also the rudiment of the soul. He suggests that body and soul are like seeds or portions of roots taken from live plants.[159] Nyssen also records the rejection by his sister Macrina of the preexistence of the soul, discounting "absurd invented doctrines which settle the souls in the bodies through evil."[160] She argues that the soul and body begin together: "Just as, when the earth receives from the farmer a slip cut off from its root . . . what is separated from a human being for the propagation of a human being is itself also in some way a soul-endowed being from a soul-endowed being, a growing being from a growing being."[161] Though all the faculties of the *nous* are not yet present, they lie in potential in this soul-endowed human scion. Without a soul, the human seed would be dead, unable to produce a new child. Thus, Macrina concludes that "a common transition into being takes place for the compound constituted from both soul and body. The one does not go before, nor the other come later."[162] Gregory of Nazianzus suggests that just as the bodies of all humans exist through a continuous connection to the first body formed from dust, so also all souls are derived from the original inbreathing of God.[163] In his homage to the martyr Julitta, Basil recounts her final words: she is from the same lump (*phyramatos*) as men; of the same race (*sungeneis*) as men in all things.[164] In these various examples, we see that Macrina and the Cappadocian fathers embrace a model in which body and soul together pass from a father to his offspring.

Beyond the Cappadocians, Macarius of Egypt also teaches that fathers beget their children from their own nature, both body and soul.[165] Anastasius of Sinai writes that God endowed Adam with a living soul, but that Eve's soul came from Adam.[166] Traducianism appears early in the Latin tradition in the writings of Tertullian, who insists that both body and soul are conceived and shaped simultaneously. He suggests that the human father passes two kinds of seed, *humor* and *calor*, mixed in the seminal fluid, which produce the body and the soul, respectively. This is sometimes referred to as *corporeal* or *materialistic traducianism*.[167] The soul, originally breathed as vapor into Adam, coalesces within a man's semen and is planted in "their appointed seed-plot" where they "fertilize with their combined vigor the human fruit out of their respective natures." Summarizing his claim, Tertullian writes, "Accordingly from the one (primeval) man comes the entire outflow and redundance of men's souls—nature proving herself true to the commandment of God, 'Be fruitful and multiply.'"[168] Tertullian's model, with its emphasis on calor as a spiritual substance, differs from other forms of traducianism that are less explicit in defining the mechanics of reproduction. However, it follows the same formula in which the souls of women nonetheless are passed from their fathers.

While never coming to a formal decision regarding the origin of the human soul, Augustine turns to the question many times throughout his career. The most protracted discussion of the origin of souls is found in *The Literal Meaning of Genesis*.[169] While he does rule out the sort of materialistic traducianism suggested by Tertullian, as well as the preexistence of souls found in Plato and Origen, the bishop of Hippo is unable to make a firm decision among three other models: *rationes seminales*, creationism, or traducianism.[170] The first option follows Augustine's teaching on the double creation of the world by which the formulas (*rationes*) of all things were created within God simultaneously during an initial episode recounted in the first chapter of Genesis, while the physical realities unfold in what humans perceive as a subsequent flow of time.[171] While Jerome championed creationism, Augustine could not reconcile this view with the declaration in Gn 2:1 heralding the completion of God's creative works at the end of the sixth day. Augustine believed that a strong case can also be made for traducianism that answers several questions in his thought about the transmission of original sin to human offspring. Seeking to be convinced, Augustine wrote to Jerome at Bethlehem, asking the monk to answer a series of questions that would allow him to adopt the creationist view.[172] However, Jerome died without responding. To the very end of his career, Augustine held open the possibilities for each of these three models, never making a final decision.[173]

In each of the patristic sources presented above, traducianism serves as the mechanism for the handing down of both body and soul to further generations of human beings. The transmission is assumed to come from the father, even if his children are female. In our own time, common wisdom about the bodily makeup of children has changed considerably, acknowledging the contributions of genetic material from two parents. And yet, this is not a full picture, either, as we will see in chapter 4. For now, I have included traducianism in this survey of patristic thought because it points to an understanding among the fathers and mothers of a common human nature, shared by all human persons, regardless of sex. This model stands in opposition to discrete, incommensurate male and female principles characteristic of gender essentialism of our own time.

Forward with the Fathers

As we saw in chapter 1, the patristic corpus plays an important role as a primary source for theological reflection within several streams within the Paris School. Yet the transmission and use of patristic texts are complex and often nonlinear. In this chapter, we have seen some instances where particular contexts are characterized by a conceptual framework (or frameworks) and a unique set of theological, philosophical, philological, and cultural resources from which an author selectively draws in the production of further reflections. These reflections in turn may contribute to an ongoing dialogue both between members of the Church as well as in broader cultural contexts. In the process, new theological reflections continue to shape the tradition passed on to future members of the ecclesial community.

The patristic authors surveyed propose a variety of anthropological models. They speculate on the structure of the rational mind, the origin of sexual division, and the nature of resurrected bodies. Their explanations differ in many details. They respond to different problems in their communities (e.g., the role of consecrated virginity, the defense of Christian marriage) and foreground particular concerns (e.g., the theodicy of corruptible bodies, the defense of women created in the image of God). The resulting conversation is messy, discontinuous, and even contradictory. But this is to be expected. Only a naïve misreading of Florovsky's neopatristic synthesis suggests that we are searching for a common core of teaching to elevate as timeless truth. Were this the case, the fathers' own unquestioned acceptance of the superiority of men over women in every realm of life—an idea which most people in contemporary society find unacceptable—would certainly qualify.[174]

Florovsky's own students questioned whether they were supposed to accept everything from the fathers, including ideas that were obviously contextually dependent, inaccurate, inadequate, or just plain wrong. His response is clear: "No. . . . the *consensus patrum* is not binding, nor can the authority of the fathers be construed as a *dictatus papae*." Florovsky describes the patristic sources as "guides and witnesses, no more. Their *vision* is 'of authority,' not necessarily their words. By studying the fathers, we are compelled to *face the problems*, and then we can follow them but creatively, not in the mood of repetition."[175] Here Florovsky holds up the fathers not as masters who have worked out all the answers to our own questions, but rather as exemplars who have asked their own questions, mapped particular trajectories (including false starts and dead ends), and embodied the practice of theological inquiry. Our task is to learn from both their successes and their mistakes.

Amid the texts we have examined, can we find a vision of the fathers, a "message of life and truth"[176] with which we may move forward? Two candidate teachings come to the fore, along with a methodology of which I wish to make sure we do not lose sight.

Image Bearers

Both men and women bear the image of God. The fathers and mothers of the Church differ on the details. But regardless of where they stake their claims, all our authors assure us that sexual difference is a matter of the flesh in which we currently live, move, and breathe. However, sexed bodies do not pertain to the image of the unseen God, who transcends male and female. Reading such anthropomorphic detail back into the divine nature is simply beyond our authors' sensibilities.[177] At the same time, we should note that the *imago dei*, while shared by all human beings, is found in each person, not in humanity collectively or in a couple consisting of a man and a woman. This will become important as we explore contemporary anthropologies in chapters 3 and 4.

Male and Female in Every Person

Second, the many allegorical readings in our survey suggest that each human being includes aspects characterized as masculine and feminine. These models are not without their problems. Gendered characterizations like Philo's chariot, describing the stallion as "proud . . . unrestrained and free" while labeling the mare as "mean, slavish, rejoicing in thievery, eating up house and home and destroying it,"[178] are plainly misogynistic. The various hierarchies of intellect over sensation, *sapentia* over *scientia*, and high spirit over desire, when attached to masculine over feminine, are offensive to modern sensibilities. Indeed, entire strands of feminist critique and gender theory have deemed the entire corpus irredeemable, and for good reason.[179] The easy association of positive spiritual traits with masculine gender norms while relegating negative traits to the feminine gender harms us all in multiple ways. Not only is it appallingly easy to signal negative worth for stereotypically feminine or "womanly" traits, reducing half of humanity to a lesser status and perceived value, but it also artificially inflates the position of men in the struggle for spiritual growth.

Some sympathetic historians and theologians have attempted to cast such discussions in a more favorable light, noting that the inheritance and reuse of terminology does not imply a wholesale agreement with earlier iterations.[180] Some of these earlier redeployments are quite progressive in their original contexts. But a contemporary constructive argument must continue questioning strengths and weaknesses grounded in gender stereotypes. It is no longer enough to assert, *pace* Nyssen, that one can choose to be spiritually born a man or a woman. Rather, the ongoing encounter with the Holy Spirit has shown the truth of Julitta's claim: we all come from the same lump, each of us is capable of the same spiritual disciplines, and each of us may aspire to the same goal of communion with God.

This is not to say that bad allegories negate the entire allegorical tradition. Beyond our valuations of sexism, there remains a useful insight in the allegorical readings we have reviewed. Whether the sensible and the intellect, or desire and high spirit, the upper and lower parts of the rational soul, both parts of each pair are found in both women and men. In this respect, the so-called male and female exist side-by-side in every human person. Likewise, the various traducian accounts offered also tend toward an understanding of a humanity that shares both a physical and psychical lineage. In some of the accounts explored above, a child's body and soul originate solely from the father, even in the case of daughters. Accounts that follow agricultural understandings of reproduction leave room for the mother's contribution to her offspring through the material drawn from the "soil" of her own body, even for her sons. The common theme of all such accounts is that the breath of life that God breathed into Adam is the common inheritance of us all, without respect to our physical embodiment.[181] These understandings, grounded in the one-sex body, are based in a human nature that is common to all humans, regardless of their biological sex or gender.

The Recovery of Allegory

In harmonizing the teaching that human beings, both male and female, are image bearers of God with the apophatic teaching that God transcends gender, patristic authors often resort to allegory. Even as they abandon some allegorical readings (e.g., the Origenian spiritualized reading of the divine command to reproduce and multiply), they continue to develop new ones (e.g., masculine and feminine passions, Augustine's explanation of the upper and lower mind). Allegory remains an important device throughout this period.

Within Orthodox theology, allegory remains an acceptable and useful tool in the Church's hermeneutical toolbox.[182] Moreover, I would suggest that even as we work to dispel the sexist allegorizations of the past, the consciousness created by allegorical readings that include both masculine and feminine elements in every human being can still serve to highlight the common inheritance of us all. Such readings may also provide frameworks that allow us to accept all aspects of our makeup without judging an element as foreign to our gender ideal. As we shall see in chapter 4, an openness to understanding each human person as comprising both masculine and feminine characteristics will help us to re-examine some of our incorrect suppositions about gender and biological sex.

A Final Note on Dogmata and Theologoumena

With the irreconcilable differences of opinion in practically every other aspect of their speculative theologies—the nonsexual or androgynous nature of the preoperative Adam, the nature of prelapsarian and eschatological bodies, the need for sexual intercourse in procreation or some ineffable, angelic alternative—all other patristic claims enjoy a status more akin to *theologoumena* or theological opinions. These claims, like all others that we might advance in a constructive theological argument, require an open conversation within the Church community. Remembering Florovsky's words, Orthodox recognize the fathers as privileged interlocutors because of their erudition in the faith and their lives of spiritual virtue. However, it is wrong to elevate their opinions to a position of unquestioned authority. In keeping with the Paris School's commitments, I am limiting the collection of immutable dogmatic definitions to those adopted by the seven ecumenical councils. While certain anthropological elements may be deduced from these teachings, particularly the Christological definitions, it is important to keep in mind that we are exploring an area in which the Church has yet to reach a formal consensus.

Conclusion

As this patristic survey ends, we are now in a better position to evaluate the claims of contemporary Orthodox thinkers that will appear in the next two chapters. In contemporary Orthodox discourse, blanket appeals to the patristic tradition often begin with the words, "The fathers say . . ." or "The fathers believe. . . ." Yet, as we have seen, patristic reflections on gender and biological sex are not univocal. Their various views tend to be informed by the one-sex model of bodies that we briefly examined in chapter 1. Beyond this, patristic reflections present a variety of speculative ideas regarding the sexing of protological and eschatological bodies, the origin and composition of the human soul, and the characterization of particular traits and parts of each human as masculine or feminine.

However, amid this patristic diversity, our sources tend to converge on a few major themes. Both men and women are created in the image of God. By God's grace and by individual ascetic discipline, men and women are called to divine-human communion and are capable of the same spiritual virtues. Finally, according to various models of the soul, all human persons, regardless of gender or biological sex, share a common set of elements, labeled as masculine and feminine.

As we turn to chapter 3, my argument will move from the patristic to the contemporary. Within contemporary Orthodoxy, a selective reading of patristic texts is sometimes offered, suggesting that gender essentialism is consonant with the teachings of the fathers. Though particular passages from patristic reflections can serve as prooftexts to support these modern conceptions, the survey of patristic authors of this chapter puts us in a better position to evaluate these claims. There is no definitive patristic teaching on biological sex and gender that supports an essentialist viewpoint. Furthermore, chapter 3 will show that contemporary Orthodox ideas about the fixed, ontological differences between men and women are not at all rooted in the patristic tradition, but rather in extra-Orthodox sources encountered in much more recent cultural contexts.

3

GENDER ESSENTIALISM IN CONTEMPORARY ORTHODOX THOUGHT

If it has not been specifically explicated and articulated in the past, it is the present task to show clearly that human community, as the created epiphany of the uncreated Trinity, is made male and female so that it can realize and achieve the divine life given to it by its uncreated Archetype.

—THOMAS HOPKO[1]

Introduction

In the previous chapter, our review of patristic teachings on gender and biological sex turned up a wide variety of conflicting viewpoints among the fathers. In this chapter, we turn to the contemporary Eastern Orthodox discussion. I have chosen to begin with the writings of Thomas Hopko. While I am focusing on Hopko's teachings on gender, this chapter's endnotes signal to the attentive reader that these arguments are presented first and foremost in the defense of an exclusively male priesthood. The question of women and the priesthood will be the focus of chapter 5.

Hopko may seem like a strange choice for focus. His audience was often more popular than academic. He was a protopresbyter of the Orthodox Church in America and a faculty member and dean of St. Vladimir's Orthodox Theological Seminary. A spiritual mentor to a generation of priests, he was also a successor to the charismatic figures of Alexander Schmemann and John Meyendorff. In the broader Christian world, Hopko was an active participant in the ecumenical discussions of the World Council of Churches. A prolific author of popular books, he was a sought-after guest speaker and the host of three podcasts. Each of these roles provided him an influential platform for sharing his views. It is exactly his reach that justifies a closer look.

Beyond the sheer reach of his influence, I have chosen Hopko for another reason. In his earliest writings on gender and Orthodoxy, Hopko points to the distinction between the *kerygmata,* or public proclamations of the Church to the world, and the *dogmata* that the Church teaches within its own ranks and which her members understand by the enlightenment of the Holy Spirit.[2] Hopko includes teachings on gender in the latter category. Nearly two decades later, in his final essay on gender, Hopko declares that though consensus has not yet been reached, in the end there can be only one Orthodox view on gender.[3] He goes on to offer what he characterizes as theses and a personal *theologoumenon* to advance the discussion.

By suggesting that in the end there can be only one definitive Orthodox view on gender, Hopko raises the stakes in the conversation. No longer an area for speculation and theological opinions, his claim would raise debates about gender to questions of ultimate concern. At first, I was dubious. Can one man control the conversation? Who decides what questions are of salvific import? But as the culture wars of broader society rage on, gendered questions of salvific import have appeared. Can a woman administer a sacrament? Can same-sex Orthodox couples be blessed by the Church? Does gender transition bar a person from communion? Gendered questions have become salvation questions. And for this reason, Hopko's theses and their subsequent use in contemporary Orthodoxy are subject to theological evaluation.

While it should go without saying, I will add a personal note. I met Father Tom only once before his death. He was a likable man, and I hold no personal animosity toward him. In what follows, I ask those who hold the man in high esteem to focus on the ideas he presented. The conversation I am advancing is about the latter only.

Throughout his writings on gender, Hopko argues that man and woman fit together—both ontologically and in their activity within the created order—to manifest the image of God the Father in ways analogous to the being and activity of the Son/Word and the Holy Spirit within the Trinity. This includes a particular order of relationships and the assignment of distinct, non-interchangeable roles and characteristics to each gender.

While outlining various resources for his theological project, Hopko claims that in addition to "the church fathers" and "the Christian liturgy," there are "several modern theological and spiritual writers" that share his "intuition" regarding the parallel between the two "modes of divine existence" within the Trinity and the "modes of human existence." However, as we will see, his most central claim concerning gender and the Trinity is simply not a part of the traditional sources of Orthodox theology.

In the first part of what follows, I provide a careful reading of Hopko's thoughts on gender. In the chapter's endnotes I trace the potential sources of his inspiration, based on his own citations and an examination of authors he claims share his view. These include his instructor and colleague Serge Verkhovskoy, his colleague and father-in-law, Alexander Schmemann, Paris School theologian Vladimir Lossky, Anglican lay theologian C. S. Lewis, German Jewish philosopher Edith Stein, and Roman Catholic lay theologian Joan Schaupp.[4] As we will see, some of these authors often take their own inspiration from Jewish Kabbalah and the archetypes of Carl Jung.

A few theologians have suggested that Hopko takes his inspiration from the work of Russian theologian Paul Evdokimov. However, in the second part of the chapter, I will show that the teachings espoused by both Evdokimov and Hopko are rooted in the Russian philosophical and theological tradition of the late-nineteenth and twentieth centuries, which found their fullest systematic expression in the works of Sergius Bulgakov. This revival in Russian religious thought was also inspired by interactions with extra-Orthodox sources. In addition to the sources listed above, the Russians were also influenced by the Lutheran mystic Jakob Böhme, German Romanticism, and the thought of Sigmund Freud.

As we have seen in the previous chapters, Orthodox tradition is not bound to the mere repetition of previous teachings. Rather, at various critical moments, leaders within the Church have appropriated concepts and language from their broader cultural contexts to formulate teachings in response to concrete issues. Stoic, Platonic, Aristotelian, and other Greek philosophical tools have each been adapted in response to theological questions. In their own work, Hopko and his predecessors have done much the same. The Russian thinkers examined in this chapter were explicitly moving beyond the Orthodox tradition. In examining these moments, my goal is to strip away the veneer of Orthodox tradition sometimes imputed to Hopko's work. In the end, his ideas are a new teaching (as he himself openly acknowledged), influenced by contemporary sources that stand on the same level as the ideas that I will present in chapter 4. As such, both sets of propositions are subject to the same possibility of critique and correction as we continue to explore new and urgent questions raised in our current cultural and ecclesial contexts.

An Invisible Paradigm Shift

Before moving to Hopko's thought, I remind the reader that the patristic sources we examined in the previous chapter are all informed by what Thomas Laqueur refers to as the "one-sex" model. In this way of thinking, based in Galenic and Hippocratic medicine, along with Platonic and Aristotelean philosophies, women are essentially failed men both physically and morally. But in the period covered by this chapter, a paradigm shift has occurred. We are now reading authors who work from a "two-sex" model in which men and women are separate, complementary beings constituting a binary. Without the awareness of the rise of the two-sex model, it is easy to fall prey to the assumption that authors have always seen the world in the categories that we take for granted. This in turn raises the possibility of misreading the one-sex accounts in the patristic period, assuming that they fit into our two-sex paradigm. As an example, both proponents and critics of Hopko's thought read the two-sex paradigm into patristic sources that describe the mechanics of human reproduction.[5]

Traces of Contemporary Orthodox Thought

Hopko begins, as do most contemporary Orthodox theologians, with the Trinity. "The Christian faith in its traditional orthodox, catholic expression has always confessed the Godhead to be a Trinity of consubstantial, coequal, and coeternal persons in perfect unity, confessing as well that true human life—*salvation*—consists in man's union with God the Father through the Son of God incarnate as a real man in Jesus Christ, that by the power of the Holy Spirit human beings might become by God's grace all that God is by nature."[6] While this opening declaration may perhaps serve as a candidate formulation of contemporary Orthodox teachings, scholars and students of the development of Christian theology will realize from the start that this compact litany of doctrinal declarations has not "always" been the expression of the catholic faith, but rather is the result of a series of controversies within the Church over the course of many years.

The Monarchy of the Father and Trinitarian Order (taxis)

Hopko continues his exposition by claiming, "The one true and living God is God the Father."[7] Tucked in this claim is the contemporary Orthodox teaching known as the monarchy of the Father.[8] To wit, adherents to this idea claim that references to "God" throughout the Bible and the subsequent tradition refer exclusively to the Father, the First Person of the Trinity. Hopko refers to the Father as *principium divinitatis*, the unique source of all that is, including the Son and the Spirit,[9] who "eternally" manifest the Father "in two forms of divine being and personhood. . . ."[10] While there is no mention of human persons in this passage, we find the first element of differentiation in what Hopko later refers to as "manner of realization" in "different forms of natural existence" as he draws his analogy below between the Son and men and the Spirit and women.[11] God is neither "one God in three persons" nor "three persons in one divine essence." Instead, "the one, true, and living God" is "the Father who has within himself eternally and, one might dare say, as an 'element' of his very being and nature, his only-begotten Son" and "his one Holy Spirit."[12] Citing dogma and the liturgical tradition, Hopko offers quotes from the Nicene Creed and the anaphora of the Divine Liturgy of St. John Chrysostom. The "one God" of the Nicene Creed is "the Father Almighty" rather than the Trinity. Hopko cites two passages from Gregory of Nazianzus to support his claim.[13] In addition, in the prayers of the Divine Liturgy, the priest addresses prayers to God the Father. For example: "for Thou art God . . . Thou and Thine only-begotten Son and Thy Holy Spirit. . . ."[14]

The monarchy of the Father establishes an order (*taxis*) within the Trinity. As sole source, the Father is identified as the First Person. However, the term *Father* is relational, making no sense without the Son, who is identified as the Second Person in the Trinity, leaving the designation of Third Person to the Holy Spirit.[15] Hopko suggests that the order in the Trinity implies a particular idea of hierarchy among the persons that does not impinge on their equality.[16] However, even as they preserve equality within the Trinitarian hierarchy, the Son and the Spirit "are personally obedient to [the Father] in their divine being and activity."[17] The idea of hierarchical order in the Trinity is essential to Hopko's thought as he turns to human relationships.[18]

Trinitarian and Human Persons

Hopko describes human persons as analogous to Trinitarian Persons: ". . . a community of coequal, coessential persons united together in exactly the same nature, whose essential spiritual freedom makes it to be reflective and expressive of God, but whose creaturely character—its open-ended temporality, incompleteness and lack of 'fullness'—binds it together in an unending process of growth and development in 'deification.' . . ."[19] As Hopko transitions from these outlines of human personhood to the goal of divine-human communion (*theosis*, or "deification" as described in the quote above), he cites the mystical writings of Gregory of Nyssa and the cosmic vision of Maximus Confessor. However, in the same citation Hopko dismisses the anthropological elements of both authors, asserting that "their views on human sexuality are at best unclear and at worst incompatible with the biblical and sacramental witness of the Church and her dogmatic and canonical Tradition, since both see physical sexual reproduction, if not sexual being itself, as created in view of man's fall into sin."[20] In spite of his rejection of these patristic reflections on the origin of sexed bodies, Hopko later affirms in the same essay that God could have made another method of human reproduction, echoing a line from Nyssen's *On the Making of the Human Being*—reiterated, as we saw in chapter 2, in works by John Chrysostom, Maximus Confessor, and John of Damascus—without ever crediting the Cappadocian bishop by name.[21] However, since Hopko has already ruled out Gregory's theodicy as an explanation for the division of humanity into male and female, he suggests that sexual dimorphism must have a spiritual purpose.[22]

Dismissal of Biblical Interpretations that Abrogate Sexual Distinctions

From his initial offering on gender, Hopko dismisses readings of Gal 3:28 and Mt 22:30 (and the parallel passages in the other synoptic gospels) that speculate on a human eschatological embodiment devoid of sexual difference (e.g., as sometimes understood to be the case in Gregory of Nyssa). In the case of Gal 3:28, he draws a distinction between human sexual differentiation as an ontological reality of the created order and nationality and slavery, which he characterizes as consequences of the fall.[23] While a case may be made for the preservation of sexual difference in the eschaton, the idea of *spiritual* distinctions based on gender is a claim that we will examine in greater detail below.

Hopko's most sustained argument against the eschatological possibility of a sexually undifferentiated, redeemed humanity appears in an essay devoted to an Orthodox interpretation of Gal 3:28.[24] In an opening footnote, he acknowledges that of the three pairs found in the passage, only the last, male and female (*arsen kai thēly*) is joined by the conjunction *and*. Though he is aware that this formulation follows Gn 1:27, he is uncertain whether this is of any didactic significance, suggesting instead that it may just be force of habit.[25] Such an interpretation is less convincing in the presence of the overwhelming number of patristic sources that misquote the passage. As the essay unfolds, Hopko states a typical Orthodox view that a host of interpretive lenses (e.g., feminist and Marxist commentary, all manner of philosophies, as well as individual religious, mystical, and sexual experiences) used by both individuals and in academic biblical studies are each subject to the "foundational, critical, and decisive hermeneutical context for reading, interpreting, and applying a biblical text" found in the Church's "lived experience of God through Christ in the Holy Spirit."[26] Yet, ironically, in his attempt to shore up his argument against the readings of his opponents, Hopko dismisses the entire patristic history of allegorical and theological interpretation of Gal 3:28, declaring that the "only way" in which the text can be examined is the general context of justification by grace through faith in Christ as the subject of the entire epistle.[27] This move is not only shortsighted in closing off access to the patristic tradition as part of the lived experience of the Orthodox Church, but also fails to take into account the full range of historical-critical methods. Hopko further argues that slaves, gentiles, and women, in contrast to free Jewish men, were not required to observe Jewish laws. While he goes on to mention circumcision specifically in his next sentence, his initial claim erases Jewish women as a category of consideration.

Moving on to Mt 22:30, Hopko suggests that Jesus's teaching that humans become like angels in the afterlife is limited in scope to neither marrying nor being given in marriage.[28] He rejects any lack of sexual differences in the resurrection. Elsewhere he claims that marriage is eternal, reopening the Sadducees' original question to Jesus: *Whose wife will the woman be of the seven as she was married to each of them?*[29]

Male and Female in the Image of God:
A Thesis with Several Corollaries

Having dismissed the most common arguments for the transient nature of biological sex, Hopko makes his major claim: "According to the catholic tradition of the Christian faith, there is a direct analogical, symbolic, and epiphanic relationship between Adam and the Son of God, and between Eve and the Spirit of God."[30] Following this assertion, he introduces a series of corollaries that warrant quoting at length:

1. As Adam is the *typos* of Him "who was to come" as the final Adam, the "high priest of our confession" and the "pastor and bishop of our salvation," so Eve is the *typos*, as the "mother of all living," of the "life-creating" Spirit who "proceeds from the Father and rests in the Son" as the personal power and life of all that exists, both human and divine.

2. What this means is that as in the Godhead there is and must be a union between the Son and the Holy Spirit for the Father to be eternally and divinely expressed, so *on the level of creation* there is and must be male and female so that the same God could be temporally and humanly expressed within the life of His creatures by His divine decision and grace communicated through His Son in His Spirit.

3. This means as well that as the mode of being and action of the Son is different from the mode of being and action of the Holy Spirit, both eternally and essentially, as well as in the dispensation of salvation—or, more traditionally put, both according to *theologia* and *oikonomia*—so, in a similar manner, the mode of being and action of the male in creation is different from the mode of being and action of the female within the same nature of created being.

4. More specifically, this means that as the Son and the Holy Spirit are not the same and are not interchangeable in their unique forms of their common divinity, so the male and female are not the same and are not interchangeable in the unique forms of their common humanity.[31]

Hopko further affirms the essential goodness and necessity of human sexuality in expressing the divinity in whose image humanity is made.[32] Without providing specifics, he lays claims to the authority of the sacraments, spirituality, doctrine, and canons of the Orthodox Church.[33] At this point we will pause to examine the extensive range of this cascading collection of assertions.

Unpacking Hopko's Statements

From the outset, it is worth noting the inherent contradictions in Hopko's claim of "direct analogical, symbolic, and epiphanic relationships between Trinitarian Persons and the Son and Adam or the Spirit and Eve."[34] Analogy makes use of inductive reasoning based on a correspondence between two things (or, in this case, persons). Symbol, instead, implies not only representation but also participation in an act. Epiphany is the revelation of something (or someone) that was hidden. It would be difficult to see how the links Hopko proposes could be described in each of these ways simultaneously.

Moving on to relationships, the first moment of note in Hopko's original assertion is uncovered in carefully reading his parallels: (1) between the Second Person of the Trinity (the Son) and the human person Adam, and (2) between the Third Person of the Trinity (the Holy Spirit) and the human person Eve. His reference is limited at this point to the two protological humans of the second Genesis creation narrative as opposed to the generic categories of male/Man and female/Woman. This level of specificity is essential for scriptural, liturgical, and patristic theological references that he links together in his first corollary.

In a move reminiscent of Irenaeus's recapitulation, Hopko alludes to Eve as "mother of all living" (Gn 3:20), coupling this reference with the "life-creating" attribute ascribed to the Holy Spirit in Irenaeus's *Against Heresies* 5.12.2 before adding an allusion to the pneumatological activity within the immanent Trinity as found in John of Damascus's *The Orthodox Faith* I.8.172–74.[35] In a footnote to the first corollary, Hopko further alludes to the connection between the New Eve and the Church found in Methodius of Olympus and the recapitulation theme of Mary as the New Eve found in both Justin Martyr and Irenaeus.[36] While perhaps unsettling to modern scholars who prefer to study each of these texts within its own context, Hopko's cascade of allusions follows a standard convention of Orthodox hymnography and liturgy in which multiple images are layered one upon another, employing an intertextual hermeneutic that evokes new associations. However, while the feminine associations in this corollary are quite traditional, the parallel set of masculine associations is Hopko's own constructive contribution. Utilizing the same typological framework, he begins his corollary with the Pauline trope of Adam as a type of the one who was to come (Rom 5:14), linking this further with passages describing Christ's salvific activity in the world as high priest (Heb 3:1), shepherd ("pastor"), and overseer ("bishop") of our salvation (1 Pt 2:25). Paul's typology of fallen and sinful humanity in the old Adam and those who are a part of the new Adam in Christ is also a favorite theme in the recapitulation teaching of Irenaeus of Lyons.[37] However, the subsequent list of descriptors, while traditionally associated with Christ, is not typically associated with the first Adam. Because the new list of masculine associations is immediately followed by a traditional set of feminine images, the novelty of the former is easy to miss if the reader is concentrating merely on the parallelism.

As we move to Hopko's second corollary, the attentive reader will notice two shifts. First, there is a transition from the protological Adam and Eve to the broader categories of male and female. Second, extending the initial typological associations of the first corollary between Son/Adam and Spirit/Eve, Hopko asserts that the economic activities of the Son and Spirit observable within the created order have an analog in the activities of male and female. While not explicitly stated in the corollary, Hopko has hinted previously at a reading of the *parallelismus membrorum* of Gn 1:27 as establishing an equivalence not between the human (*ha' ādām/ho anthrōpos*) and "male and female," but rather between "male and female" and "in [God's] image."[38] In other words, the image of God is expressed not by individual human beings, but rather in the union of the sexes.[39]

The slippage between Adam/Eve and male/female continues in the third corollary, where Hopko asserts that the intra-Trinitarian relational existence (mode of being, *theologia*) and the extra-Trinitarian activities (mode of activity, *oikonomia*) of the Son and the Spirit must also have an analog in the created world in the modes of being and activity of the male and the female, respectively. Readers familiar with the differentiation of Trinitarian Persons into three *hypostaseis* may recognize the phrase "mode of existence" (Greek *tropos tēs hyparxeōs*) as an allusion to the causes of the Son and the Holy Spirit. The Father begets the Son and emits the Spirit. Or put another way, the Son is begotten, while the Spirit is poured out or proceeds. Hopko slips between this standard usage and an idiosyncratic meaning that he never fully explicates, but that appears to be related to what he sees as activities associated with either masculinity or femininity.[40]

Finally, in his fourth corollary, Hopko follows standard Trinitarian theology by asserting that though the Son and Spirit share a common divinity (*homoousian*), their unique forms (begottenness and procession) are not interchangeable.[41] By analogy, he posits the same for the human male and female.[42] The first part of each assertion about common divinity and common humanity appear to be a restatement of the principle of *homoousia*. The word *form* is introduced without comment. It appears to serve as a shorthand for the "mode of being and action" of the previous corollary. However, here Hopko introduces a category error with his analogy between the Son and the Spirit within the Trinity and male and female within humanity. As we will see in chapter 4, the correct analogy is not between Trinitarian Persons and human sexes, but rather human persons.

Ideal Relations between Men and Women

Having laid out his initial thesis and corollaries regarding male and female in the image of God, it is now possible to examine how these propositions might play out in the Church and society. From the beginning, Hopko is quick to note that his propositions are "theological abstractions" for which there is no actual "existential demonstration."[43] Put more simply, the vision he proposes is not how the world currently works. Instead, in our current world order, both men and women compete in a manner that Hopko characterizes as the "image of the 'fallen Adam,'" an image marred by self-seeking individualism that attempts to achieve fulfillment through the quest for pleasure and power.[44] Christian men and women are called to reject this model and to embrace instead relations exemplified in the bond between Christ and the Church. Here Hopko adds another layer of imagery to the analogies of his first corollary. Male is now associated further with images of Christ, the true Adam, and the Bridegroom, while the category of female is further associated with images of the Church, the true Eve, the Bride, and through the repetition of previous links, the Virgin Mary. A footnote reminds the reader of the previously established metaphorical link between Mary, the New Eve, and the Church in the writings of Methodius of Olympus, Justin Martyr, and Irenaeus of Lyons.[45] Again, this cascade of imagery is the result of multiple images in the liturgical texts of the Orthodox Church.

Thus, "the Christian male" is called to complete, kenotic, self-emptying "in love for the good of others in spirit and in truth," to be "meek and lowly, humble and poor." Appropriating language applied to the Church in Eph 5:27, Hopko suggests that women are no longer competitors to the Christian male, but rather by means of the male's sacrificial love, women should appear to him "in splendor, without spot or wrinkle or any such thing . . . holy and without blemish."[46] Alluding to the biblical account of the creation of Eve, he asserts that "women are created and called to be men's 'helpers' in their service of self-emptying love."[47] He then connects these assertions to the Trinitarian economy by suggesting that women "are to be 'submissive' to men's love and service, and as such to enable and empower it, as the Holy Spirit, 'incarnate by grace' in saved humanity, enables and empowers Christ Himself to 'fulfill' his divine ministry in His creatures."[48] In this description the reader is finally offered a vision of the parallels Hopko sees between the activities of the Son and the Spirit within the divine economy and those of male and female in the created order. Lest anyone fear degradation in these divinely sanctioned roles, he again holds up Christ and the Holy Spirit as perfect role models. The former was not degraded by becoming a "servant to all" (Mt 21:27–28), taking on the "form of a slave" (Phil 2:7), just as the latter "is not degraded by silently, hiddenly, invisibly enabling Christ to be and to act as the Son of God and the Savior of the world, the high priest, pastor, and bishop of saved humanity. . . ."[49]

Citing the head covering controversy of 1 Cor 11, Hopko suggests that "women must be 'submitted' to men, as men themselves are 'submitted' to Christ, and Christ to God the Father."[50] This image is then united with a collage of allusions to the pastorals, other Pauline epistles, passages from Luke and Acts, and a reference to the Orthodox Hymn of Pentecost in describing the active and willing submission of women (and eventually men) to their respective headships and the power of the Holy Spirit to purge the current order in calling all to unity. "This vision of the ideal in man-woman relationships," Hopko asserts, "is applicable to human society in general, to all men and all women." It begins in the "small church" of the family,[51] is replicated in the life of Christ and the Church, the sacramental structure of the church community, and the Trinitarian economy expressed within the world. It will reach its final consummation in the marriage of the Lamb, found in the imagery of Revelation as Christ the Bridegroom and his Bride the Church consummate their love.[52] Returning to his original assertion, Hopko reminds us that this is the vision that Christians are to strive for, the eschatological vision of those who are currently living in a world shaped in the image of fallen Adam rather than the ideal for which men and women were created.

In his vision for ideal relations between male and female, we can now see the practical effects of the slippage from Adam and Eve to husband and wife and finally to all men and women. Adam and Eve are portrayed as the first wedded couple, with Adam as head and Eve as his helper who already lives in submission to her husband. Hopko's prescriptions begin by addressing "the Christian male," but quickly move to this individual's relations to all women. While the Christian male was treated as an individual, the following paragraph moves to the description of "women" who are created to be men's helpers, and finally to the idea that women in general must be submitted to men. While Hopko's vision of the Christian husband and wife is the first building block of the nuclear family as "little church," he is clear that this theocratic vision is the building block for subsequent iterations of Church, broader society, and finally the entire created order.

Initial Responses

Two years after his first reflections on the male character of the priesthood, Hopko responds to the initial criticisms that he has received. Paying particular attention to the gendered aspects that we have just explored, he characterizes the analogy in slightly different terms, this time referring to his idea as a "comparison between the Logos and man and the Holy Spirit and woman."[53] Thus, another slippage in terminology occurs, with the substitution of Logos for the Son, and introducing a third binary of man/woman to complement the original binaries of Adam/Eve and male/female.

On Hopko's own account, initial criticisms of his gendered parallels to the Trinity fall into three categories. First, some respondents suggest that the male/female analogy was incorrect because there is no sexual differentiation within God, and as such gendered categories are simply inappropriate.[54] This criticism, while raising a valid point, fails to consider Hopko's own claim in his earlier essay in which he very carefully rules out any sexual differentiation within the Godhead.[55]

However, the second criticism speaks to the points that I have raised above, even as I have laid out Hopko's arguments: the divine *hypostaseis*, as developed in the Cappadocian theology that leads to the Nicene Creed, deal with modes of existence (i.e., generation and procession) and are the marks of unique Trinitarian Persons. Thus, the human analog best suited to mirroring this phenomenon would be unique human persons (e.g., Peter, Paul, and Mary) rather than human sexes (e.g., male and female). As Hopko's unnamed critics have correctly countered, reducing all of humanity to two sexes runs the risk of occluding the particularity of each individual human *hypostasis*. As we will see in chapter 4, it also excludes the true spectrum of human biological complexity that exceeds a sexually dimorphic binary and the culturally dependent character of gender roles and expectations.

While Hopko readily agrees with the assessment that there is no sexuality in God, his response to the collapse of human persons into two categories is less satisfactory. First, he offers a concise statement with new and unsupported dimensions: "Here my own point is simply that there are, as a matter of fact, two 'modes of divine existence' within the Trinity whose hypostatic characteristics and manner of interrelating, especially as they are revealed in the divine *oikonomia* of creation and salvation, bear a striking resemblance to the 'mode of human existence' and manner of interrelating created and commanded by God for men and women in the Bible and the Church, in the Old and New Testaments."[56] This new formulation introduces the authority of divine command as transmitted through scripture and the ecclesial community as mandating a particular relationship between male and female. However, as Hopko himself points out in his first essay, we are still left with the problem of a schematization that remains (at least to him) an ideal, which no human community has ever actually embodied.[57] Here also the slippage between the Cappadocian use of "modes of existence" and Hopko's own usage is evident. To say that modes of (divine) existence are an "ideal" to which human males and females aspire is a category error. Instead, what Hopko appears to be suggesting is the actions of the Logos (which he associates with masculinity) and the Spirit (which he associates with femininity) within the economy of the created order are models of the ways in which human males and females should also act within the created order. This statement is analogical rather than literal.

Following this new assertion, Hopko goes on to reiterate each of the points raised in the previous essay, only this time more emphatically: "The Holy Trinity *is* the divine archetype for human being and life. Man *is* made in the image and according to the likeness of God, male and female. . . . The human *is* a reflection of the divine. Human nature *does* mirror divine nature." And so, he continues, ultimately returning to the original analogy, but this time introducing a new term. Just as the Father, the *principium divinitatis*, is manifested in two forms (as opposed to the earlier formulations that used "modes"), so also in the created realm, two

forms of human existence image the invisible Father.[58] Hopko briefly acknowledges the multiplicity of human persons as "a fact to be dealt with"
but one that ultimately has no bearing on his "fundamental intuition" of the
comparison between Logos/Spirit within the Godhead and man/woman
in the created order.[59] This confusion between the categories of gender and
human *hypostasis* is, indeed, more problematic than Hopko's gloss would lead
the reader to believe.

In response to Hopko's claim that Christ is the perfect role model for
men while the Virgin Mary serves as the perfect role model for women,
unnamed parties suggest that Christ is not just the perfect male, but the
perfect human who provides a role model for both men and women. Likewise, the Virgin Mary and her *fiat* are to be emulated by all Christians who
would hear the word of God and submit to it by the power of the Holy
Spirit.[60] Insisting that "proper distinctions must be made," Hopko counters
that Christ and Mary do indeed share a common humanity with all people.
Nonetheless, while participating in the same humanity, the figures of Christ
and Mary express their common humanity in dual and distinct male and
female forms.[61] Focusing on the gendered symbols previously discussed,
Hopko reiterates that "Jesus the bridegroom, head, and husband" is the pattern for males, while the Church, "imaged in the Virgin Mary, is a pattern
for females as the bride, the body, and the wife."[62] These images, drawn from
scripture and repeated in liturgical tradition and patristic reflections, serve as
the basis for Hopko's model for the roles of male and female, reflected in the
Trinitarian inner life as well as its activities within the created order.

Further Developments

Between the two scholarly essays that I have outlined above, Hopko also
released a popular volume in which he expresses a similar line of thinking.
While his original essay referred to a "speculation,"[63] his popular volume
expresses his thought in stronger terms: "I believe that God created human
beings according to his own image and likeness because of the Trinitarian character of the Divine Nature, and that the proper interrelationship between the sexes within the order of creation is patterned after
the interrelationship between God's Son and his Spirit. This divine interrelationship is the 'prototype' of the union of love between a man and a
woman in the community of marriage."[64] Turning his attention to the Trinity, he continues:

Within this "union" there is a definite "order" of relationships, which is perfectly divine, yet which includes a distinction of personal "modes of existence" in which the Son and the Spirit have a definite form of relationship, manifested to the world in the revelation of God through Christ and the Spirit in the dispensation of salvation, which is perfectly fulfilled and realized in the life of the Church. For, Christ is the King and the Spirit is the Kingship. Christ is the Anointed and the Spirit is the Unction. Christ is the Head and the Spirit fills his Body. Christ is the Bridegroom and the Spirit dwells in his Bride. And Christ and the Spirit are perfectly one in their inseparable unity in God, who is love.[65]

Several moments in this extended quote are of particular interest.

First, the concept of "modes of existence," which refers in Cappadocian theology to the cause of a particular *hypostasis* (begottenness/procession) once again acts instead as a shorthand for the economic activity of the Trinitarian Persons in the created order. Or in other words, the modes of existence are no longer applied to the inner life of the Trinity, but rather to their actions in the world. This is problematic because traditional Trinitarian theology ascribes co-activity to the Trinitarian Persons in all things exterior to the Godhead, a point that Hopko himself makes elsewhere in another argument dealing with modern attempts to substitute non-gendered names for Father, Son, and Holy Spirit in theology and liturgical texts.[66]

Second, the roles that the two *hypostaseis* fill are not parallel, but rather express a variety of relationships. Thus, the king is joined with his kingship, his anointing is joined with the unction poured out upon him. In the first the Son acts as a person, while the Spirit characterizes a state, but in the second the Son is symbolized by a characteristic as the Spirit is characterized as an object. The incommensurability of the metaphors continues in subsequent pairings between Christ as Head and Bridegroom. The logical pairings are Body and Bride, respectively. However, Hopko chooses to pair Christ in these two roles with the Spirit which fills the Body and dwells in the Bride. In the end, these various distinctions are all rhetorically subsumed into the unity of the Godhead, leaving the reader with a dazzling array of fleeting images.

While not mentioned by name, Hopko's work appears in a resource published in 1980 by the Orthodox Church in America in response to a World Council of Churches' study on the roles of women and men in the Church.

Here we find a final and instructive expansion of the paired images offered in Hopko's work to date, summarized in the following pairs: Jesus/Mary, man/woman, male/female, Bridegroom/Bride, husband/wife, king/queen, son/daughter, eternally masculine/eternally feminine,[67] servant/handmaiden, Head/Church, Word/Wisdom, *Logos/Sophia*, Son/Spirit.[68]

However, amid this barrage of images, Hopko associates Mary with the *typos* of mother, a word for which there is no corresponding masculine counterpart associating Jesus with the *typos* of father. This is consistent with what we know of Jesus's status within the Christian tradition as a single man, but it is also consistent with doctrinal teaching that reserves the attribute of fatherhood to the First Person of the Trinity. I highlight this lack of parallel in the proposed imagery for two reasons. First, it complicates the argument for the masculine Logos and feminine Spirit and the image of God as expressed in the human male and female with which Hopko began this line of reasoning. Second, as we will see below, this problem is characteristic of another slippage that periodically occurs in the authors that Hopko alludes to as justification for his thinking. In several of his sources, the parallel between the masculine Logos and the feminine Spirit breaks down at the pairing of father and mother, where the Father displaces the Son. In his later works on gender, Hopko makes the analogy between male and the Father himself.[69]

Cherry-Picking: The Problem of Unsupportive Biblical and Patristic Texts

Hopko and his source materials tend to focus on scriptural, liturgical, and patristic references that identify the Spirit with ostensibly feminine characteristics. However, other passages incorporate more masculine imagery. Within the New Testament alone, the Holy Spirit is symbolized by tongues of fire (Ac 2:3). It is referred to as "the power of the Most High" (Lk 1:35), "the power of the Lord" (Lk 5:17), the vindicator of Christ (1 Tim 3:16), and "Lord" (2 Cor 3:18; 2 Thes 3:5). Likewise, the Nicene Creed refers to the Holy Spirit not only as "the giver of life," but also as "Lord," while the prayers that begin the daily cycle of divine services typically begin with a prayer that addresses the Spirit as "Heavenly King." It is only by selective readings of both scripture and liturgy that Hopko's exclusively feminine associations can be maintained.

A variety of problems are also found in additional patristic sources quoted by authors whose works have inspired Hopko. While Wisdom is sometimes associated with the Spirit, there are also ante-Nicene authors (e.g., Philo of Alexandria, Justin Martyr) who associate Wisdom with the Logos instead. Within Schaupp's work, other patristic references also complicate Hopko's schema. For example, in Origen's nuptial imagery, all souls are female as brides of Christ,[70] subsuming all humans into the category of the feminine in relation to God. Origen provides no exceptions for priests or all men more generally.

Likewise, a small set of patristic images seems at first to provide interesting analogies between the procession of the Holy Spirit and the procession of Eve. However, Methodius's procession refers to the Holy Spirit as the "rib of the Word," an image that only works if the Spirit proceeds from both the Father and the Son—an idea more at home in Western theology where the *filioque* is the norm than within the boundaries of Eastern Orthodox thought. Meanwhile Gregory's analogy addresses the consubstantiality of the Father and the Spirit in a way that is mimicked in the image of Adam and Eve yet falls short of the eternal procession ascribed to the intra-Trinitarian relations of the Godhead.[71]

Among Hopko's conversation partners, we also find attempts to link the Wisdom tradition and ante-Nicene fathers with the Spirit and femininity by casting a wide net of associations. For example, in Si 24:3–4, Wisdom personified covers the earth like mist. A similar image is found in the hymnody of Ephrem the Syrian, where air is used as a symbol of the Spirit of God, and Adam's breathing is equated with suckling.[72] Among the ante-Nicene fathers, Theophilus of Antioch equates *ḥokmâ*/wisdom in the Hebrew scriptures with the Holy Spirit.[73] Irenaeus similarly links Wisdom with the Holy Spirit and the Word with the Son.[74] The Hebrew *rûaḥ* and *ḥokmâ*, "spirit" and "wisdom" respectively, are grammatically feminine, lending themselves to poetic and allegorical readings.[75] Schaupp's discussion of femininely gendered vocabulary also extends to the Hebrew root *rāḥām*, related to the noun "womb," which in verbal forms is used for "compassion" or "love."[76] While aware of these associations, Hopko himself does not use arguments from grammatical gender to support his claims. He appears to avoid these arguments for two primary reasons. First, he wishes to avoid reading any gender back into the immanent Trinity. Second, since the writing of Sergius Bulgakov (discussed further below), Wisdom is uncomfortably associated with sophiology for many Orthodox theologians.[77] While not overtly stated, Schaupp's association of the Holy Spirit with love appears to be connected with the Augustinian vision of the Holy Spirit as the *vinculum caritatis* (or "bond of love") between the Father and the Son.[78] Elsewhere in the text she makes reference to Augustine's analogy between separate elements of the human person and Trinitarian Persons: memory to the Father, understanding to the Son, and will to the Spirit, a schematization which Hopko finds problematic in other contexts.[79]

Extra-Christian Sources

Finally, Hopko ignores two lines of argument advanced in Schaupp's work that rely on traditions beyond Christianity: the archetypes of Carl Jung and the male and female emanations of God found in Kabbalah.[80]

In the first of these arguments, Schaupp takes her inspiration from the work of Jungian philosopher and psychologist Erich Neumann, who associates the Holy Spirit with the highest symbolism of the Great Mother or the Eternal Feminine.[81] Schaupp uses Neumann to reinforce her associations between the Holy Spirit, *Ecclesia*, *Sophia*, Mary as Mother of God, together with eternal life, as various images of the upper or positive aspect of the Great Mother.[82] Neumann's own work opposes these tropes to a lower or negative aspect that includes the images of the Jaws of Hell, Death, Medea, and other negative images that lure down into death.[83] For Jung, each human being contains a polarity, both a masculine *animus* and a feminine *anima*, which find balance in the healthy person.[84] Schaupp suggests that the *animus* and *anima* are mirrors of an "essential twinness of God, revealed in the Trinity," in the persons of the Word and Love. In place of Hopko's idea of the human male as image of the Son/Word and the human female as the image of the Holy Spirit, Schaupp instead suggests that each human individual is an expression of the Trinity, containing within him- or herself both the Word and Love.[85] Her formulation more closely follows Jungian psychology than Hopko's gender complementarity.

Schaupp further connects the Jungian concept of *animus* and *anima* with masculine and feminine aspects of the image of God found in Jewish Kabbalah, associating the *Shekinah* or Presence of God with the Holy Spirit as the feminine aspect of the Godhead.[86] She references the work of J. Massingberd Ford to suggest that a man is incomplete if he does not take a wife.[87] Drawing on a Kabbalist interpretation of Gn 2:18, Ford suggests that the complete image of God is found in the joining of husband and wife. Here Schaupp suggests that the spousal relation is not the exclusive locus of the image of God in male and female. Rather, she suggests, both men and women need relationships with friends, coworkers, and associates of the opposite sex to bring them balance.[88] As we shall see in the second half of this chapter, Schaupp's insights gleaned from both Kabbalah and Jungian psychology are shared by various Russian religious philosophers and theologians that Hopko rejects in his own work.

Holes in the Argument

However, what is thus far missing from the authors that Hopko claims share his intuition is also instructive. Among the various authors, we find little reference to the ideas that the image of God is revealed in the relationship between male and female. In all the sources referenced, this idea appears only in the writing of Joan Schaupp. However, Schaupp draws the idea not from scripture, Orthodox liturgy, or patristic sources, but rather from Ford, whose argument hinges on her reading of *Zohar*, a thirteenth-century Jewish mystical text that will appear again in the next section.[89] Another potential source for Hopko's claim that male and female together constitute the image of God is found in the work of evangelical theologian Paul K. Jewett, who occasionally appears in Hopko's footnotes. However, the source of Jewett's claim is not patristic either. Rather, Jewett borrows the idea from the great Swiss theologian of the Reformed Tradition, Karl Barth.[90]

Also nearly absent from the thought of the authors Hopko mentions is support for his claim of a connection between the Son/Logos and men. As I noted above, the associations Hopko draws between Christ, Adam, the shepherd, and the high priest are not a part of Orthodox tradition. Rather, they are his own formulations that parallel traditional feminine imagery. While Orthodox theological sources are replete with instances that reinforce the association between Eve, Mary, the Church, and the Holy Spirit, masculine parallels are missing from the male side of the equation.[91] Biblical sources attest that the incarnate Logos, Jesus Christ, took on a particular male form,[92] while the trope of recapitulation that draws an association between Adam and Christ begins even in the Pauline corpus.[93] But the suggestion that there is a link—analogical, epiphanic, symbolic, or otherwise—between the Second Person of the Trinity and all humans of the male sex is not a primary concern of the authors under review. Whence then does Hopko draw inspiration for his intuition?

The Unacknowledged Sources of Hopko's Thought

In the first half of this chapter, we have examined Hopko's major claims regarding human gender, including his proposed analogy between male and female modes of human existence and the activities of the Logos and the Spirit respectively in the Trinitarian economy. I have attempted to identify the potential texts that Hopko has used to support his model, based on allusions in his work to a list of thinkers that he claims share his intuition. But Hopko's intuition is simply not a part of traditional Orthodox theology. As we have seen, patristic evidence to back his claim is scant, while many of his modern sources use materials that are part of larger systems of thought that are problematic for Hopko's Orthodox framework.

As we enter the final section of this chapter, I propose that Hopko's initial model is much more closely aligned with the thought of several Russian religious philosophers and theologians of the late-nineteenth and twentieth centuries than with the sources that he has named. Much controversy has been associated with these thinkers. While we cannot know Hopko's motivations for avoiding mention of these authors, it is plausible that his silence regarding the overlap between their thought and his stems from the scandal their names evoked in the period in which Hopko wrote.[94]

Paul Evdokimov

Several theologians have associated Hopko's gender essentialist claims with the thought of Russian émigré theologian Paul Evdokimov.[95] To be sure, many of the themes found in Hopko's work have antecedents in Evdokimov. However, even ideas that the two theologians have in common often turn out to be derived by very different means. While some of Evdokimov's work appeals to traditional Orthodox authorities beyond the scope of Hopko's project, he also incorporates extra-Orthodox sources that would be difficult to justify from Hopko's perspective. Let us briefly examine both the points of confluence as well as the critical points at which the two men's thoughts diverge.

In a line of thought that should now sound quite familiar, Evdokimov suggests that man alone does not represent the full image of God, but rather one divine Person. He further proposes that just as the Son and the Holy Spirit reveal the Father, so also the Father is revealed in the conjugal relationship between man and woman.[96] In their joint revelation of the Father, the man once again is analogous to the Son and the woman to the Holy Spirit.[97] While Evdokimov spends very little time on establishing an analogy between the Son and men, he offers various connections between Eve, Mary, the Church, the Holy Spirit, and women.[98]

Like many thinkers previously explored in this chapter, Evdokimov links his own spousal imagery with the metaphor of Christ and the Church in Eph 5. However, in reinforcing his various associations, Evdokimov offers the icon of the Christ Child seated on Mary's lap in support of his argument.[99] The icon has a twofold meaning. First, it functions Christologically as a depiction of the Incarnation, with the Theotokos representing the human nature and the Christ Child representing the divine. However, Evdokimov goes on to suggest that on the Trinitarian level, the Word is represented in the Child, while the Holy Spirit is represented in his mother.[100] To Evdokimov, the icon depicts a spousal relationship. Evdokimov suggests that the Holy Spirit plays a pivotal, spiritual role in the birth of Eve and in the birth of Jesus. Eve, "child of Adam," is born of Adam's side and becomes his spouse. Mary, as God-bearer, contained within herself humanity, the universal soul, the Church. She is Mother of God and Bride of the Lamb. The unity between Mary and Jesus Christ is embodied in her participation in the Incarnation.[101] Evdokimov connects the Virgin with the Mother of all the living, the life-giving Source, and also with the Holy Spirit.[102] His various connections between the images of husband and wife, Christ and the Church, and Christ and the Theotokos result from a type of intertextual reading common to the Orthodox tradition that we have already seen in Hopko's work.

Relying on the trope of recapitulation, Evdokimov continues his argument by suggesting that Calvary recovers the symbolic order of Genesis. While Eve, mother of humanity, was born from Adam's side, blood flows from the side of Jesus, a Eucharistic sign of both eternal life and the birth of the Church. Christ further announces to John the Beloved, who stands in for all of humanity, "Here is your mother," establishing Mary's universal maternity, a quality she in turn shares with the Church.[103] From here, Evdokimov returns to the Bridegroom and the Church of Eph 5, noting that there is a succession of images, each revealing the Father: the Word and the Spirit, the Incarnate Word and his Body/the Church, and finally in Christ and the Theotokos. Each, he suggests, is a spousal union, joining together two parties who become an image of the invisible Father.[104]

Like many other thinkers, Evdokimov's primary concern is to associate women with the Holy Spirit. As we have seen before, there is very little evidence in the historical tradition for Hopko's assertion that men are linked with the Son. Here Evdokimov offers some support. In a subsequent work, Evdokimov returns to his previous analysis of the icon of the infant Christ seated on the lap of the Virgin. As before, the Virgin and Christ Child taken together are an image of the Incarnation, "the human united with the divine." But he also extends his Trinitarian reading: "[the] Virgin is the place of the presence of the Holy Spirit, and the Child, the place of the presence of the Word. Together, the two make human the mysterious face of the Father."[105] Continuing his argument, Evdokimov turns to a second image, a second-century fresco from the Callixtus catacombs, depicting a scene from the Eucharist. Here, a man, whom Evdokimov identifies as a bishop, stands before the altar, his hand extended over the bread. A woman stands on the other side of the table (or "in the background" in Evdokimov's description), her hands raised in the *orans* prayer position. Evdokimov suggests that, taken in isolation, each figure is but a fragment. They must come together to form the Eucharistic whole.[106] Suggesting that these images exemplify the distinct and complementary masculine and feminine charisms embodied by men and women, respectively, Evdokimov then makes a claim crucial to Hopko's own argument: "If woman is linked ontically to the Holy Spirit," a claim that is echoed throughout the works that we have already examined, "this relationship acquires universal value and meaning only if man is likewise linked ontically to Christ."[107] Taken together, these two images—the Theotokos and the Christ Child and the depiction of the Eucharistic celebration that includes both a male and a female figure—provide Evdokimov's basis for an anthropological methodology that he explores in both the current and subsequent texts.[108]

Even this brief overview of Evdokimov's texts shows a broad overlap between his conceptions and the framework that Hopko offers. Yet Hopko makes scant reference to Evdokimov in his own writing.[109] I suspect that there are two primary reasons. First, Evdokimov uses Jungian archetypes and the work of Johann Jakob Bachofen as the basis of many of his claims for the proper roles of masculine and feminine.[110] The prominent use of these extra-Orthodox authorities would only be problematic for Hopko's arguments, which he attempts to couch in terms of traditional Orthodox sources for theological reflection. Second, while Evdokimov offers a Trinitarian analogy between the Son and the Spirit and the masculine and feminine, much of his work is devoted to a second, Christological analogy based on his reading of the *Deisis* icon. Here, he proposes the Virgin Mary and John the Forerunner as the archetypes of femininity and masculinity, respectively, and as the role models for women and men. As we will see below, precedent for Evdokimov's thought appears in the work of Sergius Bulgakov. This novel reading removes emphasis from the Son/Christ/man link previously established in favor of an alternative model of masculinity that emphasizes the life and activity of John. However, a closer look at Evdokimov's own inspirations within the Russian religious and philosophical renaissance will reveal the true sources of Hopko's intuition.

The Russian Religious and Philosophical Renaissance

While today's Orthodox theological discourse is still dominated by a "return to the fathers" initiated decades ago by the exponents of the neopatristic synthesis, the pre-revolutionary Russian religious landscape was quite different. The Russian intelligentsia, like many of their counterparts in Western Europe, were fascinated with occult knowledge, freemasonry, theosophy, spiritualism, Jewish and Christian mysticism, and a mix of themes tracing their roots to the classical period.[111] This environment gave rise to a new school of theosophical and theological thought that articulated all of the key elements of Hopko's own intuitive speculations.[112] For our purposes, let us begin with the thought of Vladimir Solovyov, the father of Russian sophiology.

VLADIMIR SOLOVYOV

Solovyov drew on a host of sources within various religious, philosophical, and mystical traditions to formulate his ideas. Among the key elements of his system are the primordial androgyne, its division into male and female principles resulting in estrangement, and the reconstitution of androgynic humanity (and with it the Divine image) through erotic love shared within the marital bond. Solovyov's ideas are a mixture of elements taken from the writings of Kabbalists, Jakob Böhme, Plato, and the German Romantics.

From Kabbalah, Solovyov drew the idea that the *sefirot*, emanations from the Divine, were gendered principles, interacting to form the creation.[113]

In Lurianic Kabbalism, the *sefirot* were mapped onto the image of *Adam Kadmon*, or the primordial man—an androgynous image containing both masculine and feminine attributes.[114] Christian Kabbalists adopted the concept of *Adam Kadmon*, associating him variously with the Logos and the pre-incarnate Christ. Solovyov adopted this principle also, using *Christ* and *Adam Kadmon* as synonyms, distinguishing this figure from Jesus, the incarnate God-Man.[115]

Kabbalistic teaching also holds that when souls come to earth, they split into separate masculine and feminine elements, which are then born into separate human beings. These elements are brought together again in the union of husband and wife. Kabbalah holds sexual union to be sacred. When a Jewish male has sex with his wife, the two form a mystical bond that allows them to interact with the Shekinah, another divine emanation with female qualities.[116] *Zohar*, used by Schaupp and Ford above, describes the descent of paired human souls, male and female, into the world where they are born into separate male and female bodies. Later, the pairs are joined again in marriage, forming "only one body and one soul."[117]

Solovyov was also well acquainted with the works of Jakob Böhme, the father of modern sophiology.[118] Influenced by themes from Kabbalah, Böhme wrote of a primordial human, an androgynic being or "youth-maiden" (*männliche Jungfrau*), who lived in eternal bliss with Virgin Sophia.[119] However, the human's eye wandered from Sophia, resulting in the fall. The Virgin Sophia flew away, while the androgynic youth-maiden was fractured into two principles, male and female, which gave rise to men and women.[120]

Böhme's androgyne is taken into the works of the German Romantics where its influence takes on various forms. Novalis, Franz von Baader, and Friedrich Schlegel tend to follow Böhme's understanding of the reunion of the masculine and feminine principles as a salvific return to a pre-sexed wholeness. In contrast, F. W. J. Schelling envisions a more tragic narrative in which male and female attempt to overcome their separation, but instead produce more offspring that also fall back into being either male or female.[121]

Solovyov mixes these various sources to produce his own view. He draws on Plato's themes of the androgyne and the unitive force of eros,[122] but he also includes elements taken from Böhme, filtered through German Romanticism.[123] Solovyov argues that the union of male and female is independent of the mechanics of sexual intercourse. No love is required in lower, sexed organisms, whose offspring are the most plentiful. In contrast, the greatest human sexual love often results in no offspring at all.[124] Following Schelling, Solovyov suggests that sexual intercourse, rather than achieving a unity of principles, results in offspring who remain sexed and incomplete like their parents. Combining these various elements, Solovyov creates his own unique reading of Gn 1:27: "Eternal God created the human being, in his image and likeness created it: husband and wife, created them."[125] He continues, noting that the image and likeness of God is found not "in half a person, not in sex," but in "the whole person," "in the union of the male and female principle."[126] The path to reunification is through "sexual love," a love that need not be physical, but can only be experienced by persons of opposite sexes. Love, Solovyov tells us, "compels us to affectively acknowledge in *another*, with all our being, the unconditional central significance that, on the strength of egoism, we sense only in ourselves."[127] Sexual love, in turn, is the extraordinary (exclusive) love between two people of different sex who may come together as husband and wife. This love is "separate from the physiological side of the matter." It is independent of biological reproduction and, in fact, can be foreclosed if a couple moves too quickly to sexual intercourse.[128]

For Solovyov, the image of God in humanity is fractured into imperfection and the beginning of death. Human beings in their current state are lopsided. Only together do they manifest the image of God. Solovyov looks to "sexual love" as the remedy for humanity's current "discord and disintegration."[129] In his exploration of sexual love, he draws a series of analogies between the creation of male and female in Gn 1:27, the mystery of Christ and the Church represented by the husband and wife in Eph 5, and the relationship between God and creation. In each image, he sees a hierarchical relationship in which the first partner in the pair shapes and molds the second.[130] Within the spousal relationship, both husband and wife can receive, through the grace of adoption, both the integration of their human nature and the restoration of the image of God.[131] Here, in the Russian tradition, we find Hopko's teaching that the image of God is expressed in the union of man and woman. However, we must look further for the relationships he describes between male and female and Trinitarian Persons.

NIKOLAY BERDYAEV

Our short survey of Russian religious thinkers would not be complete without a brief examination of a few key motifs in the work of Nikolay Berdyaev. Berdyaev's contributions to Hopko's thought are indirect at best.

However, I briefly linger over his works to shed some light on the latter portion of the genealogy presented here. Berdyaev provides elements that appear both in the thought of Paul Evdokimov and in the thought of Sergius Bulgakov, whom we shall take up shortly as the thinker whose thought foreshadows Hopko's theological project. Like Solovyov, Berdyaev posits an initial androgynic state of humanity that has been fractured by the fall and is manifest in the reality of separate man and woman.[132] Berdyaev takes his own inspiration from Böhme's sophiology and Bachofen's gender archetypes, mixing them with Solovyov's own quest for reunification of male and female in the spousal bond. This synthesis produces its own interesting results. Berdyaev writes that the human is "a complete, masculinely feminine being, solar and telluric, logoic and cosmic at the same time." Echoing Böhme, he connects original sin with the fall of the androgyne into divided sexes and "the formation of the bad masculine and the bad feminine." In chastity, the human is perfectly whole. But as a sexual or halved being, it is "not chaste, not wise, is doomed to disharmony, to passionate longing and dissatisfaction."[133]

Following Solovyov's narrative from *The Meaning of Love*, Berdyaev also explores humanity's futile attempts to reunite in primordial wholeness through sexual intercourse. While providing fleeting moments of union, these physical relations cannot effect the mystical union, "the permeation of every cell of one being into every cell of another," that the couple seeks.[134] The ultimate sign of love's failure becomes the birth of another sexed child who also experiences the polarized existence of male and female. Berdyaev offers an interesting embellishment to Solovyov's work, arguing that both masculine and feminine principles exist in each human being.[135] Biological sex is an expression of the dominant principle. Following Freud, Berdyaev suggests that humans are fundamentally bisexual beings with both masculine and feminine elements. He goes on to suggest that every spousal union, in fact, has four parts, bringing together the feminine aspect in the woman with the masculine aspect in the man, as well as her recessive masculine aspect, which is drawn to the man's recessive feminine aspect.[136]

Finally, Berdyaev draws a distinction between the androgynic state to which humanity aspires and the monstrous, hermaphroditic state he sees embodied in feminism and the emancipation movements of his time in France.[137] Here we find descriptions, now familiar in the works of Evdokimov and Hopko, of women who reject their natural, feminine roles, seeking rather to emulate the image of fallen Adam in a competitive spirit.

SERGIUS BULGAKOV

With our brief excursion into the works of Solovyov and Berdyaev, we are now in a better position to appreciate the work of Sergius Bulgakov. As will become evident, both authors influenced Bulgakov's theological reflection. We will also see that Bulgakov's thought is a direct antecedent to Hopko's work, matching it much more closely than Evdokimov's.

Bulgakov's first foray into the questions of sex and gender appeared in an essay in which he explores the opposing views of Gregory of Nyssa and Augustine of Hippo.[138] He subsequently expanded this material to include overviews of both Jakob Böhme's androgyne and Kabbalistic mystical teaching of the union of husband and wife in one body and soul and incorporated this revised material into his first major tome on theology.[139]

Following his various sources of inspiration, Bulgakov concludes that the full image of the human being is contained in the spiritual-corporeal marriage of a man and a woman. However, he theologically also affirms that even in isolation, each half-human being is still a full person (*hypostasis*) with its own spiritual fate. Following Berdyaev, he further suggests that each outwardly single-sexed human being is inwardly two-sexed, knowing within itself the erotic tension of (feminine) creation and (masculine) creative activity.[140] Traces of Berdyaev's thought can also be found in Bulgakov's early work in his claim that every cell of the human body has the nature of sex.[141] In a break from his interlocutors—he names Gregory of Nyssa, Maximus Confessor, and Eriugena—as well as his Russian antecedents, Bulgakov argues that sexual differentiation is not a tragic state to be overcome. Rather the female sex (and specifically motherhood) is blessed by the Theotokos in her giving birth to Christ, while the male sex is glorified in the presentation of Christ in the Temple on the eighth day as firstborn son to be consecrated to the Lord.[142]

Rejecting the primordial androgyne of his interlocutors, Bulgakov offers a new model in which Male and Female stand as complete and separate principles, originating in the Godhead and manifesting in human beings.[143] Attempting to work from the top down, Bulgakov suggests that the Second Person of the Trinity is called Son first according to his generation from the Father. In the Incarnation, he is also born male. The male principle, Bulgakov argues, enters the Godhead as a personal property (*idiōma*) of the Son.[144]

At this point, Bulgakov introduces the distinction between the male principle and the male sex of the corporeal nature that humans share with animals. While the two categories are separate, biological sex is a physical manifestation of the spiritual principle.[145] The male principle is not a half, but a whole. At the same time, it is relational. Just as the Son exists hypostatically only in relation to the Father and vice versa, the Son as Absolutely Male exists only in relation to the Holy Spirit as Absolutely Female. The Son is revealed in the economy of the created order in the Incarnation as the male principle in the image of the male sex. The revelation of the Holy Spirit is related to the female nature. The Holy Spirit chose a woman as a vessel: "a woman, the 'new Eve,' the Ever Virgin, the Church."[146] Here we find the first links between the masculine and feminine principles and the Second and Third Persons of the Trinity, respectively.

The essay in which Bulgakov worked out these details remained unpublished until 2003.[147] However, he lays out his themes publicly over the course of his minor trilogy.[148] Bulgakov's first public attempt to differentiate principle, gender, and biological sex—an exercise undertaken in relation to Sophia and the feminine—proved inscrutable to his readers. The feminine as a spiritual principle, Bulgakov explains, refers to "a reciprocal treatment, a passive love, outside any relation to [biological] sex." He continues, "Therefore, femininity in this context has no relation to womanliness, and even less to woman."[149] Likewise, Bulgakov's use of the word *sex* (Russian, *pol*) can also be confusing, as for example in his earliest formulation concerning Christ who was "a man, but in no way in the sense of human sex."[150] While first appearing to refer to biological categories, Bulgakov's usage refers less specifically to markers of sexual dimorphism (in his own day, external genitalia and internal reproductive organs), and rather to the fallen human state in which humans thirst for one another, seeking out marriage and sexual union.[151] Later he describes the sexual state in humanity as one in which sex was awakened as "a rebellious, autonomous element" of "desire and passion," not subject to the spirit, but rather subjecting the spirit to itself. As a result, the woman desires her man (Gn 3:16) and he her.[152]

Key to Bulgakov's developing thought is the concept of ever-virginity, a state which Christ enjoyed by nature, having taken on the entire human nature except for sin. In contrast, the Virgin Mary and John the Forerunner were born as other humans but achieved ever-virginity through grace. More than simply abstaining from sexual intercourse, all three were free from sex and its ardors, which Bulgakov associates with the fallen, sinful nature.[153] Here Bulgakov notes the association drawn by the Church between Christ, Mary, and John as the exemplars of perfected humanity in the *Deisis* icon. This is the source of Evdokimov's inspiration and his reason for associating the masculine principle with John (rather than Christ) as the model for perfected manhood.

However, as the minor trilogy progresses, Bulgakov continues to refine his articulations. In a particularly lucid passage, he presents his thought:

> Male and female in themselves, outside of the fall, are in no way already biological sex, however afterward they provide the bases for two sexual modes of human nature. In the beginning they were spiritual principles, some sort of spiritual qualifications. Inasmuch as the male principle is determined by the primacy of intellect and will over sensation as the power of unmediated experience, so the female principle manifests a primacy of sensation, of experience over intellect and will. The male is truth in beauty, the female beauty in truth: truth and beauty are indivisible and of the same essence, but together they also differentiate as two images of a single principle, the revelation of the one Father, begetting the Son and issuing the Holy Spirit. Both images belong to the fullness of the Divine image in the human. In the Holy Trinity, the Father begets the Son and issues the Holy Spirit; He reveals Himself in a single and eternal act of hypostatic tri-unity. In the monohypostatic human being, this dual image is revealed as a dyunity, as two possibilities, two images of human essence, neither of which independently expresses its fullness. The human being is not only the male or only the female principle, but it contains in itself one and the other, and what's more, not as biological sex, i.e., halfness, unfullness, but exactly as the fullness of its own being.[154]

In this new formulation, Bulgakov touches on each of the themes of his emerging thought. First, he harmonizes his own idea of inherent sexual principles in man and woman with Gregory of Nyssa's account of the sexual attributes associated with the garments of skin worn after the fall. This new formulation allows for a reading of Nyssen's works that affirms biological sexual distinction and the need for the present reality of sexual reproduction, while maintaining masculine and feminine principles in the resurrected state. While alluding to the ancient Greek characterizations of masculine reason (Russian *razum*, corresponding to the Greek *nous*, *logismos*) and feminine sensation (Russian *chuvstvo*, Greek *aisthēsis*),[155] he further posits a union of both male and female principles as the precondition for the human expression of the *imago dei*. Just as the Logos and the Holy Spirit reveal the image of the invisible Father, so also do the male and female principles in their unity.

Having touched more fully on the difference in his thought between femininity as a principle and womanliness as associated with biological sex, Bulgakov returns to his Mariology. He writes that while existing as a female being, the Virgin and Mother, Ever-Virgin is not a woman in the sense of sex. Likewise, Christ possesses a masculine nature, but possessing ever-virginity, is not a man in the sense of sex.[156] Here Bulgakov teases out his sexual distinctive, which is not primarily a *biological* difference between man and woman, but rather "the condition of man and woman turned towards each other" as "the lot of the whole fallen human race."[157] Bulgakov postulates that, by grace, both Mary and John the Forerunner achieve a state of original ever-virginity. In this state, the male and female natures are not destroyed. Rather, both natures were primordially created, and only in their union is the image of God expressed.[158] Expanding on his initial treatment of the Virgin Mary as a human being possessing a female nature, but not a woman in the sense of sex (*v smysle pola*), he suggests that "just as the Lord is of the male sex (*est' muzheskago pola*), but also not in the sense of the [male] nature connected with sinfulness (*v smysle svyazannago s grekhovnost'yu estestva*), so the Forerunner of the Lord was of the male sex (*muzheskago pola*), but he was not a male in the fleshly [or *carnal*] sense (*ne byl muzhem v plotskom smylse*), for he was clothed in virginity."[159] Here the word *sex* in the first reference is used as before when Bulgakov speaks of the Virgin Mary. However, as he turns to Jesus and John, he deploys the word in its more usual sense—both Jesus and John are of the male biological sex, with reference to Lk 2:23 and Jesus's consecration to God as first-born. In this case, he substitutes the phrase "in the fleshly sense" to describe the fallen sexual state of humanity, a state avoided by Mary, Jesus, and John.

In the final volume of his minor trilogy, Bulgakov returns to the masculine and feminine principles. Following Berdyaev, he posits that both male and female principles are present in the human soul, filling one another. One is always predominant over the other.[160] Bulgakov now ties these again to Truth and Beauty, arguing that the primacy of Truth and the primacy of Beauty are both equally subordinated to the primacy of the Good. Bulgakov has not referenced the origin of these three now capitalized principles;

however, one can see that they are related to earlier philosophical discourses on the Good (*agathon*), the True (*alēthes*), and the Beautiful (*kalon*). Having brought in all three categories, Bulgakov now turns to the Trinity in which he associates Truth with the Logos, Beauty with the Holy Spirit, and Good with the Father. The Logos became incarnate in Christ, while the Holy Spirit indwelt the Virgin Mary. Now publicly, Bulgakov suggests that "the fullness of the human image in the heavens is Jesus-Mary."[161] Building on the idea that the image of God is found in the union of man and woman, he goes on to suggest that the icon of the Virgin Mary and the Infant Christ together, the Pneumatophore and the incarnate Logos, displays the revelation of the invisible Father.[162] In Bulgakov's schema, Mary undergoes a type of adoption in the moment in which the Holy Spirit descends on her, making her into "a receptacle, an absolutely spirit-bearing creature, the Pneumatophoric Human."[163] Here we find the source of two of the recurring themes in Evdokimov's writing. First, we have the icon of the Theotokos and Christ Child as the complete image of God in humanity.[164] Second, we have the identification of Mary as the complete spirit-bearing or pneumatophoric person, which Evdokimov applies more broadly to the feminine polarity.[165]

Hopko's idea of subordination or order in Trinitarian and human relations respectively are also addressed in Bulgakov's work. First, Bulgakov argues that the Spirit is subordinated to the Word in activity *ad extra* in the world. The Word *reveals* the Father, while the Spirit *accomplishes* this revelation through the manifestation of his beauty or glory. The actions of the Spirit are dependent on those of the Son, suggesting an ontological priority of the Son.[166] In humanity, the male has primacy both in the order of creation (Gn 2:23) and in being head of the female (1 Cor 11).[167] This argument, in which Bulgakov collapses male and female into the persons of Adam and Eve, is the basis for a final argument, also found in Hopko's work. Bulgakov argues that in their fulfillment of the divine command to be fruitful and multiply, the children of humanity appear in only two forms, male and female, manifesting the male and female spiritual principles, but never any other form. All male *hypostaseis* possess a multi-unity whose center is the *hypostasis* of the Logos. Likewise, all female *hypostaseis* possess a single center, the Holy Spirit. As such, every creaturely *hypostasis* shares in a supra-eternal proto-image in either the Second or the Third Person of the Trinity.[168] Here Bulgakov originates a claim like the error we see in Hopko. Bulgakov predicates masculine and feminine principles first to the *hypostaseis* of the Trinity and subsequently to human *hypostaseis* where Hopko predicates these attributes to the sexes. The result is the same, collapsing all men into one category and all women into another. As we will explore more fully in the next chapter, divine hypostatic identity is unique only as an indicator of that which is not shared within the Godhead. While the Father is not the Son or the Spirit (and all other statements *mutatis mutandis*), the three Persons nonetheless share all else in common by virtue of their *homoousia*.

Elisabeth Behr-Sigel and the Personalist Turn

No discussion of Hopko's theological anthropology would be complete without examining the response of French Orthodox theologian Elisabeth Behr-Sigel. In the year following Hopko's initial reflection on gender, the World Council of Churches sponsored a conference to discuss the role of women in the Orthodox Church. Behr-Sigel was asked to deliver the keynote address.[169] While she had never addressed the topic before, Behr-Sigel was widely versed in Orthodox thought of nineteenth- and twentieth-century Russia and the diaspora population that had relocated to Paris.

Behr-Sigel's address provides a charitable exposition of Evdokimov's ideas of gendered charisms. At the same time, she is critical of the ways in which the idealization of feminine roles, particularly motherhood and the central position as "heart and soul of the family," can be used to cover over legitimate concerns.[170] One of the hallmarks of Behr-Sigel's work on gender from this earliest presentation is her tempering of romanticized notions of femininity with concern for the lived experiences of actual women. Thus, even as she champions Evdokimov's cause, she also points out the fact that the biblical tradition lacks both a theoretical exposition on the nature of women and any mention of particularly feminine charisms.[171] Finally, she asks some open-ended questions that require fuller reflection: Do men and women have different and complementary missions or vocations? Or do they share the same task, fulfilling it in different ways?[172] Turning to questions of women and the ordained priesthood, Behr-Sigel notes that priesthood is a charism, granted by God. She suggests that a woman might also receive this charism regardless of her gender. She ends her talk on a warning about the danger of subordinating grace to biological determinism.[173]

In a longer reflection published after the conference, Behr-Sigel articulates her ideas more fully.[174] Evdokimov's ideas run the risk of exchanging, real, concrete persons—both men and women—for concepts of masculinity and femininity and even outright cultural stereotypes. Behr-Sigel takes exception to Evdokimov's claim, borrowed from Berdyaev, that femininity is identified with birth-giving, while masculinity is related to cultural production.[175] She suggests instead that every human person is a composite, with both men and women carrying the image of Christ, who is the image of the Father. Key to her emerging thought is an idea she refers to as *biblical personalism*. "The Lord," she writes, "calls by name. . . ." Each person has a unique vocation and is gifted with personal charisms. Each is called to self-realization. However, this is accomplished only in communion with other persons.

As her thought continues to develop in subsequent essays, Behr-Sigel rejects outright Evdokimov's schema that associates the feminine with the Holy Spirit and the masculine with the Christic male. She argues, rather, that the fathers affirm the Logos not as the model of the human male, but as the image and likeness in which all humanity, male and female, are created.[176] She initially argues from scripture. Using Gal 3:27–28 she claims that all, without distinction, are baptized into Christ, while Paul's discussion of spiritual gifts in 1 Cor 12 and the image of the Church in Eph 4:1–7 suggest to her that charisms are distributed throughout the Body of Christ without being designated as either masculine or feminine. Over time Behr-Sigel expands her arguments to include patristic sources. She rejects Gregory of Nyssa's double creation as being too dualistic.[177] Elsewhere she claims, like Hopko, that Nyssen's double creation "has not been taken up generally by the patristic tradition."[178] However, in Basil of Caesarea, Behr-Sigel finds an ally who seems to defy the gender norms of his time by heaping both traditionally masculine and feminine attributes on his portrait of a Christian woman.[179] Gregory of Nazianzus offers affirmation of equality between men and women who share the same creator, are made from the same lump, will share the same experience of death, and will be glorified in the same resurrection.[180]

From her keynote address in 1975, Behr-Sigel had been familiar with Hopko's first essay on gender and the priesthood. She had even selectively quoted from it, while registering in her footnotes disagreement with his conclusions.[181] Though her initial critiques and questions addressed Evdokimov's work, they are also relevant to Hopko. On the 1983 release of *Women and the Priesthood*,[182] Behr-Sigel takes the opportunity to address Hopko's thought directly. Her diagnosis of the central problem in both Evdokimov and Hopko agrees with one of Hopko's initial anonymous respondents: each confuses the human person with the category of sex.[183] In her review of Hopko's ideas, she writes: "The mystery of each person's unique relationship with the living God cannot . . . be reduced . . . to the Platonic reflection of some masculine or feminine archetype."[184] Attempts to do so violate the essential gospel message, resulting in persons being subsumed under and mixed with the category of sex.[185] While affirming Hopko's observations regarding differing modalities of masculinity and femininity within humanity, Behr-Sigel cautions against reading these back into the Trinity. Analogy must be used wisely and soberly, she suggests, or risk introducing anthropomorphism into the ineffable Godhead.[186] Further, modalities change, depending on culture and era. But most importantly, she notes that the Church has traditionally affirmed human persons in transcending and transforming these norms as they fulfill their personal vocation.[187] From her earliest work she justifies this claim by pointing to the freedom from the expectations of marriage and family offered by consecrated virginity and the monastic life.[188]

Throughout Behr-Sigel's critiques, we find multiple appeals to *persons* and the language of *personal* charisms and vocations. The Cappadocians, she writes, did not extend the idea of persons (or *hypostaseis*) to humanity, but only to the Godhead. However, she continues, the modern concept of the person developed out of Christian Trinitarian theology.[189] In her most mature writings she calls for "a deeper study of the understanding of the person." Here again she refers to "the personalism of the fathers" and the work of Vladimir Lossky.[190] Yet within her own work, Behr-Sigel never provides a systematic exposition of this personalism. In the next chapter, we will take up her call.

Conclusion

As we saw in the previous chapter, there is no consensus teaching on gender and biological sex within the patristic tradition. We can now see that the gendered theses espoused by Thomas Hopko are only partially grounded in traditional sources of Orthodox teaching. Hopko's use of patristic sources can be problematic when his prooftexts are examined in their original contexts. Further, he selectively highlights scripture references and liturgical texts that support his arguments to the exclusion of those that do not. Moreover, several elements of his thought simply are not found within the tradition. Where these ideas appear in Hopko's acknowledged conversation partners (e.g., the image of God expressed in the union of male and female) they are drawn from Kabbalah and Jungian archetypes. While some of his sources have argued for a connection between women and the Holy Spirit, none have offered an argument for linking men and the Logos/Son. While the many new images that he offers are all traditional, their association with one another is a novelty—one that must be evaluated in light of Hopko's contention that we must come to a single Orthodox view on gender.

Within the broader, unacknowledged context, theologians and religious philosophers of the Russian religious renaissance draw on many of the same sources used by Hopko's interlocutors, as well as the thought of Jakob Böhme, German Romanticism, and Sigmund Freud. These medieval Jewish and late-modern sources turn out to be the only sources that support Hopko's overall argument.

My goal has not been to discount Hopko's arguments based on his use of extra-traditional resources. From the very beginning, Orthodox thinkers have drawn on ideas from their broader cultural settings as resources in their theological reflection. However, borrowed concepts and terminology are traditionally subject to critique and refinement. To this end, I have sought to highlight those borrowings so that they may be examined in the light of the tradition. Once we can critically examine his ideas, we find that Hopko's understanding of masculine and feminine "modes of being" rooted in persons of the Trinity and encompassing all men and women is a category error that obscures the uniqueness of each human person. As Behr-Sigel suggested, what is called for is a more in-depth look at the human person. In the following chapter, we will turn to the concept of personalism, exploring this line of theological anthropology with particular attention to the roles of gender, biological sex, and sexualities. Like Hopko's own constructive theological reflections, personalism is also informed by sources beyond traditional Orthodox theology. As such, it is also open to scrutiny and refinement. But in my counterproposal, I will show how personalism offers an alternative to the gender essentialism of the Russian religious renaissance—one that allows us to formulate a theological anthropology that considers the personal, physiological, and cultural diversity of gender and biological sex.

4

PERSON, GENDER, SEX, SEXUALITY

To proclaim with Scripture that humanity—that is to say man and woman—are created by God "in his image and likeness" is to affirm, in the words of [Vladimir] Lossky, that both are persons. This implies that each . . . is also a totality: mysterious, unique, unclassifiable, and free—according to their vocation. At the same time [each is] called to a relationship of communion with the other, totally different and totally similar. The unique person is irreducible to any category, such as sex, where one would be tempted to confine them.

—ELISABETH BEHR-SIGEL[1]

Introduction

At the end of the previous chapter, we saw a critique of gender essentialism offered by Elisabeth Behr-Sigel in response to the writings of her friend, Paul Evdokimov, and to similar essentialist arguments offered by Thomas Hopko to support a male-only priesthood.[2] Behr-Sigel argued that a gender essentialist anthropology obscures the unique charisms and vocation of the human person, subsuming it under biological and cultural determinism. To remedy the problem, she called for an in-depth exploration of personalism in the development of a theological anthropology.

Since the mid-twentieth century, Orthodox theologians have shown renewed interest in the idea of personhood. Vladimir Lossky, whom Behr-Sigel references above, is among the first Orthodox theologians to make this anthropological turn, defining the human person as a free being that exceeds—rather than being determined by—its nature.[3] In this chapter I wish to examine some of the unexpected points of confluence between Lossky's idea of the human person and the destabilization of essentialist understandings of gender, sex, and sexuality that have unfolded in contemporary gender and queer theory. Taken together, these ideas highlight instabilities in the culturally dependent categories that authors such as Thomas Hopko and the Russian religious thinkers before him take as God-given and immutable. Such an approach rejects the limitations of essentialist labels, accenting the plentitude within collective humanity and the personal freedom to transcend and transform ways of being and acting in the world. In the place of prescriptions, Lossky's anthropology points to an apophatic understanding of the human person who may be described by a collection of attributes, but never reduced to them.

We begin this chapter with a close reading of several of Lossky's works. I have chosen to focus on Lossky's thought for three reasons. First, though other Orthodox theologians have reflected on human personhood, Lossky provides the foundation from which many begin.[4] While his observations are tentative and not fully developed, they offer useful guiding principles for the elaboration of an apophatic theological anthropology within the Orthodox tradition. Second, Lossky insists on a "top down" approach, firmly dependent on Trinitarian and Christological dogmas. He suggests that since human persons are created in the image of the Triune God, it stands to reason that the intra-Trinitarian life should inform our thought about what it means to be human persons. Christological dogmas that establish the full and perfect humanity of Christ add another dimension to his arguments. This line of reasoning is consonant with an immanent critique of Orthodoxy's recent turn to gender essentialism. Third, Lossky resists the trap of premature certainty by embracing an apophatic understanding of both God and humanity. Acknowledging that God exceeds the limits of human language, he elaborates his thought while maintaining a relationship of humility to *theologia* proper (i.e., the contemplation of God in Trinity). Unlike others who have come after him, Lossky's thought regarding Trinitarian inner life and its relation to the world is thoroughly grounded in the acknowledgment that no human language can contain God.[5] While we may speak cataphatically about God, using analogies derived from that which we know from our experience of the world, we must also speak apophatically, denying that we can reduce the *Deus absconditus* who always exceeds our labels to any of the attributes we might wish to essentialize. Beginning from Lossky's own observations, I will argue that the apophatic safeguard so central to Lossky's Trinitarian theology also carries over to any anthropology rooted in his work. While recognizing our common human nature, we nonetheless affirm the freedom of each person in pursuit of our joint vocation, uniquely contributing to the whole of God's creation.[6]

After briefly exploring Lossky's reflections on what it means to be a human person, I turn to explore key insights from contemporary discourses on gender, biological sex, and sexuality. Using gender and queer theory, I will show that gender, biological sex, and sexualities each consist of schematizations that are culturally bound and molded. These schemas seek to order vast arrays of individual characteristics into unified categories, which we can understand as meaningful. However, in so doing, they too can obscure the uniqueness of persons.

This exploration has two primary purposes. First, a personalist approach suggests that human individuals may express a variety of the characteristics found in other human individuals. But the elevation of any one of these characteristics to the level of an ontological principle obscures the absolute distinctiveness of each human person, particularly regarding their freedom to exceed our common nature in uniquely fulfilling their vocation. Second, on closer examination, we find that the categories used in gender essentialist arguments—masculine and feminine, male and female, man and woman—are not actually fixed ontological principles (Sergius Bulgakov, Evdokimov) or even modes of being (Hopko). Rather, they consist of a multitude of variations that must be constantly monitored, massaged, and regulated to maintain the illusion of a stable either/or binary. Formulated another way, gender, biological sex, and sexualities are categories that describe elements of our shared human nature. But they do not exist as ontological realities; rather, they are expressed by unique persons, whom we encounter as gendered and sexed individuals. To understand that statement will require a brief overview of Lossky's anthropology and its dependence on philosophical personalism. But to set the stage, we must first briefly return to Sergius Bulgakov.

Setting the Stage

In the previous chapter, we traced the development through Bulgakov's minor trilogy of his thought regarding masculine and feminine principles. With the publication of *Lamb of God*, the first installment of his major trilogy, Bulgakov again connects the divine *hypostaseis* of the Son and the Spirit with masculine and feminine principles and then further with the incarnate Christ and the Theotokos.[7]

As we previously saw, what begins with Christ and Mary is further extended to all men and women at the hypostatic level. The masculine and feminine principles manifest as the visible image in humanity of the invisible God in a way analogous to the Son and the Spirit who manifest the image of the invisible Father. Key to Bulgakov's argument is a reading of Gn 1:27 that interprets the "image of God" as synonymous with "male and female." For Bulgakov, the duality of masculine and feminine principles, taken together, constitutes the *imago dei* borne by humanity.[8] As we saw in the previous chapter, this reading exists among a line of Orthodox thinkers down to our own time that includes Vladimir Solovyov, Bulgakov, Paul Evdokimov, and Thomas Hopko.

It was this formulation of Bulgakov's developing system of masculine and feminine principles, associated with both the Trinity and humanity, which drew official censure from Sergius (Stragorodsky), Acting Patriarchal *Locum Tenens* of the Moscow Patriarchate. In his condemnation of elements of Bulgakov's theological project, Sergius notes that Bulgakov's teaching on masculine and feminine principles in the Godhead offers a temptation to deify the sexual life as had some early gnostics, "spiritual Christians," and secular authors.[9] Though Bulgakov had not gone down this path, "what the teacher leaves unsaid, the student can finish, coming to conclusions that the teacher, with horror, had attempted to avoid." Bulgakov's teaching, Sergius proclaims, "has nothing in common with Church tradition and does not belong to Christ's Orthodox Church."[10]

Building on Sergius's condemnation, Vladimir Lossky joins the debate the following year with a treatise titled *Controversy concerning Sophia*.[11] In his own argument, Lossky accuses his opponent of a category error: Bulgakov has confused the personal with the natural, or to use more common metaphysical terminology, that which belongs to the *hypostasis* with that which is common to a shared nature or *physis*.[12] Lossky supports this claim with two arguments.

First, turning to Gn 1:27, Lossky asserts that the proper reading of
the passage affirms that both male and female are created in the image
of God. Rather than pointing to masculine and feminine principles within
the Godhead as Bulgakov suggests, the passage affirms that the *imago
dei* is shared by each human *person*, just as much in female as male, despite
the different created forms of the (common) *nature* of Adam and Eve.
Both Adam and Eve, and by extension all human persons, are created in
God's image.[13]

An analogy, Lossky reminds us, is fitting only when it is correctly qualified. To illustrate his point, he turns to an oft-repeated analogy between
the Trinity and the first human family. As the Son is begotten and the Spirit
proceeds from the Father, so also a human son is born and Eve is drawn
from Adam's rib.[14] The analogy illustrates how various persons can share a
common nature.[15] However, if taken too far, this analogy also produces
a category error, confusing that which is proper to divine *hypostaseis* (the procession of the Spirit from the Father) with that which is proper to the
common human nature (the derivation of Eve from Adam).[16] Bulgakov's
own confusion between hypostatic and natural qualities is the result of just
such an incorrect analogical formulation.

Second, Lossky claims that Bulgakov has transferred a quality of the
Second Adam (maleness, or more generally, sexedness) to the qualities of
the Second Hypostasis of the Trinity.[17] Bulgakov has forgotten, Lossky
claims, that sex is predicated of human nature, a nature that Christ shares
with the rest of humanity.[18] However, sex has no place in the divine nature.
Lossky argues that this becomes clearer when we recall that the hypostasis
of Christ is the hypostasis of the Logos. In Christ there is no human hypostasis. Since there is no sex in the Godhead, Christ's sexedness must be
predicated of his human nature rather than his divine hypostasis.

At this point, some readers are probably scratching their heads and
wondering what just happened. To understand Lossky's point, we must first
understand the way in which he is using the terms *person* and *hypostasis*.
While in English these two words have long been used as synonyms in
Trinitarian theology, the term *hypostasis* when used to refer to human beings has, in general, simply meant a concrete instantiation of the otherwise abstract human nature. However, Lossky and many other thinkers
of his milieu use the language of philosophical personalism to get at an aspect of human existence they claim has been obscured with the rise of
Western discourses.

Personalism

Personalism, like the gender essentialism examined in the previous chapter, has its roots in modern philosophical traditions. It developed in response to both individualist and collectivist political notions that appeared in the nineteenth and twentieth centuries.[19] According to the personalists, individualism prioritizes the autonomy of the individual above any group or society. Individualism's fruits include the systemic late capitalism in which most of us now live. In opposition to individualism, various collectivist philosophies prioritize groups of people over the individual. On the right, collectivist philosophies have appeared under the guises of Nazism and Fascism, on the left as Marxism. Each is willing to sacrifice the person for the sake of the collective values the system promotes. Personalism suggests that there is a middle way between the rampant egoism of individualism in which personal desires reign supreme and the collectivist philosophies that prioritize the state, a particular people group, or the workers' paradise with little regard to unique persons.[20] In resistance to the advances of dehumanizing technologies and ideologies, personalism emphasizes the unique and unrepeatable existence of each human being, "the boundless and indeterminate character of creativity," and the priority of nondiscursive ways of knowing such as intuition, perceptual experience, and mystical encounter that go beyond rational experience.[21]

Lossky draws on many sources, synthesizing elements of prior personalist models with overtly Christian categories to outline a new theological anthropology. In addition to Russian philosophical personalists such as Nikolay Berdyaev and Vladimir's own father, Nikolay Lossky, the younger Lossky also draws on the French personalists of his new homeland.[22] Like his earlier teacher Lev Karsavin, he frames his understanding of human persons in parallel to the divine Persons of the Holy Trinity. And with inspiration from both neo-Thomist conversation partners such as Étienne Gilson and Jacques Maritain and the neo-patristic synthesis of Georges Florovsky, Lossky formulates his personalist insights in the language and concepts of both late-antique and medieval theologians.[23]

While personalism itself is an admittedly new philosophical system worked out in response to nineteenth- and twentieth-century exigencies, Lossky attempts to show how Christian anthropology is consonant with a personalist worldview, even in its biblical and patristic roots. From the first creation story in Genesis, the personal God pauses at the pinnacle of creation to deliberate among the Council of Trinitarian Persons, saying: *Let us cre-ate the human being in our image and likeness.*[24] "Made in the image of God," Lossky writes, "the human is a personal being confronted with a personal God. God addresses them as a person, and the human answers Him."[25] This call and response is illustrated in God's walks in the garden with Adam and Eve in the cool of the evening. "A personal Absolute who enters into relationships with human persons;"[26] who calls chosen human per-sons by name: Abraham, Isaac, Jacob. Implicit in Lossky's description are the unique and non-interchangeable relationships of each human person with God and with one another.

While sketching the outlines of a personalist anthropology, Lossky frames his work with three observations. First, unlike the dogmas concern-ing Trinitarian Persons articulated by the ecumenical councils, the fathers do not provide exact teachings regarding human persons.[27] Second, what the fathers did write about personhood tends to address Christological con-troversies. As such, their teachings normally concern the person of Jesus Christ, without much thought for the implications for the rest of human-ity.[28] Third, the language used in these discussions, when applied to human persons, is often freighted with philosophical meanings that must be care-fully examined and, often, deconceptualized in order to clearly and pre-cisely indicate what we are talking about.[29] With these caveats in mind, a brief foray into Trinitarian theology will help us set the stage for an explo-ration of the human person.

Trinitarian Persons

In the standard account of the fourth-century Trinitarian controversies, the writers of the Creed of Nicaea adopted the term *homoousios* to express the divinity shared by the Father and the Son. This shared divinity was eventually extended to the Holy Spirit as well.[30] The essence of the Trinity is not divided among the Three, a move that would result in tri-theism. Rather they are a Tri-Unity, without separation or division. The words *ou-sia* and *hypostasis* were synonyms, borrowed from Neoplatonic and Stoic philosophical systems, respectively. The genius of Cappadocian theology is in the emptying of these two terms of their previous metaphysical as-sumptions so that they could be vested with new meanings. *Ousia* came to describe the essence shared by the Father, Son, and Holy Spirit, while *hypostasis* was redeployed to designate the characteristics unique to Father,

Son, and Holy Spirit that can be attributed exclusively to one divine Person: paternity, generation, and procession. No longer synonymous, *hypostasis* became a sign that points to that which cannot be generalized to all three Persons. *Hypostasis*, Lossky claims, points to the "radically personal character" of God.[31] Henceforth, *ousia* and *hypostasis* are used to describe what Lossky refers to as the antinomy of one and three in Trinity without emphasizing one over the other.

Hypostasis and Person

Can Lossky's human person be mapped to the classical metaphysical term *hypostasis*? The brief response is no. Lossky occasionally does use *hypostasis* as he attempts to talk about the human person.[32] However, this only works when his reader understands the usage as being analogous to Trinitarian Persons, as we will see below. Lossky's human person, like its Trinitarian prototype, is not a limited, concrete instantiation, a chip off the block of essence, but rather is the entire human nature, undivided, yet is irreducible to it. However, the commonly accepted usage of *hypostasis* when discussing human beings refers to a real or concrete instantiation. Lossky's person and the common understanding of a human *hypostasis* do not refer to the same subject.

This infelicitous confluence of terminology is the result of an encounter between the vocabularies of two disparate discourses. Within theological discussions, *person* has already been used to render two Greek terms: *hypostasis* and *prosōpon*. French theologians, like their anglophone counterparts, use the terms *hypostase* and *personne* interchangeably when discussing the Trinity. French philosophical personalists, not particularly worried with the patristic tradition, also adopted *personne* to name the concept they sought to explore. Thus, Lossky's attempt to map philosophical personalism in theological terms results in a collision between these various terminologies.[33] What he means when he refers to the human *person* was in his own day largely unexplored.

The Concept of Human Persons

Returning to anthropology, Lossky makes a series of arguments to elucidate the theological concept of a human person. He first turns to the early sixth century, when Boethius defines a *person* as "an individual substance

of a rational nature."[34] Later theologians took exception to this definition
as it applied to Trinitarian Persons, since an *individual* substance would
violate the understanding of an undivided divine essence. While subsequent theologians propose new definitions for divine Persons that account
for both the *homoousia* of the Trinity and the *hypostaseis*, Boethius's definition is never questioned in its application to *human* persons. Lossky concludes that this has resulted in a situation in which the definition of the
human *person* is indistinguishable from the human *individual*.[35] But what
does he mean?

A further key to understanding personalist arguments is the distinction
between the *person* and the *individual*. In English, we use the words *individual* and *person* as synonyms, when in fact, Lossky asserts, they are near
opposites.[36] "The word *individual* expresses a certain mixture of the person
with elements that belong to the common nature, while *person*, on the
other hand, means that which distinguishes it from nature."[37] The human
individual, like the human *hypostasis*, is a concrete instantiation of the
human nature. But while *hypostasis* is a value neutral term, the *individual*
of philosophical personalism has a negative connotation. More than just a
collection of characteristics, the individual is cut off from collective humanity, turning inward in isolation and staking a claim as sole possessor
of what is, in fact, ontologically shared by collective humanity. The individual pits this "me" against others, confusing nature and person—what
is common or shared versus what is completely unique. Individuals are
known by the collection of attributes that they draw from the common
nature: hair and eye color, height and body type, a combination of gestures, talents, and skills. For example, many individuals may have brown
hair, favor their left hands, and cock their heads to one side when they
encounter something new or unexpected. These characteristics are not
unique to any one individual. Instead, they are drawn from possibilities
within the plentitude of our shared human nature. Given enough human
beings, no individual is unique, as the collection of attributes they possess
can eventually be found in another individual. In theory everyone has a
doppelgänger. In contrast, the human *person*, like its Trinitarian counterpart, references the one who exceeds the common nature. Just as the Father
is not the Son or the Spirit, so also Paul is not Peter, and neither is Mary.
And should I meet my double, there is a difference: I am not he, nor is he
I. This is where we discover personhood. Though each human shares a common nature and may even overlap in the characteristics expressed in their

individuality, each is personally "always unique and incomparable" by virtue of not being the other.[38]

To show that the human *person* cannot be synonymous with the human *individual*, Lossky turns to the logic of Chalcedon. The fathers of the Fourth Ecumenical Council declared that Jesus Christ is truly human (*anthrōpon alēthōs*), having a rational soul and a body (*ek psychēs logikēs kai sōmatos*). Like Boethius's definition, Christ has a rational nature. However, according to the Chalcedonian Definition, Jesus Christ is acknowledged in two natures (*en duo physesin*), concurring in one *hypostasis* (*eis . . . mian hypostasin syntrechousēs*). This one *hypostasis*, however, is not human, but rather the divine *hypostasis* of the Son, the Second Person of the Trinity. While we commonly refer to the union of God and human in Jesus Christ as the *hypostatic union*, Lossky prefers to say that the human nature is *enhypostasized* by the Son.[39] This expression, borrowed from Leontius of Byzantium, helps Lossky to stress that the *hypostasis* of Jesus Christ is the preexistent *hypostasis* of the Logos. It is not human, for there was no preexistent human *hypostasis* to which the Son joined Himself.[40] The consequence of this move is that the rational soul and body possessed by Christ cannot be attributed to a human *hypostasis* or *persona*, as Boethius's definition suggests. Rather they must be properties of Christ's *human nature*. Or, to use Lossky's own elegant distinction: "The *hypostasis* of the assumed humanity cannot be reduced to the human substance, to that human individual who was registered with the other subjects of the Roman Empire under Augustus."[41] Lossky here argues that the imperial census of the Lukan narrative counts individual human *bodies*, but not human *persons*. While Lossky is clear that this distinction between the *hypostasis* and the individual applies specifically to the limit case of Jesus Christ, it is enough to highlight the problem within Boethius's definition.

As previously mentioned, Latin medieval theologians also raise objections to Boethius's definition when it is applied to Trinitarian Persons. First, there is the problem of the individual substance when speaking of persons who share in undivided consubstantiality. But moreover, Richard of St. Victor observes in his twelfth-century treatise *On the Trinity* that *substance* answers the question *what*, while *person* answers the question *who*. Since we are dealing with persons rather than things, Richard offers a new definition in relation to Trinitarian Persons: "A divine Person is the incommunicable existence of the divine nature."[42] Here the word *incommunicable* refers to that which cannot be shared: again, paternity, generation, and procession.

While Richard's definition refers specifically to divine Persons, Lossky affirms the Victorine's distinction between *who* and *what* and adopts it for his candidate definition of the human person, as we will see below. But first let us explore one more possibility for defining the human person.

Before moving to his own definition, Lossky turns to Gregory of Nyssa. Gregory describes the *nous* as the rational seat of liberty (*autexousia*) and the faculty within the human being that rules over the animal body.[43] For Gregory, the *nous* is the element in humans that is created in the image of God, distinguishing us from other created beings. However, Lossky argues that the human person cannot be associated with the *nous*. In light of the Chalcedonian Definition, we are faced with the specter of a Christological heresy.[44] Jesus Christ has but one *hypostasis*, which Chalcedon teaches is divine. If the *nous* were to represent the hypostatic element within the human being, then the humanity of Christ would be devoid of a human *nous* in favor of the rational mind of the *Logos*. Christ would not have assumed the fullness of humanity, including its *nous* or rational soul (*psychē logikē*).[45] Lossky correctly identifies this proposition as the error of Apollinaris of Laodicea.[46] Thus, the human person or *hypostasis* cannot be equated with the *nous*. Not only would this scenario violate the dogma of the Chalcedonian Definition, but it would also go to the heart of the question of human salvation. For according to the maxim of Gregory of Nazianzus, whatever is not assumed is not redeemed.[47] It is for this reason that the Christological dogma insists that Jesus Christ is perfect in his humanity (*teleion . . . en anthrōpotēti*), which includes both body and rational soul.

With these limit cases in place, Lossky offers his candidate definition for the human person:

> *Person* signifies the irreducibility of the human to its nature— "irreducibility" and not "something irreducible" or "something which makes the human irreducible to its nature" precisely because it cannot be a question here of "something" distinct from "another nature" but of *someone* who is distinct from their own nature, of someone who goes beyond their nature while still containing it, who makes it exist as human nature by this overstepping and yet does not exist in themselves beyond the nature which they "enhypostasize" and which they constantly exceed.[48]

Lossky's definition follows his general apophatic method. Having offered and negated a series of positive attributes associated with the common human nature or essence, he gestures beyond to one who exceeds the common nature. In keeping with Richard of St. Victor's distinction between *substantia* and *persona*, he notes that the human person is not *something*, but rather *someone*, a move consonant with Lossky's personalist values. With a nod to the usage of Leontius of Byzantium, he speaks of the person as enhypostasizing—or to anglicize the term, *personifying*—the common human nature.[49] Finally, in a move parallel to the use of *hypostasis* to signify that which is incommunicable between Father, Son, and Holy Spirit, the word *person* here is decoupled from the word *individual* to instead point to the uniqueness of the one who exceeds the common human nature.[50]

The appeal of Lossky's argument for Elisabeth Behr-Sigel in opposition to the essentialist paradigm explored in chapter 3 should be clear. Rather than assigning and forbidding roles and behaviors based on gender or biological sex, Lossky's claim—that the human person is the one who exceeds our common nature—opens avenues for unique, new, authentically human actions that go beyond the properties that we all share.

The essentialist arguments of the previous chapter suggest that humans fall into one of two categories, male or female. Essentialists then further assign different ontological attributes, spiritual charisms, and roles within the created order, based on the perceived sex of the individual. Lossky's distinction, in contrast, predicates sexedness to the shared human nature. Human persons (*hypostaseis* in the sense previously applied only to Trinitarian *hypostaseis*) possess within themselves all that is a part of the common nature but also transcend the human *homoousia*. As we saw previously, Behr-Sigel identifies two ways in which this transcendence can readily be seen. The first is in the free choice of consecrated virginity that defies social convention and biological imperatives. The second is in the assertion that charisms (including the ordained priesthood) are not bound by sex or gender. In the concluding chapter we will explore several other ways this freedom can and should inform some of the thornier issues of our own day. But before we can do so, we must further explore the ways that gender, biological sex, and sexualities are related to theological personalism.

The Indeterminacy of Gender, Sex, and Sexualities

We turn now from Lossky's definition of the human person to examine a series of parallel moves in contemporary gender and queer theory. Before I begin, it is important that I point out that Lossky was no fan of "secularized" anthropology. He writes: "Scientific anthropology, based upon observation of concrete facts, can have only an accidental value for theology. Theological anthropology must be constructed from the top down, beginning from Trinitarian and Christological dogma, to discover in human reality the unity of nature and the multiplicity of created hypostases. . . ."[51] It is for this reason that I have gone to such lengths in the first part of this chapter to explore theological anthropology from above.

However, a commitment to Orthodox dogmatic teachings is insufficient grounds for refusing to interact with the findings of contemporary scientific and philosophical discourses. As Kallistos Ware suggests, "Orthodox need to explore, with a rigor and a humility that we have not so far displayed, the characteristic insights of contemporary medicine, psychology, and sociology." He is quick to add two caveats. First, these disciplines will not supply "ready-made answers." Second, the Orthodox attitude while engaging these discourses should be "one of openness," but not of "abdication" of distinctive Christian affirmations.[52] Elsewhere, Ware echoes Behr-Sigel's earlier observation: personhood cannot be deconstructed and reduced to the facts of various sciences.[53]

With these caveats in mind, I now use the "observation of concrete facts," taking several concepts in turn and showing how—as they are applied to human nature—each has been "essentialized"—a term that still bears witness to its origin in the word *essence*. Such elements are considered necessary and ontologically fixed, rather than simply being accidental to individuals. I will begin with gender and gender roles—concepts that many of us have come to see as largely culturally defined. I will follow up with two more categories: biological sex and sexuality or sexual orientation. For various audiences, these latter categories may be deemed more essential or ontological in nature. However, as we will see, these categories are not nearly as stable as many have assumed. Instead, they appear to be dependent on historical and cultural conditions. Rather than being based in immutable metaphysics, they turn out to be the products of cultural and scientific discourses. Applying Lossky's insight into the human person to these various categories, I hope to show how an apophatic anthropology opens the way for each human person to transcend the shared human nature. While manifesting a variety of attributes from the plentitude of our shared human nature, each human person is always more than these attributes, unique in relation to God and other human persons, gifted with personal charisms and called to their own activities in our joint vocation.

Before proceeding, it is important to note that much of what follows was unknown to the authors explored in the previous chapter. I am not suggesting they should have known, nor am I impugning their personal character. However, their ideas, especially as they are to inform an Orthodox theological anthropology, must be evaluated in light of these discourses. Let us turn now to gender.

Gender

As we saw in chapter 1, the English words *gender* and *sex* are used largely interchangeably. But since John Money, the two words are sometimes used to refer to different concepts. In exploring the nature of intersex conditions, Money turned to philology, borrowing the word *gender* to signify "a person's personal, social, and legal status as male or female without reference to sex organs." He coined the term *gender role* to denote "the things a person says or does to reveal him- or herself as having the status of boy or man, girl or woman." Finally, Money coined the term *gender identity* to refer to the subjective experience of gender.[54] This opened the possibility of reorienting the word *sex* to refer only to the biological characteristics that separate male and female: hormones (and pubertal differentiation), chromosomes, gonads, internal reproductive structures, and external genital morphology. While many within our larger culture may not have given much thought to the distinction between biological sex and gender, the different elements are easy to draw attention to by referencing our cultural tropes of the manly man, the sissy, and the tomboy. The first of these aligns biological sex with socially acceptable or expected gender roles while the latter two refer to people who transgress the gender roles commonly associated with their perceived sex. Second-wave feminists adopted this distinction between gender and sex to differentiate what is socially constructed and what is biologically bound or determined. Vested with this distinction, *sex* allowed for the idea of a group of humans called *women* who could contest the *gendered* conditions of their lives, especially areas of inequity and oppression, as things that can be changed rather than simply accepted as immutable or preordained. However, the distinction between gender and biological sex is not a completely new phenomenon.

In the ancient world, being born with a particular set of genitalia was not necessarily indicative of one's gender. As we saw in chapter 1, Greco-Roman doctors searched for explanations for the traits they observed by positing an essential nature influenced by various combinations of moisture and dryness or heat and cold. Ancient medical treatises attribute some behavioral characteristics to the types of seed contributed by an individual's parents as well as hypothesizing about the effects of gestation within a particular quadrant of a mother's womb.[55] Astrologers turned to the heavens, claiming that the conjunctions of various celestial bodies at the time of a person's birth result in particular personality types that hew more and less closely to gendered norms.[56]

But even after being born male, men of the ancient Mediterranean world were constantly subject to scrutiny, rumor, and rhetorical battle within a zero-sum game. Their masculinity was under constant observation and evaluation. Manhood was difficult to achieve and had to be vigilantly maintained. Physiognomists were in demand for their ability to determine an individual's actual manliness regardless of biological sex. They created an entire occupation of observing a man's physical characteristics, way of holding himself, and gait to uncover those who were secretly inclined to odious behaviors that undermined their masculinity.

In the Greco-Roman context, a man could be deemed womanly by at least two different (though sometimes related) avenues. First, an over-emphasis on self-presentation in the pursuit of pleasures could result in accusations of being soft or effeminate (Greek *malthakos/malakos*, Latin *mollis*). This could include the use of cosmetics or the removal of body hair to be more attractive to one's sexual interest.[57] Second, both Greek and Roman cultures paid particular attention to the mechanics of who penetrated whom in sexual acts. The male citizen could penetrate his wife, a courtesan, or male or female slaves.[58] He might also penetrate his enemy taken in combat, humiliating him by stripping him of his masculinity. A man who voluntarily allows himself to be penetrated in the pursuit of pleasure was deemed a *kinaidos*, an ancient Greek scare-figure adopted by the Romans as the *cinaedus*. Promiscuity, receiving payment for sexual favors, and passivity were all elements of this unmanly trope.[59] Through his sexual proclivities, the *kinaidos* forfeits his masculinity by assuming the role of a (feminine) sexual object.

Other examples of the separation between gender roles and biological sex, this time in the allegorical realm, are evident in our patristic sources from chapter 2. Both Augustine's masculine-upper and feminine-lower faculties of the mind and the Philonic model of masculine high spirit and feminine desire within the human soul demonstrate a distinction between biological sex (male or female) and the gendered elements (masculine and feminine) that constitute all human persons. A different model demonstrated by Gregory of Nyssa speaks of the choice to be born female (of the world) or male (of the spirit). Using his sister Macrina as an example, Nyssen contends that though she is biologically female, her spiritual identity is male. These examples of gender roles and expectations from various historical cultures help us to see our own understandings of gender, gender roles, and cultural expectations. They can also be useful in highlighting the distinctions in Lossky's thought. In the cases of the composite human soul (masculine *thymos* and feminine *aisthēsis*) and mind (masculine *sapentia* and feminine *scientia*), the emphasis is on elements of our common human nature. In Nyssen's description, the focus is on the transcendence of biology in the fulfillment of spiritual vocation. All three examples speak to the makeup of and options available to all human beings.

Increased exposure to different cultures has also made the fluid nature of gender norms much more apparent in most quarters. In some cultures, men embrace, kiss, and hold hands, while in others such behaviors are considered effeminate. Some modern gender theorists speak of gender as a performance, something we "do" with varying degrees of success.[60] Gender theorist Judith Butler has coined the term *performativity* to describe this phenomenon. But Butler differs in her evaluation of gender from both the ancient rhetoricians and moralists and contemporary theologians who claim a core masculine or feminine essence in that she denies an ontological source of maleness or femaleness. For Butler, a gender performance successfully passes for male or female through repetition of previous performances. While repetition (*iterability*) is key, a given performance will always be different in some way from those that preceded it (*alterity*). Over time minor changes may be acceptable, and the accretion of variations may even alter the criteria by which gendered performances are evaluated. But too much difference too quickly results in failing "to pass."

The Orthodox theologians and religious philosophers reviewed in chapter 3 theorize separate male and female natures, created by God, which manifest in masculine and feminine genders with separate, complementary charisms and roles.[61] However, even among essentialists, opinions vary about exactly which elements of gender roles are essential and which are matters of cultural contingency. For example, most contemporary Orthodox theologians who address the issue argue that there is something distinctive between men and women that excludes women from ordained ministry, a topic to which we will return in the next chapter.[62] Other gendered expectations differ over time, such that even proponents of an essentialist view of gender are sometimes willing to concede that not all gender roles and expectations are divinely mandated. Examples of such changes include discussions concerning women, menstruation, and communion, or the practice of veiling.[63] However, while these changes are often couched in the language of social custom, some of these changes in practice also include a change in the understanding of human physiology, or arguments from nature (Greek *physis*) as found in Paul's writings in the New Testament.

Many of the tropes of manliness in ancient sources are still recognizably masculine by today's standards. Yet the categories are also dependent on particular conceptions of what it means to be masculine or feminine within the cultural contexts in which these ideas circulated. This in turn leads us back to the instability of gender categories across time, culture, and locale. What is manly for the ancient Greek citizen is not always the same as what is manly for the twenty-first-century cosmopolitan male. While the modern man, we are told, looks out for his partner's sexual gratification, the ancients would see such a man as effeminate.[64] Likewise, the modern preoccupation with bigger and stronger erections that last longer was a characteristic relegated to the mythical satyr of ancient Greece and quite unbecoming of the citizen male who held disciplined control over both his body and his passions. Such demonstrable differences in the understandings of what are appropriately masculine and feminine illustrate the nonessential nature of these categories. In personalist terms, human persons present to us as concrete, gendered individuals. But in their personhood, they are free of any determinism that would suggest that they are bound to an essential set of gendered characteristics and activities.

Up until now we have primarily focused on concepts within a *cisgender* (sometimes shortened to *cis*) essentialist binary, meaning an individual's gender identity aligns with the sex they were assigned at birth. We have also briefly examined the policing of gender norms in cases where external observers deem an individual's actions or presentation incongruent with the individual's perceived sex (e.g., the sissy, the tomboy, the *malakos*). Before moving on to the next section, I wish to briefly introduce several terms related to *transgender* (or *trans*) individuals as those whose gender identity does not match the sex they were assigned at birth. Rather than an external judgment, the emphasis in both cisgender and transgender terminology is on the subjective experience of the individual. Trans people may still fall within the binary. For example, a *trans man* is assigned female at birth but has a male gender identity. Likewise, a *trans woman* is assigned male at birth but has a female gender identity. The older term *transsexual*, originating in clinical usage, is still sometimes preferred by individuals who have taken (or wish to take) steps to bring their bodies into line with the gender expectations of their gender identity. However, this term is currently contested, as many trans people and their supporters associate it with medical pathologization and gatekeeping protocols that have historically limited access to hormone replacement therapy and surgeries to individuals whose experience and presentation match particular narratives.

Our exploration has also focused primarily on binary designations. However, in recent years the number of nonbinary and agender trans-identifying individuals has grown significantly.[65] In both cases, greater sophistication in the language we use to describe personal subjectivity has opened avenues for articulating a lack of fit experienced by some individuals when faced with a strict gender binary. Here, Berdyaev and Bulgakov offer a useful model. If we conceptualize male and female or masculine and feminine not as poles on a single continuum, but rather as wholly separate categories, we can then see that each individual can express both in greater and lesser degrees. Agender persons would characterize their subjectivity as being low or nonexistent for both categories, while nonbinary, trans individuals experience both masculinity and femininity in degrees resulting in a gender identity that is neither male nor female, man nor woman.

The language of the previous paragraph breaks with the conventions I have observed throughout this book, referring to male and female, man and woman in places where gender designations would normally be described as masculine or feminine. This reflects the diverse language usage within the trans community. However, no one in the conversation seriously contests a statistical bimodal distribution of physical characteristics that we commonly identify with the male and female sexes. What is at stake is the recognition of gender identities that exist outside of an overly determinative either/or binary.

In more recent usage *transgender* operates as an umbrella term that also includes a variety of non-binary gender identities and expressions, including individuals who identify as some combination of male and female, agender, or of another gender falling outside of the binary. The term *genderqueer* has also been adopted by some individuals whose subjective gender identity is non-binary, regardless of their assigned biological sex. As more individuals choose from a variety of options (e.g., manner of dress; hormone replacement therapy; and various surgeries to reshape the face, vocal apparatus, chest, and genitals), the number of bodies that do not strictly adhere to the binary model continues to increase.

While our broader society becomes more aware of both transgender and genderqueer individuals, the Orthodox ecclesial context is less informed. Orthodox scholars and hierarchs often recognize binary transgender phenomena, but non-binary or genderqueer identities are largely absent from church experience. Reluctance to accept trans people is justified primarily by framing trans subjectivity as a mental disorder while asserting that gender identity should properly be dictated by biological sex. With this in mind, let us turn from our exploration of gender to examine the underpinnings of biological sex. We will discover that sex, much like gender, is vastly more complicated than the essentialist paradigm would lead us to believe.

Biological Sex

As we saw in chapter 3, some Orthodox thinkers refer to the embodiment of human persons as male and female as ontological "modes of being" or "modes of human existence." Our everyday experience shows us these two modes in the form of women and girls, men and boys. However, the idea that biological sex with its attendant descriptions is a stable fact is questionable from several angles. Already we have explored the distinction between biological sex and culturally conditioned gender that allows us to critique the idea that biology is destiny. Going a step further, some gender theorists argue that just as gender roles and identities are socially constructed, so also are the categories of biological sex.[66] Rather than immutable, ontological principles, our ideas about what constitutes the categories of biologically male and female are constituted by a range of culturally dependent discourses within the biological and medical sciences.

With an idea as ingrained as the male/female binary, many people balk at the suggestion that these designations are arbitrarily constructed rather than essential aspects of human nature. After all, it is as plain as the genitals between a newborn's legs. With the advent of ultrasound technology, we can make sex determinations while the child is still in the womb. The presence of a penis indicates that a child is male, while a vagina characterizes the female sex.

But like gender performances that prove unintelligible (or *illegible*) in the absence of categories through which to perceive them, so also bodies that fall outside of the normative parameters of male and female can prove difficult or impossible to truly see. Specialists in the field of gender and sex have identified no fewer than seven different indicators of biological sex and an additional five categories around gender roles, forming a matrix of possibilities that extends well beyond the easy classification of male and female, masculine and feminine.[67] But our preconceived categories directly affect what we are able to perceive.

Since the 1950s, the biological sex binary has been reinforced through the application of medical protocols developed for the "correction" of infants born with internal and external structures that confound the dimorphic model. In cases of sexual ambiguity, doctors are trained to quickly assess the range of possibilities and attempt through surgery to fit the newborn infant into either the male or female category. Researchers estimate that from 0.373 to 1.7 percent of the population are born outside of the strict male/female binary.[68] While the percentage is small, as the human population approaches 8 billion, this still comes to between 29.8 and 136 million people worldwide. Gender theorists point to intersex persons as the limit cases that expose the inadequacy of the predominant concept of biological sex.

With the advent of the microscope, scientists identified male and female gametes. Subsequent discoveries have led to our understandings of DNA, chromosomes, and the roles played by genes. The typical human possesses twenty-three pairs of chromosomes in most cells that make up their body, one chromosome of each pair originating from each of the individual's parents. The chromosomes contributed from each parent are identical in structure for pairs one through twenty-two. However, in the twenty-third pair, some variation occurs. While the mother contributes an X-chromosome, the father may contribute either an X or a Y. Scientists designate children possessing a Y-chromosome as chromosomally male.

Until recently, scientists assumed the female sex to be the default morphological form for the human species, while thinking the male sex to be the result of an active process of development. However, beginning in the 1990s, the discovery of separate networks of gene activity has led to the understanding of two opposed processes that lead to the development of male and female sexes. Yet in an interesting parallel to the personalist view of a common nature, scientists have discovered that each typical embryo, regardless of later assigned sex, begins from a common cellular configuration, and begins its development in the same way.

Each developing human possesses a genital tubercule that will develop into a phallo-clitoral body. Each has the same gonadal tissues that can develop into ovaries or testes (or sometimes both). Each has both Müllerian and Wolffian ducts. In the presence of estrogen, the Müllerian ducts develop into fallopian tubes, a uterus, cervix, and upper portion of the vagina, while the Wolffian ducts that would have otherwise formed male urogenital structures wither away. In the presence of testosterone, a different process unfolds by which the Wolffian duct develops into the structures that will eventually produce and transport semen. Testosterone also triggers the production of another hormone that causes the regression of the Müllerian ducts, resulting in the cessation of development of female urogenital structures. Each fetus also develops a set of labioscrotal swellings that will eventually form, as their name implies, either the labia majora or fuse to form a scrotum. Each embryo also develops two separate tissues that form various elements of the typical female and male urogenital tracts. The atrophy or continued development of these common elements is governed by two distinct and competing sets of genes. By the time most babies are born, they clearly fall into a bimodal distribution of physical traits that we commonly identify as male and female. Yet each begins with a common genetic inheritance, differentiating into a unique, embodied human being as they develop.

But human development can be more complex than the account I have just described. In the most readily visible cases, a child may be born with ambiguous genitalia. A child may externally present as one sex while internally possessing the reproductive structures associated with the other—or even both—sexes. Some babies are assigned female at birth, only to discover at puberty that they are male when their testes descend and they exhibit secondary sex characteristics associated with men. Some babies are designated female at birth but possess a Y-chromosome and lack internal female reproductive organs. Though chromosomally male, they look like girls and develop outwardly as women, they have a feminine gender identity, and they may even marry men. Without gynecological examination or genetic testing, such women can go through life without anyone questioning their sex. Others may be chromosomally female and nonetheless develop a typical penis.

In addition to these differences in sexual development, recent advances in genetic analysis have revealed to us a world of genetic mosaicism within some human individuals. This happens when two or more separate genetic lines (e.g., two or more fertilized eggs) merge to form a single body in which the different genetic inheritances form various organs. A similar phenomenon known as microchimerism occurs when cells pass between a mother and her unborn child. Researchers have identified XY (chromosomally male) cells that remain with a mother, taking up residence in her organs and incorporating into her body as though they were her own. Twins, whether identical or fraternal, swap cells during gestation that become a part of their sibling. Likewise, successive children born of the same mother can inherit cells left behind by previous occupants of the same womb. The lines between bodies and sexes again become blurred in these instances.

Common wisdom might also point to some hormones as a distinguishing feature of the sexes. Estrogens are associated with women. Androgens, including testosterone, are associated with men. The researchers who first isolated these compounds thought they had identified substances exclusive to each sex. Their preconceptions were so strong that when they discovered estrogen in samples from stallions and human males, they suspected contamination rather than immediately coming to the truth. Not long afterwards, testosterone was found in females. While the ratios of these hormones are different from individual to individual, both estrogens and androgens are typically found in us all. Both are necessary and play key roles in regulating a variety of bodily processes regardless of assigned biological sex. What's more, there are females with higher testosterone levels than some males and males with greater estrogen levels than some females. Though the distributions of various characteristics associated with biological sex tend to cluster within a population around two statistical norms, there is overlap between the sexes that undermines a simple either/or binary.

Estrogens and androgens also play key roles in two other processes. During gestational development, these hormones play crucial roles in prenatal brain development. Researchers hypothesize that either the lack of hormonal production or the inability for receptors to process these hormones may result in differences in brain development resulting in transgender children whose gender identities do not match their assigned biological sex. The secretion and reception of estrogens and androgens also regulate the production and activities of reproductive cells within ovaries and testes. Finally, recent studies at the cellular level suggest that cells involved in the production of sperm and ova exist in a delicate balance as either female or male. Ovaries contain granulosa cells, which provide nourishment to developing ova, while Sertoli cells found in testes nurse the development of sperm cells. A shift in the hormonal balance within the cell can result in a shift in the cell's "sex" as expressed in terms of form and function. Bathed in testosterone, granulosa cells appear and function as Sertoli cells, while the deactivation of a single gene results in the reprograming of Sertoli cells to become granulosa cells. These discoveries have led to the understanding that, at the cellular level, sex is not an immutable characteristic, but is a constant balancing act in which two competing processes, both pro-grammed into the same DNA, are regulated by genes that maintain a particular environment. Once again, these findings indicate a deeply shared commonality between male and female that goes even further than we had previously imagined.

But what does all this information mean to a theological anthropology? Are we not at risk of falling into a trap like essentialist arguments that emphasize biology as destiny? Despite what gender essentialists might sug-gest, there is no clear-cut line between the sexes. Whether the criterion is external genitalia, internal morphology, chromosomal makeup, hormonal environment, or even cellular composition, many human beings manifest characteristics that are more complicated than a simple male-female binary can accommodate. Following Lossky's arguments, we encounter human persons as sexed individuals. All these differences in sexual development are variations found in human individuals among the expressions of our common human nature. However, the human person is neither defined by nor limited to any of these criteria, either singly or in combination. Rather, the person continues to transcend the common human nature as the one who exceeds what is shared and is thus unique and unrepeatable. So far, we have seen how this is the case for gender and biological sex. As we will see, the same can be said of sexual orientations.

Sexualities

We turn now to the concept of sexuality, most commonly described under the rubrics of *heterosexuality* and *homosexuality*, with the occasional acknowledgment that some people fall between these poles (*bisexuality*), while others may see themselves nowhere within this polarity (*asexuality*).[69] We live in a time of heated debate over these labels. Their meanings are often contested. Some suggest they refer strictly to sexual acts, while others use them to describe affective attraction.[70] Arguments also rage over cau-sation, be it learned behavior, genes, differences in the hypothalamus or amygdala, or the hormonal environment during fetal development or in adult life. As we proceed, I first point out that this section complicates not only essentialist categories, but also the common wisdom about sexual orientations.

Like the previous exploration of shifting descriptions of gender roles and the ambiguities of biological sex, a closer examination renders the categories of sexuality much less stable and more historically dependent than most people are aware. At an elementary level, modern sexualities depend on the binary of biological sex for their meaning. Heterosexuals, for example, are either sexually involved with or romantically attracted to individuals who fall on the opposite side of the biological sex binary. Yet the previous discussion of the ambiguities of biological sex surely complicates such a simplistic coupling.

Beyond the biological debates, Michel Foucault presents us with a genealogy of the development of the modern concept of sexuality. While homogenital activity has been around at least as long as written records, Foucault argues that the notion of assigning an identity to an individual based on their sexual desire—on the content of the individual's inner thought life rather than observable practices—is a distinctively modern social construction. He traces the development of sexual identities through a series of historical phenomena that includes the medieval practice of confession and the subsequent forms of self-disclosure cultivated in modern medical and psychiatric disciplines. As part of the movement to label, categorize, and cure a variety of sexual pathologies, nineteenth-century professionals formulated new identities: the hysterical woman, the masturbating youth, and the sexual deviant.[71] This last identity, as Foucault describes it, is one of gender inversion in which the masculine and feminine interiority of the subject is the opposite of the subject's biological sex.[72]

Building on Foucault's discussion of the rise of the homosexual identity, other scholars continue to highlight the constructed nature of sexualities through the examination of sexual categories in cultures both historical and contemporary. While it is true that Foucault's particular brand of psychological subjectivity is necessarily dependent on modern psychiatric discourses, Mark Jordan suggests that in the medieval discourses around *sodomia*, something akin to a full-fledged Sodomitic identity already begins to emerge in the eleventh-century writings of Peter Damian and continues to develop in the work of medieval Christian authors to include "remarks on Sodomitic anatomy and physiology, personal history, and secret community." A medical identity, adopted from Arabic medical texts, is already in evidence from the thirteenth century.[73] Jordan's corrections serve as refinements to

Foucault's thinking, fleshing out the latter's gloss regarding juridical and canonical subjects to reveal the role of the Sodomite in preparing the way for the easy acceptance of the modern homosexual subject.[74]

Literary critic and queer theorist Eve Kosofsky Sedgwick offers an additional corrective to Foucault's inquiry. Observing the metanarrative of historical progression in which the discourses of sexuality appear to displace older categories and understandings of same-sex relations, Sedgwick argues that our modern understandings of sexualities are more akin to accretions atop the previous categories.[75] Integrating this insight into his own work, David Halperin maps older categories of same-sex relationships, both erotic and philial, that continue to exist within our own frame of reference and influence our conceptions of sexuality. These ancient categories—same-sex friendship, the lover (*erastēs*) and beloved (*erōmenos*) of ancient Greek pederasty, the dissolute *kinaidos/cinaedus* who gives up his identity as a man in order to experience the pleasures of being sexually penetrated, and the soft or effeminate dandy (*malthakos/mollis*) who modifies his appearance and behavior to gain the attentions of women and boys—are the tectonic plates on which the structures of contemporary sexualities shift and rock.[76] To Halperin's list we may also add the Sodomite, whose resurgence is a centerpiece of current movements in Orthodox Christianity against same-sex marriage and anti-discrimination protections for LGBT citizens and the invert highlighted in Foucault's study.

In our own era, anthropological accounts of other cultures offer a window on acts that through our contemporary lenses of sexuality fall under the rubric of homosexuality. In their own context, these acts are not described in the language of desire, but rather as rituals of initiation into manhood.[77] Even within our own context, popular accounts of sexualities are contested through both an examination of sexual fluidity among women and new studies that focus on the intersection of gender and race that show how self-identified straight white men engage in sexual activities with other men without identifying as homosexual or gay.[78] Like the awareness of the variations in gender roles and expectations across cultures, knowledge of alternative sexual practices and identities highlights the dynamic nature of the categories that many in the modern West take for granted and read anachronistically into other cultures across time.

In another critique of the current paradigm of sexualities that aligns in some ways with the personalist critique of gender essentialism offered by Elisabeth Behr-Sigel, feminist author and social activist bell hooks suggests that the act of labeling a woman as heterosexual declares her willing or open to sexual advances from any man.[79] The inverse of her claim can be observed when, on discovering a man is gay, many other men—both gay and straight—assume themselves automatically to be the objects of the first man's desire by virtue of also being men. However, neither of these scenarios should be assumed. hooks observes that as women assert their right to choose their sexual partners, they "challenge the assumption that female sexuality exists to serve the sexual needs of men."[80] We will explore how her claims are supported by a personalist anthropology in chapter 6.

In summary, the discourses of sexuality that permeate our current understandings of erotic bonds are problematic on several levels. Most basically, they depend on essentialized understandings of gender and biological sex. However, gender categories vary according to culture and era, while our understandings of what makes a person biologically male or female become more complicated with each new scientific discovery. In addition to these instabilities, lived experience continues to show that a variety of erotic affections and sexual practices simply cannot be accounted for by a strict heterosexual-homosexual binary. Further, self-identification tends to blur the lines, suggesting that either sexuality is fluid over time, or that some sexual liaisons may be rationalized as temporary (e.g., acceptable experimentation while in college) or situational aberrations (e.g., hazing rituals, sexual acts in segregated environments such as prisons, military service, or educational institutions). Whatever the case, essentialized sexualities, like essentialized genders and biological designations, are apt to obscure the freedom of the human person, who transcends these descriptions.

Conclusion

In chapter 3 we saw how Elisabeth Behr-Sigel developed and applied insights she gleaned from Lossky's personalism in her critique of the gender essentialist ideas advanced by her friend Paul Evdokimov, as well as similar arguments by Thomas Hopko. By assigning fixed and separate sets of charisms to men and women, these models threatened to eclipse the unique and irreplaceable contributions offered by each human person to the broader project of God's creation. Working from a personalist anthropology, Behr-Sigel stressed that characteristics such as "the capacity of reception, openness to others and the Other, openness to transcendence of all humanity," and "the virility of 'the violent that take hold of the Kingdom of Heaven'" are not exclusive to a single sex.[81] At the same time, she proposed instead that the human person is a mysterious, unique, unclassifiable, and free totality who cannot be reduced to or confined by any particular characteristic. Her argument used words like *sex* and *sexuality* interchangeably rather than with the different conceptual categories explored in this chapter. But regardless of the lack of conceptual delineation between the cultural and the biological—let alone any thought of sexual orientation—Behr-Sigel's initial argument points the way for analogous arguments across the various areas of differentiation that we have explored in this chapter.

Behr-Sigel drew her argument from the personalism developed by Vladimir Lossky. In his own work, Lossky differentiates between the individual—one who manifests a set of characteristics drawn from our common humanity—and the person—the *who* that is completely unique, unrepeatable, and free to transcend our common nature. While sharing in our common humanity, the person fulfills its own unique vocation in communion with other human persons. From his earliest writings, Lossky saw sexedness as a characteristic of the common human nature, something all persons share but also exceed.

The risk we run in our classification of humanity into two biological sexes both parallels and overlaps with the dangers inherent in the schematization of gender into the opposition of masculinity and femininity. In both cases, the danger lies not necessarily in the label in and of itself, but in the occlusion of the human person as the price paid while forming and maintaining categories into which unique persons are not easily fit. The results are twofold. First, hard-and-fast categories hinder deep relationality by leading us to make assumptions, often incorrectly, about persons with whom we interact—assumptions about their innate capacities, their abilities, and the roles they play in the world. Instead of seeing the actual person, we see only an interchangeable member of a larger group. Second, these assumptions are connected to the doors of vocation, access, and opportunity that are opened or closed to those who bear a particular label. What is at stake is the ability to fulfill one's call, to fully contribute to God's work in the world according to one's particular combination of talents, abilities, and charisms.

In the second movement of this chapter, we have explored the categories of gender, biological sex, and sexualities. Under closer examination, these categories turn out to be historically and culturally dependent conceptual schemas rather than ontological principles as they are characterized in essentialist arguments.[82] The sexual binary, so completely engrained in our thinking as to be considered self-evident or natural, is confounded by those human individuals whose anatomy, or biochemistry, or chromosomal makeup cannot be analyzed and neatly assigned to one of the two commonly available categories of biological sex. While many theological anthropologies are completely unaware of these complexities, others discount their value, relegating them to signs of a fallen world.[83] The tendency to dismiss variations in biological makeup as abnormal can be traced to an Enlightenment practice of associating statistical norms with the nature that God intended. This worldview continues in the medical community with pathologization of naturally occurring variations within the human population.[84] Such valuations are strengthened by the tendency in modern medical discourse to pathologize atypical cases rather than accept them as infrequent but non-threatening variations in the human population. Advances in modern biological and medical sciences have allowed us to look beyond the macro level to identify many finer differences between individual human bodies. At this more detailed level we continue to find new variations that exceed the boundaries of the typical developmental process outlined above.

Further, the purported rationale for the division—the ability to procreate for the continuation of our species—is simply not guaranteed by the label assigned to each body. While the typical male may produce sperm from puberty until his death, the window of fertility for the typical female closes with the onset of menopause. But, for a variety of reasons, not all men and women possess the same procreative capacity. From the personalist perspective, the ability to procreate has absolutely no bearing on the category of the human person. Clearly other forms of relationality must count in the various personifications of our shared human nature. If this were not the case, then infertility would prove an automatic disqualification for personhood, as would the conscious embrace of celibacy, that noble vocation of so many saints of the Church. In short, there is more to being a human person than the capacity to physically procreate new human beings. Again, procreation is an element of the common human nature rather than the property of the human person.

The personalist approach outlined by Lossky allows us to move beyond the well-trodden arguments of fertility to integrate into our picture what we know of non-binary bodies. In a creative appropriation of Julitta's common lump,[85] we can reconceive the clay of her metaphor to encompass our common inheritance of flesh and blood. From our conception, we all follow a common developmental pattern. We all possess both Müllerian and Wolffian ducts. Each of us forms the same genital tubercle and labioscrotal swellings with their raw potential to develop in a variety of configurations, including those that exceed the easy binary classification of male and female. This common embodiment, our shared birthright, is the strongest argument in opposition to the essentialization of a particular characteristic. At the same time, the personalist emphasis on totally unique and unrepeatable *hypostaseis*, called to live out their vocations in communion with one another, serves as a safeguard against versions of collectivism that would reduce groups of people to interchangeable units for industry, economies, and nation building. Instead, each person with their unique and unrepeatable combination of relationships, charisms, and activities, contributes to the whole in ways no other can.

In the chapters that follow, we will examine various ways that a personalist approach might inflect responses to the questions with which this book began: women and the priesthood, a constellation of questions around homosexuality (same-sex attraction, sacramentality of same-sex relationships, and sexual activity), and care for intersex, transgender, and gender nonconforming individuals within the parish. As previously noted, initial Orthodox responses to these questions have tended to rely on arguments informed by gender essentialism. Using a personalist anthropology, I argue not simply for plausible alternatives but for what I hold are better, more correct responses to each question. Let us turn first to women and the priesthood.

PART II

5

WOMEN AND THE PRIESTHOOD

The question of the ordination of women to the priesthood has only recently been asked. For us Orthodox, the question comes "from the outside." It must become for us a question that is asked "from the inside." This question requires of us all an interior freedom and a deep communion with the vision and will of God, in a prayerful silence.

—ANTHONY BLOOM[1]

Introduction

First among the contemporary questions related to sex and gender mentioned in chapter 1 is the theme of women's ordination. In his exploration of feminine charisms, Paul Evdokimov asserted that a woman, by her very nature, is ontologically incapable of serving in the role of ordained priest. Indeed, he suggested, it would be "a betrayal of her being."[2] At the time of his claim, there was not even a question in the Orthodox context concerning the possibility of clergywomen.[3] However, the intra-Orthodox conversation changed in 1976, when the question of women's ordination was raised during a conference on Orthodox women and their role and participation in the Orthodox Church, sponsored by the World Council of Churches. In her keynote address, Elisabeth Behr-Sigel asked whether the current arrangement excludes women with a priestly vocation from the charism of the priesthood, "subordinating grace to a biological determinism."[4]

Once the question was raised, various Orthodox thinkers began to speak. The question of women's ordination has come alive among laity, priests, and episcopal authorities alike, signaling a new question that the tradition can no longer afford to ignore.[5]

The Argument from Tradition

The first response offered in defense of current practice is an argument from tradition, which is, at the same time, an argument from silence, as there are no records indicating that a woman has ever held the position of presbyter or bishop. For a religious tradition that prides itself on continuity with ancient practice, the argument that "we've never done it that way" has a particular appeal. However, an appeal to past practice is not enough. The argument is more negative than positive. Moreover, there is a great deal of variation in Orthodox practices around the world, suggesting that, in various contexts, congregations have responded to particular needs by instituting practices that, at one point, were also not a part of Orthodox tradition.[6] While the argument from tradition is powerful, most Orthodox thinkers, aware of new Orthodox responses formulated to address new circumstances, do not stand on tradition alone, which is after all mostly silence. Thus, we move on to other arguments that have been offered.

Rights vs. Vocation

A second argument that we should address before moving into more complex theological territory is a straw person fallacy often set up by opponents of women's ordination. Taking the feminist language of *equal rights*, the argument suggests that women are demanding the "right" to ordained ministry.[7] These observations often echo arguments suggesting that women today seek to remake themselves in the image of fallen Adam as opposed to their God-given feminine nature.[8] This characterization of feminism, while applicable to some strands of the broader feminist movement, cannot be used as a blanket characterization for all feminists. Within the Orthodox Church, advocates for the recognition of the priestly vocation among women eschew the use of "rights" language.[9] Appealing to a more personalist approach, advocates of women's ordination focus on vocation. They fully recognize that not all women are called to the priesthood, just as all men are not. They simply reject the modern essentialist claim that a particular masculine charism, a penis, or a Y-chromosome is necessary to the fulfillment of the priestly office. Rather, they argue that God calls unique *persons* to serve as priests. An essentialist response again asserts that only men are called. To support this claim, some essentialists offer a set of theological arguments from scripture, as well as constructive theological work based on Trinitarian and Christological dogmas. To these we now turn.

Scriptural Qualifications of the Bishop/Presbyter

A third argument against women's ordination stands on the requirements for an overseer (*episkopos*) as set forth in 1 Tm 3:2, where the writer of the epistle insists that candidates for this position should be the husband of one wife (*mias gynaikos andra*). Thomas Hopko, for example, argues for a literal interpretation of the sex of the candidate (*anēr* vs. *gynē*), as opposed to the exclusive, relational nature of the spousal pairing (i.e., being espoused to only one person).[10] However, within the broader Orthodox tradition, the accent lies on the monogamous commitment of the pair. Canon law dictates that priest and spouse must be married only once, to each other.[11] The same demand for literal interpretation on which Hopko's argument rests falls away in relation to unmarried clergy who fill the monastic and episcopal ranks. Here, the qualifications dictated by scripture have been augmented within the history of Orthodox tradition. If a man is unmarried at the time of his ordination to the diaconate or priesthood, he is expected to take a vow of celibacy.[12] Marriage after this vow results in his removal from the sacerdotal ranks.[13] While 1 Tm 3:2 allows a bishop one wife, it has been Orthodox tradition since the Quinisext Council that bishops are required to cease to live with their wives.[14] For this reason, bishops are normally selected from the ranks of celibate monks. Lifelong celibacy of unmarried priests and bishops is not required by scripture but has nonetheless become the practice of the Orthodox Church.

The fact that Orthodox tradition has chosen to interpret the qualifications for both priests and bishops in a way that exceeds the letter of the biblical texts undermines Hopko's argument in two ways. First, the critical reception of a scripture passage is subject to changes in interpretation that reflect the experience of the Church. Qualifications for sacerdotal ministry join countless other instances in which Orthodox traditions depart from the literal meaning of the scripture. Thus, a prooftext from scripture alone cannot act as an argument without taking into consideration the interpretations offered within the tradition. Second, this example of divergence between scriptural guidelines and legal-canonical directives provides a precedent that shows it is indeed possible to rethink the qualifications of the presbyteral and episcopal offices originally given in scripture. In the spirit of the original passages, the qualification of having only one spouse may still be observed. In the same vein, bishops may continue to be selected from the ranks of those without a spouse. If biological sex is no longer a limiting factor, then candidates could include widows or nuns who meet all other criteria for the office.

Heirs to the Paris School tradition, including Hopko, are aware of Orthodoxy's history of providing multiple interpretations for scriptural passages. As with Hopko's reading of Gal 3:27–28,[15] however, it seems the meaning of a passage becomes unusually restrictive only when other readings prove favorable to a non-essentialist position.

Christological Arguments

In addition to arguments from historical practice, several Orthodox thinkers have offered theological arguments for their positions. In each case, the roles of presbyter and bishop are associated with Jesus Christ. The unifying factor in each argument is an emphasis on Christ as male. Let us explore each in turn.

Trinitarian Argument Redux

As we saw in chapter 3, Hopko's response to the question of women's ordination was a novel theological reflection that combines traditional Orthodox tropes with a new set of gendered associations. Hopko used existing associations between Eve and Mary, Mary and the Church, and the Church and the Holy Spirit to construct a new set of male-centered associations between Adam and Christ, Adam and men, and men as shepherds (pastors). He further argued for analogical links between women and the Holy Spirit and men and the Son in both ontology and activity in the created world. These themes had already been explored in great depth in the works of Sergius Bulgakov and modified in the writings of Paul Evdokimov. These Paris School authors, in turn, had drawn inspiration for their claims, especially as they relate to gender complementarity, from various sources: Kabbalah, Jakob Böhme's mysticism, German Romanticism, and psychoanalytic discourses. Hopko did not reference these Russian theologians directly. Bulgakov's theological project was tainted by the scandal aroused by his sophiological speculations. Evdokimov, while attempting to make Bulgakov's work more palatable, reinforced the idea of complementary male and female principles by turning to the works of Bachofen and Jung. In contrast, Hopko attempted to cobble together a collection of more traditionally acceptable authorities—scripture, liturgy, prooftexts from the fathers—to support his claims. However, there should be no mistake that his "intuition" was something not found in the ancient traditions. Rather, it was assembled from a collection of elements that he read through the modern lenses of the two-sex body model and a Romantic view of gender complementarity.

Hopko's argument was immediately criticized for collapsing men and women into two essential forms at the level of the human *hypostasis*. While he acknowledged the critique—once in print—he nonetheless continued to repeat his initial claims throughout his career. However, the mere repetition of an erroneous hunch does not make it any more correct. In the end, Hopko's gendered schema obscures the human person, predicating an essentialist set of charisms and activities to each human individual based on their assigned sex.

In addition to the claim of a Trinitarian analogy with the sexes, Orthodox thinkers have offered several other Christologically focused arguments to which we now turn.

In Persona Christi *and the Iconic Argument*

In the apostolic and patristic periods, many authors suggested that the priest (or bishop) acts in the person of Christ.[16] This argument has come to a renewed centrality in Christian thought since the middle of the twentieth century in the Roman Catholic tradition.[17] In his original exploration of women and the ministerial priesthood, Hopko takes up this line of thought, arguing that "[a] bishop or presbyter in the Church never 'represents' another; he is always the sacramental presentation of Christ Himself."[18] Each of these instances points to the idea of the priest as an icon of Christ. While the idea of the priest making Christ present has been a part of the Church from early on, the focus on Christ's maleness as an explanation for the requirement that a priest also be male became an issue only with the question of women's ordination.[19] Within the Paris School tradition, the argument is stated succinctly by Alexander Schmemann: ". . . if the bearer, the icon, and fulfiller of the unique priesthood is *man* and not woman, it is because Christ is *man* and not woman."[20] But the introduction of a correlation between the maleness of the incarnate Christ and the priest/bishop is new and problematic for three reasons.

First, since Georges Florovsky's critique of the pseudomorphosis of Orthodoxy that resulted from the wholesale adoption of Roman Catholic theological categories in the seventeenth century, it would seem fraught to unreflectively borrow the iconic argument developed in *Inter Insigniores* in defense of an exclusively male priesthood. Again, the adoption of extra-Orthodox sources requires theological reflection, testing any new doctrinal formulation against accepted Orthodox teaching. However, such reflection has not been carried out.

Second, the *in persona Christi* argument of Roman Catholic theology suggests that the priest acts in the person of Christ throughout the Eucharistic celebration. However, Orthodox theology here differs. While, as John Chrysostom notes, the priest offers his hands and tongue in the service of Christ, this representation occurs only at moments when the priest addresses the congregation (e.g., blessings, the offering of the Eucharistic gifts).[21] In the remainder of the liturgy, the priest acts *in persona ecclesiae*, facing the altar with the congregation.[22] For this reason, Behr-Sigel asks (and Kallistos Ware repeats): Can not a woman offer her hands and tongue to serve in these moments?[23] To this we might add the question: Are hands and tongues sexed in any meaningful way?

Third, we must turn to what the tradition teaches about icons. In his discussion of the iconic argument, Ware provides four historical, theological criteria that work in favor of a non-sex-specific argument for how a priest iconically represents Christ. (1) An icon is not identical with its subject, thus there is no identification between the priest and Christ. They need not share the same essence (be *homoousioi*).[24] (2) Further, an icon does not represent its subject in a naturalistic or real sense. It is neither a portrait nor a photograph. Nor does a priest don a costume to look like Christ.[25] Thus, no natural likeness to Jesus Christ is required of a priest. Historically this has allowed for priests of various ages, ethnicities, and body types.[26] (3) Next, Ware quotes from Basil of Caesarea: "The honor shown to the icon is referred to the prototype."[27] This teaching, adopted later by Nicaea II, is companion to the first point.[28] Because there is no identification between Christ and the icon, the latter is not worshiped in itself, which would constitute idolatry. Whatever veneration may be directed toward the priestly icon (for example, reaching out to touch the priest's vestments during liturgical procession[29]) passes on to Christ. (4) Finally, an icon functions by making present a higher spiritual reality. The priest does not stand in as a deputy or surrogate of Christ, but rather makes Christ present.[30] None of these four criteria require that a priest be male, just as they do not call for sharing a common essence or physical resemblance.

However, Ware adds a fifth criterion to his list, suggesting that the maleness shared by the priest and the incarnate Christ facilitates identification in a way that femaleness cannot. Only this final criterion for the iconic argument has a particularly gendered component. But here the argument no longer stands grounded in traditional Orthodox theology. Rather, Ware relies on Schmemann's comment, quoted above, to support his claim, amplifying it with the words of Maximos Aghiorgoussis who writes that the symbolic and iconic value of the male priesthood is intimately related to both the maleness of Christ and the fatherly role of the Father in the Trinity.[31] What are we to make of the claim that maleness is essential to the ability of the priest to iconically represent Christ? By the lights of the Orthodox tradition, such an argument fails on three counts.

First, several commentators have noted that an undue stress on the assumption of maleness risks the exclusion of women from the salvific effects inaugurated in the Incarnation.[32] While Orthodox agree that Jesus Christ was born male, the patristic tradition tends to emphasize Christ's status as the true human over the fact that he was a man (*anthrōpos* vs. *anēr*). The Nicene Creed declares that the Son was made flesh (*sarkōthenta*) and became a human being (*enanthrōpēsanta*). The *horos* of the Seventh Ecumenical Council declares that representational art provides confirmation of the becoming human of the Word of God (*tēs theou logou enanthrōpēseōs*). A personalist anthropology, in consonance with the tradition, understands women and Christ to share in the exact same human nature. The burden of proof that the maleness of Jesus Christ is essential to the economy of salvation falls upon those making such a claim.

Second, at the core of the iconic argument is the claim that a woman's flesh is incapable of serving as a medium for making Christ present. Here we have a fundamental failure to fully grasp Orthodox teachings concerning images. Basil of Caesarea in his *On Baptism* argues that the baptized share the image of Christ as members of his body, regardless of ethnicity, class, and gender.[33] All the baptized share in the same priesthood, while particular persons are further called to the vocational priesthood. The priestly vestments begin with a white baptismal robe that is worn by every baptizand on the day of their baptism.[34] Basil makes no distinction based on the sex of the baptizand. Second, the icon depicts not a nature (*physis*), but a person (*hypostasis*). For this reason, the image and the subject need not share the same essence.[35] Thus, the bishops of Nicaea II affirmed traditional images that are "painted, made of mosaic, or other suitable material."[36] To their list, we may add human flesh, not only following Basil's declaration that the baptized share in the image of Christ, but also in recognition of the Incarnation itself in which the Son assumed the flesh of Mary to become a human being. As we have noted many times, sex is a property not of the *hypostasis*, but of the nature shared by all humanity. To insist that the maleness of a priest or bishop must match the maleness of the incarnate Christ confuses the point of correspondence between the image and its subject. The person of Christ is made present not in the person of the priest, but in the priest's human nature. In that moment, the unsexed *hypostasis* of the priest is not front and center. Rather, the flesh of the priest makes the divine *hypostasis* of the Son present. As the flesh assumed from Mary (a woman) served to make the person of Christ present in the Incarnation,[37] so also the flesh of the priest, as well as all the baptized, may be the medium of making Christ present. Each is an image of Christ. The sex of the flesh is of no consequence, just as biological sex is inconsequential when the medium of representation is wood, paint, stone, or the words of the Gospel book. All are icons of Christ, their natures transformed as a consequence of the Incarnation.

The third failure of the iconic argument lies in the claim that the priest stands in for the fatherly role of the Father in the Trinity.[38] While the incarnate Christ is an image of the invisible Father, Orthodox tradition forbids images depicting the Father, who remains uncircumscribed. Only the Son may be depicted as a consequence of the Incarnation.

As we can now see, the gendered condition introduced into the iconic argument does not hold up to theological scrutiny. It violates both Basil's claim that all the baptized image Christ as well as the theological principle behind the Seventh Ecumenical Council and the broader Orthodox teaching concerning icons.

On a final note, Ware's quotation from Aghiorgoussis focuses solely on small passages that support the claim that the maleness of the priest is critical to making Christ present. However, what is not quoted are Aghiorgoussis's own warrants for making this claim. In the original text, Aghiorgoussis ties his claims to the analogical link between men, a male principle, and the Logos and the parallel link between women, the female principle, and the Spirit—the gendered model we examined in chapter 3.[39] Thus, what is assumed to be a deeply traditional stance once again is rooted in extra-Orthodox sources and the complementarity of the two-sex model of human embodiment. Once the link between the male principle and Christ is established, Aghiorgoussis goes on to support his argument by drawing connections between human maleness and the tropes of Christ as the Bridegroom and fatherhood.[40] To these metaphors we now turn.

Christ the Bridegroom

A related objection to women serving as priests suggests that a female cannot fulfill the image of Christ and the Church found in Ephesians 5. According to this argument, the priest must be male to serve as the visible icon of Christ, the Bridegroom. As a variation on the iconic argument, all the previous objections raised above also apply. In his later deconstruction of the iconic argument, Ware suggests that while some will immediately suggest that a woman cannot serve as a symbol of Christ the Bridegroom, others will not see in this proposition any "intrinsic absurdity" as long as latitude is observed in which the "subtlety and polyvalence of symbols" may be appreciated.[41] If a woman is incapable of imaging Christ, then what do we say of the many men in the Body of Christ—including its priests act-ing *in persona ecclesiae*—who join in representing the Bride?[42] If we follow the same logic, men would be incapable of this gender-bending feat. At this point, the theological implausibility of an insistence on a gendered correlation to the metaphor should be clear.

Christ as Pater Familias

Finally, Lawrence Farley offers a fourth argument, also couched in Chris-tological terms. Farley breaks from the reasons offered by Hopko and Ware that focus on Christ's priestly role. According to his argument, we com-monly think of priests as those who perform liturgies within the gathered church community. Because of this liturgical role, we further think of priests as heads of the community. Farley inverts this order, arguing that the primary role of the bishop and presbyter in the early church was oversight, and from this oversight flows the role of presiding over liturgy.[43] Clergy are thus primarily rulers over the people, an idea he supports by noting that the prayers of ordination do not reference the liturgical functions of the priest, but rather the task of governance.[44] While Farley agrees that the priest represents Christ, it is not Christ as priest, but Christ as authority. In his own take on the *in persona Christi/ecclesiae* discussion above, he affirms that the priest stands *with* the people in the liturgy, but *over* them as ruler.[45] Thus the priest is an icon not of Christ as high priest, but of "divine rule and fatherhood, the spiritual authority which governs, defines, and protects." Farley concludes his argument by suggesting that priests must be men, "because gender is not irrelevant to fatherhood."[46]

Farley's argument suggests that authority is an exclusively masculine attribute linked with fatherhood. Such a claim rests not on biblical principles, but squarely on the Greco-Roman tradition of the *pater familias* who governs his household and family as absolute ruler. It neglects instances, both biblical and within the history of the Church, in which women have held authority over men. Further, as Christ himself demonstrated again and again in the Gospels, divine authority is marked not by the trappings of earthly power. Rather, Christ embodied servant leadership in which those who would be first must serve the lowliest. The image of Christ as leader is embodied in his stripping his outer robe and kneeling to wash the feet of his disciples.[47] Finally, as discussed in chapter 2, the fathers appropriated motherhood as a masculine quality, receiving instruction in the womb of their minds to give birth to a proper theological word. We may go back even further to scriptures where Jesus worries over Jerusalem like a mother or Paul uses birthing and nurturing imagery to describe his relationship with the churches of Thessalonica and Galatia.[48] Though gender is typically relevant to fatherhood and to motherhood, it is not the case that these motifs are bound exclusively to one sex or the other.

Thus, I contend, none of the common Christological arguments for an exclusively male priesthood are convincing. The new iconic argument shifts the focus from the patristic emphasis on Christ's humanity to a more restrictive emphasis on Christ's maleness. In altering the traditional focus, modern theologians raise unintended consequences for both the doctrine of the Incarnation and the related questions of soteriology and divine-human communion. In the end, it is the flesh of the Theotokos that Christ assumes in the Incarnation. Modeling the ineffable alternative manner of human begetting without seed, molding the flesh of a woman to form the body of a man. What the Holy Spirit can accomplish with actual human bodies should certainly open the possibilities for a woman to symbolically represent Christ and for a man to join in representing Christ's Bride. Finally, the *pater familias* of Greco-Roman culture is antithetical to the servant leadership embodied by the Christ of the gospels. In short, each of these three arguments fails to consider the full breadth of Christology.

A Personalist Response

Returning to the personalist anthropology explored in the previous chapter, we find that it is not abstract sexes of male and female, but rather unique persons who are gifted with unique combinations of charisms and called to particular vocations. In terms of this immanent critique, I argue that failure to recognize a human person's call to ordained ministry is detrimental on two counts, both related to the sacramental aspect of the priesthood. First, it is not the act of laying hands upon the ordinand, but rather the living out of the priestly vocation that serves as a vehicle for grace in the movement toward divine-human communion. Thus, failure on the part of the Church to recognize the charisms and vocation of priestly service within a particular human person denies personal participation in a sacrament, placing a stumbling block in the individual's path to theosis. This first tragedy, in turn, creates an absence or vacancy in the Body of Christ itself that leads to the second tragedy. The priest serves many functions within the Church: offering sacrifices, presiding at the Eucharist, caring for those in need, and embodying Christ to the congregation. Thus, the failure to recognize Christ made present due to a preconceived notion of what a presbyter must look like closes off a sacramental channel of grace offered both to the local parish and as an aid in the Church's mission in the world.

If my various premises are correct, then the Church impedes both particular persons and the collective body in the ultimate aim of ever fuller participation in divine-human communion. In doing so, we corporately sin against the individuals whose God-given vocation we deny, against our own corporate body the Church, and against those whom the Church may not otherwise reach. What then is called for is repentance, coupled with recognition of those women who are personally called to the priestly vocation but who have been previously blocked because of their biological sex. By embracing these women and their presbyteral and episcopal vocations, we more fully cooperate with God's activity in the world, expanding avenues for divine-human communion for both the individual women and those in relationship with them within the sacramental bonds of the Church.

This personalist approach was Behr-Sigel's argument from her very first position paper written in response to the invitation to the Agapia conference. Most ironically, it comes very close to the mature position espoused by Hopko himself in his final sustained discussion of the matter. "Persons, not natures or genders, have callings from God," he argues. While acknowledging that there may be collective vocations, he writes that, "ultimately . . . and most radically and profoundly, only persons—with their particular genders, nationalities, races, relationships, theological convictions, characteristics, qualities, talents, and faults—have specific callings." He goes on then to argue that not all men are called to the vocations of presbyter and bishop. However, citing Orthodox tradition, he again reiterates his earlier position that they must be either once-married or celibate *men*."[49] As we saw above, this final argument, focused on the *maleness* of the candidate for service, comes across as a desperate last stand. Ignoring the ways in which the biblical criteria for overseer have been modified in canon law and Church practices, the insistence on a literal reading for this single point rings hollow. What's more, underlying Hopko's argument is an exercise in question-begging in which he assumes the current state of practice as the only way things can legitimately be as an element of his argument. In so doing, he and other essentialists attempt to limit God with respect to whom God may call to the priestly vocation. This, in the end, is the nub of the issue. From the personalist perspective, a personal God is free to call whomever this God so desires to the vocational priesthood. These called persons are, in turn, free of any constraints of our common human nature in the choice to answer (or reject) God's call.[50]

6

HOMOSEXUALITY

> . . . God does not make human beings "homosexual." God makes men and women to live human lives of love through their complementary communion with each other on all levels of human being and life: physical, emotional, spiritual, *and* sexual.
>
> —THOMAS HOPKO[1]

Introduction

Like the question of women's ordination explored in the previous chapter, sexual orientation, particularly homosexuality, has become a highly controversial topic within contemporary Orthodoxy. Two primary factors have catalyzed this reaction. First, Orthodox parishes have received an influx of both laity and clergy leaving other Christian traditions in which acceptance of LGBT members and the ordination of openly gay clergy have become more acceptable. Second, in response to the recognition of same-sex civil marriage in an increasing number of locales, various Orthodox synods and lone bishops have issued statements reiterating traditional Orthodox stances on sexual activity outside of the marriage bond between a man and a woman.[2]

It is no secret that Church teachings, both within Orthodoxy and in other Christian traditions, have historically prohibited all sexual acts outside of a monogamous marital relationship between a husband and a wife. However, several factors have contributed to changing attitudes and new questions. First, an increasing number of Orthodox have interpersonal relationships with family members, friends, and colleagues who identify as gay, lesbian, or bisexual. These experiences lead them to question the stereotypes often associated with traditional teachings. This dynamic is coupled with the rise of modern discourses of sexuality that have led Orthodox thinkers, like many other Christians, to differentiate between same-sex love or erotic attraction and same-sex genital acts (also referred to as homosexual or homogenital acts). This distinction is rooted in discourses of pathology that remove orientation from the realm of sin and personal culpability. Many Orthodox Christians suggest that a person cannot be held responsible for their sexual orientation, even as they continue to condemn all same-sex erotic relationships and genital acts. In this section, I wish to observe this distinction for the sake of addressing the discrete conversations centered on each point.

It may come as a surprise to some readers, but I am in at least partial agreement with the epigraph by Thomas Hopko that heads this chapter: God does not make people homosexual. However, contrary to the gender essentialism that undergirds many of the ideas I will explore in this chapter and the next, God does not make people heterosexual either. In chapter 4, we briefly explored the rise of discourses of sexuality, which ultimately hinge upon essentialist ideas of gender and biological sex. In addition to highlighting the instabilities in these categories, we also saw that understandings of the immutability of sexual orientation are now being questioned within the social sciences, even as the biological sciences have provided insights that complicate a strict binary between male and female. The personalist model I propose does not deny that same-sex attraction exists. Rather, it focuses on the dynamics between persons, always embodied with a collection of physical characteristics drawn from our common human nature, who enter unique interpersonal relationships with other embodied human persons. Like biological categories of sex, the categories of sexuality are imprecise labels by which we attempt to classify persons. However, because of the personal freedom to transcend the common human nature, these labels cannot ever fully capture the complexities and potentialities of the persons they attempt to describe. In the following discussion, I will use labels such as homo- and heterosexual to describe dynamics between persons who bear particular medically assigned sexes. However, in using these labels, I am in no way indicating any sort of ontological foundation for either sex or sexual orientation. At most, these labels may be applied as situational identities describing a particular configuration of affective preferences and concrete relationships. This applies even more to labels like *gay* and *lesbian*, which refer not only to sexual acts, relationships, and affections, but to social subcultures that vary across time and locale. By drawing this distinction, I am in no way implying a ready and easy capacity for change in the dynamics I describe, though I do recognize that, for many, there is a certain degree of plasticity in both relationships and desires.

With these qualifications in place, I wish to examine Orthodox contributions to the discourses of sexuality. We will begin with the psychoanalytic discussion of homosexuality as conceived by Orthodox theologian Elizabeth Moberly. Amid earlier questions of pastoral care for gay, lesbian, and bisexual parishioners, Moberly emerged within certain Orthodox circles as an expert on the formation of gender identity and sexuality.[3] While her name is not common in today's conversation, her writings contribute to what has come to be known as reparative therapy.

Moberly made her debut in 1982 with an essay for general readers.[4] In the following year she released two books focused on homosexuality, one formulated in the language of the psychoanalytic tradition and another that explores the theological dimensions to her argument.[5] Let us explore moments of each in turn. As we will see, Moberly's psychoanalytic claims are based in a gender essentialist paradigm. Her theological arguments, informed by the same essentialist notions, are problematic in several ways.

Psychogenesis

As we saw in chapter 4, researchers have raised multiple theories regarding the causes of human homosexuality (e.g., hormones, genes, environmental factors, etc.). Moberly rejects these lines of inquiry, focusing exclusively on early developmental problems between a child and their same-sex parent.[6] She defines heterosexuality as "the ability to relate to members of the opposite sex as a psychologically complete member of one's own sex,"[7] while characterizing homosexuality as "same-sex ambivalence."[8]

Unlike most Orthodox thinkers, Moberly sees homosexual love as a normal and healthy part of early childhood development, necessary for the acquisition of a child's gender identity. To support her claims, she draws on and modifies Freudian theory, hypothesizing a new model of psychosexual development. In his mature work, Freud theorized that a mother fulfills the role of first love-object for her children, regardless of the children's biological sex. Freud further suggested that to reach mature heterosexual identification, a girl must reject her first love-object, transferring her affections to a man. A boy also begins with his mother as his first love-object, but while he transfers his affections to another woman, the dynamic of his opposite-sex love remains unchanged. Moberly argues that Freud misses a step in gender identity formation. In her own model of psychosexual development, she agrees with Freud concerning an initial stage of attachment to the mother for both girls and boys. Moberly further theorizes a subsequent stage of gender identity development that requires an attachment to a same-sex parent. Once a child's gender identity has been formed, he or she may then successfully enter a heterosexual relationship. Thus, contra Freud, Moberly argues that a girl's development is simpler than a boy's. Both boys and girls begin with an attachment to their mother. However, the girl, in this initial love-object attachment, already experiences the necessary relationship for the development of her gender identity. Once this identity is fully formed, she may eventually enter opposite-sex relationships. But a boy, to fulfill the early stage of gender identification, must exchange his attachment to his mother for a same-sex love-object, his father. Once the boy matures, he again transfers his love to an opposite-sex partner.[9]

For Moberly, homosexuality is the result of incomplete psychosocial development, stemming from an early childhood trauma related to the same-sex parent. The trauma may be the result of either intentional or unintentional behavior on the part of the parent, resulting in a multistage process with the child. The process includes initial anger, followed by mourning the loss of the same-sex love-object, and then a subsequent defensive detachment, which in turn blocks the development of the child's gender identity. Moberly hypothesizes that the same-sex love expressed by the adult homosexual is *reparative*, an unconscious attempt to reestablish the same-sex bond to make up for earlier developmental needs. The reparative impulse and its concomitant same-sex relationships themselves are a natural and healthy response. However, Moberly characterizes eroticization of the relationship, resulting in sexual expression, as unhelpful. She argues that sexual expression belongs to the sphere of adult relationships, making sexual acts inappropriate within a relationship that seeks to fulfill childhood developmental needs.[10] In Moberly's framework, bisexuality is the result of an incomplete, but more fully formed, gender identity. For both the bisexual and the homosexual, she cautions against entering a romantic heterosexual relationship before developmental deficits have been met and a truly heterosexual identity has been achieved.[11]

Reading Freud Back into Orthodox Tradition

In her writing for a theological audience, Moberly takes a different tack, reading her Freudian-inspired understanding of psychogenesis back into the first creation account. Highlighting that male and female are created in the image of God (Gn 1:27), Moberly insists that God's will for the human species and God's very image are displayed in the gender complementarity of the man-woman relationship. She posits "God-given laws for human development" that culminate in the full expression of the *imago dei* as a heterosexual couple.[12] Thus we move from psychoanalytic theory to a divinely ordained process of maturation that results in the capacity to relate to the opposite sex as a heterosexual. Once again, we find ourselves in the complementarian reading explored in chapter 3. As we saw there, the idea of the image of God being expressed within the spousal relationship between a man and a woman is not a traditional element of Orthodox theology. Rather, it is an idea first found in Kabbalah, incorporated into the mystical teachings of Jakob Böhme, and subsequently reproduced in various German Romantic and Russian religious projects. However, Moberly's inspirations are not Hopko or the Paris School thinkers or even Freud. Rather, her ideas come to her indirectly from Karl Barth.[13]

In addition to biblical exegesis, Moberly attempts an appeal to Christology to support her theory, though here her work takes an odd turn, as she speaks to unnamed interlocutors, defending Christ's heterosexuality. Heterosexuality, she writes, is the intended state for all of humanity. It should not be confused with sexual acts. Rather it is a core gender identity, independent of any sexual activity.[14] For Moberly, even developmentally mature celibates are also heterosexual. Jesus Christ, who enjoyed "close and deep communion with his heavenly Father," had no "deficit in relation with the same-sex parent" and thus no "drive to make good this deficit."[15] While the sudden defense of Christ's heterosexuality is unexpected, it nonetheless offers an opportunity to explore some of Moberly's theological reasoning.

Moberly reads gender identity, if not physiological sex, back into the Trinity, specifically predicating masculinity to the Father as a necessary condition for Jesus's own gender identity formation. This claim cannot be made on three counts. First, in the Orthodox tradition, the Incarnate Christ is born without seed and without a human father.[16] However, the seedless conception of Christ does not imply that God the Father serves as Jesus's biological father. Rather, the incarnate Christ, like the first Adam, simply does not have one.[17] Second, the suggestion that God the Father can act as the same-sex love-object of the God-man, Jesus Christ, is a category error, resulting from a mixing of the two natures of Christ in a way that is excluded by the Chalcedonian Definition. The relationship between the Father and the Son is a quality of the modes of being of the First and Second divine *hypostaseis*. In contrast, the physiological sex of Jesus Christ is a quality not of his divine, but his human nature.[18] Finally, the apophatic tradition holds that the essence of God is inaccessible to the created order. We may contemplate God through a threefold process of cataphatic predication, apophatic negation, and an acknowledgment of transcendence. For example, we may say that the Son is masculine (for he is called "he"). The Son is not masculine, for the Son is beyond masculine. I have chosen the Son for this example. Similar examples can be constructed with the Father and the Spirit.[19] However, the essence (*ousia*) of the Godhead remains inaccessible to the creation. Though Moberly seeks to ground her psychoanalytic theory in a theological framework for her Orthodox audience, her attempts are ultimately superficial. Her complementarian claims are rooted in extra-Orthodox sources, whether those that have previously been used to interpret Gn 1:27 or the same cultural trends that shaped the two-sex model that informed Freud's worldview. Further, Moberly's Christological justifications are poorly formulated, violating established Orthodox principles related to both the two natures of Christ and his seedless conception, as well as the apophatic principle that safeguards our language around the inaccessible and ineffable Godhead.

Reparative Therapy

Though Moberly's theological underpinnings are highly dubious, her therapeutic methods have nonetheless been recommended by Orthodox thinkers who share her gender essentialist views. Thus, a brief examination of her therapeutic recommendations is in order. According to Moberly, the drive toward love relationships with members of the same sex is reparative. Rather than perversion, the drive is a natural and healthy response to childhood trauma that has stunted the full development of a gender identity. The pathology lies not in the love, but rather in the lack of completion of early developmental goals. To correct the earlier deficit, Moberly proposes a treatment now known as *reparative therapy*.[20] If, as she hypothesizes, homosexual desire is the result of a deficit of relationship with the same-sex parent, then the cure is to form same-sex relationships in which early developmental needs can be satisfied. To this end she recommends a therapeutic relationship with a therapist of the same anatomical sex as the patient. The therapeutic relationship is intended to set up a transference from the same-sex parent to the therapist, forming a bond through which same-sex love needs can be fulfilled as the prerequisite to the development of a heterosexual orientation. Moberly notes that the therapist may also be homosexual, and that this might even be useful. Such a therapist would have a better understanding of the issues faced by the patient. However, this would also mean that the therapist suffers from the same deficiencies, so a relationship with a heterosexual therapist would be "more stable."[21] The therapeutic relationship may also be supplemented with additional same-sex friendships in the effort to make up for early childhood relational deficits. However, Moberly warns that all these relationships should exclude sexual activity. As previously noted, she suggests that to eroticize the same-sex relationship is to introduce adult sexual dynamics that are inappropriate to childhood developmental needs.

For her religious audience, Moberly emphasizes that the homosexual *condition*, as opposed to homosexual *activity*, is not "reprehensible." She laments the homophobia, reluctance, and antipathy that members of the Church display against homosexuals because these responses can only block healing.[22] Within the healing ministries of the Church, she recommends creating opportunities to engage in nonsexual relationships with members of the same sex.[23] In an interesting redeployment of biblical allusions, she notes that the male homosexual requires a "male helper," while the female homosexual requires a "female helper." Attempts to bypass developmental deficits are characterized as "contrary to nature."[24] Because her theory is based on making up for the love lost from a parent, Moberly suggests the biblical directive to care for the orphan should frame the Church's response to homosexuals. As no one should seek to punish a child for being an orphan, so also should punishment be ruled out as a proper response to a person who experiences homosexual feelings.[25]

In addition to therapeutic relationships, Moberly also advocates spiritual counseling that may be offered in religious contexts. Here she emphasizes prayer and listening for the Holy Spirit. Moberly cautions against praying for the end goal of a heterosexual orientation. Instead, the suppliant should ask for the fulfillment of homosexual developmental needs.[26] To address the original detachment mechanism, which Moberly claims is still present whether active or latent, she counsels forgiveness of the same-sex parent. This includes steps of praying for the ability to let go of past resentments and petitions "for the wellbeing of the person to be forgiven."[27] As with therapists, Moberly advises that spiritual counselors should be of the same sex as their counselees if they are to help with fulfilling relational deficits.[28] She couches this in gender essentialist terms: ". . . a woman cannot be a father" and, *pace* Paul, "a man cannot be a mother."[29]

Moberly's reparative therapy has enjoyed some popularity within Orthodox circles. Both Thomas Hopko and Basil Zion have endorsed her work.[30] Moral theologian John Breck, while recognizing multiple factors in the formation of a homosexual orientation, also references Moberly.[31] The appeal of the reparative therapy narrative is easy to see. In a culture such as our own, fathers are often absent during the developmental period of same-sex attachment that Moberly theorizes. Job demands, military deployments, and even hospitalization of infants are all opportunities for the trauma that can result in detachment.[32] Look hard enough at anyone's past and an episode can be identified that might serve as the source of a person's same-sex ambivalence. Thus, Moberly's theory is easy to back up with anecdotal evidence that a priest might hear in conversation with a parishioner. However, in the decades since Moberly's work was popularized, the broader therapeutic community has taken a decisively negative view toward reparative therapy. Despite the rosy outcomes that Moberly theorized in her books, the lived experiences of many Christians who experience same-sex attraction have often proven more complicated than the model.[33] Many have reported depression and suicide attempts. Others have succeeded in ending their own lives. In response to the countless failures experienced by those who have sought to change their sexual orientation, Exodus International, one of the most well-known groups to advocate for reparative and other conversion therapies, issued a public apology before shutting down its ministry.[34] In spite of the claims of psychoanalytic models like Moberly's reparative therapy, the reality is that the affective attractions of most adults appear to be largely set and unresponsive to therapeutic conversion.[35] In addition to the sea change in the mental health field, Moberly's theological framework, as I argued above, is problematic. Though her compassionate approach characterizing homosexuals as orphans to be cared for is well-intentioned, Moberly nonetheless rejects all etiologies that exceed her psychoanalytic framework. Further, as she applies her theory to Christ, she violates several theological principles, attributing gender to

God the Father and to the Son while violating the boundaries of the Chalcedonian Definition. In the end, Moberly's model is neither psychoanalytically nor theologically sound.

Narcissism

In addition to Moberly's reparative theory, another Orthodox model for homosexuality, also couched in psychoanalytic theory, uses the term *narcissism* to suggest that participants in same-sex erotic relationships are not looking for a complementary other, but a copy of themselves. The correlation between homosexuality and a narcissistic personality was first theorized by Freud. Among his explanations for the origins of male homosexuality, Freud proposes that in their childhood, homosexual men experience a short, intense, erotic fixation on a woman, usually their mothers.[36] After this experience, "they identify themselves with a woman and take *themselves* as their sexual-object. That is to say, they proceed from a narcissistic basis, and look for a young man who resembles themselves and whom *they* may love as their mother loved *them*."[37] Freud characterizes this dynamic of turning to the self as a love-object as a reversion to the auto-eroticism of an earlier developmental stage when the infant's survival needs and erotic attachments were intertwined in acts of feeding, care, and protection.[38] Rather than transferring his love for his mother to another female love-object, the homosexual represses his love for his mother, taking on her role and seeking boys like himself to love. Homosexuality thusly viewed is a symptom of arrested psychosexual development. In the underlying dynamic, the invert runs away from other women, remaining faithful to his first love-object by assuming her role.[39]

In the hands of Orthodox thinkers less familiar with Freud's theories of psychogenesis, the word *narcissism* takes on a new set of connotations. Interpreting Freud's idea of self-love through the polemic of Romans 1, they suggest that homosexuality is idolatry, an expression of self-worship.[40] A second line relates Freud's concept of self-love to the Orthodox suspicion of *philautia*.[41] Rather than seeking out difference, identified within a gender essentialist binary with sexual difference (and purported, concomitant differences in psychological and spiritual makeup), the homosexual is characterized as seeking sameness. The complex interactions of each unique interpersonal relationship are effectively reduced to the genital configuration of the couple.

Personalist Response

Both Moberly's psychoanalytic model of heterosexual psychical maturity and claims that narcissism is a search for sameness in a partner are grounded in a modern paradigm of gender complementarity, informed by a two-sex body model and a strict male-female binary opposition. From a personalist perspective, the labels employed in these paradigms obscure the unique human persons they attempt to classify. In doing so, they also mischaracterize unique human relationships by assuming they should all follow the same heteronormative paradigm. For the reparative therapist, all same-sex relationships are subsumed under the category of childhood development and evaluated according to the criteria of healthy maturation into adulthood. For those using the language of narcissism, the anthropological error committed is the assumption that two persons with similar genitals are somehow fundamentally the same. Both approaches fail to make room for the unique character of each person and their particular interpersonal relationship. Moberly's model fails to account for same-sex attraction between psychosocially mature individuals, while the narcissism model misses the multitude of other variable characteristics that attract two people and subsequently bond them together as a couple. A personalist account, in contrast, recognizes the unique configuration and dynamics of each relationship without essentializing the sexes of the partners as a necessary condition of complementarity.

Orthodoxy still possesses centuries of teaching around same-sex genital acts, condemning them based on a long history of interpretation of biblical passages, patristic references, and legal-canonical proscriptions. Observing the distinction between same-sex erotic love and sexual activity, I will address in the next chapter two more pressing issues within the current Orthodox context. Can Orthodoxy support same-sex marriage? And is there any context in which same-sex genital activity could be seen as anything other than sinful? I will begin with the question of marriage.

7

MARRIAGE

THE SACRAMENT OF LOVE

Can one write, except in the case of special revelation, something correct about one's opposite where neither agenda nor resentment, neither illusion nor theory intervenes? It is not appropriate for the married to discourse on the monastic life, nor does it suit the unmarried to construct a phenomenology of Eros.

—PAUL EVDOKIMOV[1]

Introduction

With the growing legal recognition of same-sex couples, Orthodox have taken up the question of how to respond, with both synods and individual bishops releasing encyclicals.[2] These initial responses adamantly oppose the recognition of same-sex marriage. However, some theological responses have suggested a distinction be made between legal recognition of same-sex relationships and the Orthodox understanding of a sacramental union witnessed by the Church.

In this chapter, I will explore several themes related to same-sex relationships. These include the distinction between civilly recognized unions and Orthodox sacramental marriage, the potential for recognizing the sacramentality of particular same-sex relationships, and a final discussion of traditional Orthodox limits on sexual activity. It is with a certain sense of irony that I have quoted Evdokimov above. After all, I am not by Orthodox standards (or any other, I hasten to add) a married man. However, I wonder if, in the spirit of Evdokimov's admonition, one might also assert that hetero-sexuals with no experience of same-sex love and commitment are ill-suited to the task of exploring the themes of this chapter. May we all tread lightly.

Marriage: Legal Construct or Sacrament?

Taking up the first topic, for Orthodox Christians there is a clear distinc-tion between civil marriage and the sacramental union recognized by the Church. Indeed, in many countries where clergy do not act as authorized agents of secular government, civil and church services are two separate events. Civil governments have one set of requirements related to the recognition of domestic partnerships, civil unions, and marriages. On the other hand, the Orthodox Church maintains a separate set of conditions for marriage in the Church whose most striking distinction is that both bride and groom must be baptized members of the Orthodox faith. Generally, Orthodox do not make a habit of denigrating the marriages of opposite-sex couples married outside of the Orthodox Church, including those who observe some form of religious service and have a theological understanding in an extra-Orthodox tradition.[3]

Orthodox thinkers have taken various stances regarding same-sex rela-tionships, even bracketing, as we have here, the question of sexual activity. Some categorically reject recognition of same-sex couples not only within the Church, but within the larger civil society. For example, Elizabeth Moberly rules out same-sex marriage for several reasons. First, she notes that one or both partners will have developmental deficits that make them very needy, so much so that an individual may have difficulty satisfying their partner's demands. Second, it seems unlikely to Moberly that the partners can help each other due to their own same-sex love deficits. Third, Moberly argues that the original defensive detachment mechanism respon-sible for the rejection of an individual's same-sex parent and the subsequent lack of identity formation can resurface at any time, introducing emotional distance that can sabotage a same-sex relationship. Finally, Moberly sug-gests that once childhood relational deficits have been eliminated, a same-sex relationship will automatically dissolve. Thus, the relationship, which was only a step on the path to adult heterosexuality, is not suited to the lifelong sacramental covenant of marriage. Orthodox theologians Basil Zion and John Breck offer theological arguments against same-sex sacra-mental relationships, which we will explore below. Others have argued for the recognition of a distinction between civil and sacramental marriage. Orthodox lay theologian David Dunn notes the dangers in turning to the state to protect the sanctity of sacramental marriage, noting that *sanctity* signals a shift from the civil to a theological context. Dunn further argues against any action that would place the state in a position of making pronouncements on the sacramental validity of marriages.[4] Most surprisingly, before his death, Thomas Hopko argued for the state recognition of civil unions or domestic partnerships, along with equal access to "housing, employment, police protection, legal justice, tax benefits, and visitation privileges at institutions that all members of society possess and enjoy."[5] While Hopko recognizes a secular / sacramental distinction, he cautions against a battle over words, rightly noting that attempts to deny the use of the word *marriage* in relation to same-sex partnerships "will almost always be construed . . . as expressing hatred and contempt."[6] In these reflections we see Hopko's pastoral insights tempering the zeal with which some Orthodox theologians condemn both homosexuals and same-sex eroticism.

With the *Civil Marriage Act* in Canada and the *Obergefell v. Hodges* decision in the United States, the recognition of a civil / sacramental distinction has become the law in North America, opening a space in which the Orthodox Church must acknowledge same-sex relationships in civil society even as it decides internally how to relate to same-sex couples whom the state recognizes as married. But what of sacramental recognition? This question moves us to the second theme.

Same-Sex Sacramental Relationships?

Current Orthodox practice recognizes no sacramental value in any civilly recognized same-sex relationship, whether it be a domestic partnership, civil union, or marriage. Historically, Orthodoxy has treated only the marriage between a man and a woman as a sacrament. But what are the reasons for this? In this section I will examine common Orthodox objections to the recognition of same-sex relationships. For now, I will continue to bracket the question of sexual activity, which will be explored further below. From a theological perspective, multiple arguments have been offered in opposition to same-sex marriage. These include the biblical metaphor of "one flesh" and the divine command to "be fruitful and multiply," both taken from the Genesis creation narratives, and the nuptial imagery of Eph 5. The remaining arguments tend to focus on same-sex genital acts rather than the broader relationships in which these acts appear. I will address those arguments below. As we will see, essentialist readings narrow the range of acceptable interpretations of these passages. Let us examine each in turn.

"One Flesh"

Several Orthodox thinkers have argued that same-sex relationships are a parody of the "one flesh" idiom found first in the creation narratives and redeployed by Jesus and Paul in the New Testament.[7] In this reading, "one flesh" refers to a mystical union of husband and wife, through which, Paul argues, we catch a glimpse of Christ and the Church.[8] While this is a long-standing interpretation within the Orthodox tradition, its exclusive application misses the metaphorical meaning of the original Semitic idiom. In the creation account of Eve, the accent is not, as an essentialist reading would suggest, on the opposition of male and female. Instead, the narrative indicates that God prescribes as a remedy for Adam's aloneness a helper "like unto him" (*homoios autōi*).[9] Adam's own cry of "bone of my bone and flesh of my flesh" upon seeing Eve is a recognition of an essential *sameness* that the two share. She is neither bird of the air nor beast of the field, but *human*, made of the same material (or, in the later Greek metaphysical tradition, sharing a common essence). The subsequent explanation in which husband and wife become "one flesh" is a description of the dynamic in which a man forsakes the priority of his previous familial bonds with his parents to form a new family to which he gives his allegiance.[10] Read in isolation, these references to flesh and bone are taken as unique identifiers of the spousal bond. However, the same Semitic idiom of kinship is again repeated in other Yahwist passages of Genesis. Laban accepts Jacob as his son-in-law, exclaiming "you are my bone and my flesh." Judah reminds his brothers of the kinship they share with Joseph: "He is our brother and our flesh."[11] The Hebrew idiom includes a variety of familial relationships beyond the spousal pair. As such, the "one flesh" of Genesis 2:23 extends beyond marriage. Over time the "one flesh" metaphor gains an additional connotative meaning, associated directly with sexual intercourse. This is especially true in the New Testament. However, the nature of the bond itself is quite indiscriminate. Paul warns the Corinthians that a man even becomes one flesh with a prostitute through sexual union.[12] Taking this broader view, we see that the scriptures themselves move beyond husband and wife to include a variety of familial relationships as well as more fleeting encounters in the metaphors of flesh and bone.

"Increase and Multiply"

A second theological objection to same-sex relationships, also grounded in the creation narratives, argues that a same-sex relationship cannot be compared to a marriage because the former lacks procreative potential.[13] This argument emphasizes the divine command to "increase and multiply and fill the earth."[14] However, a straightforward proof-texting argument from scripture fails to take into account both the Orthodox tradition of interpretation, as well as the lives of Orthodox Christians. As we saw in chapter 2, John Chrysostom declared the task of filling the earth already complete in the fifth century.[15] In the Latin tradition, Augustine of Hippo makes a similar case for the end of the command to procreate. He suggests that the patriarchs begat children in response to divine command. But after the birth of the Messiah, there is no longer any need for human procreation. Citing Eccl 3:5, Augustine suggests that the time to embrace has ended.[16] Further, the ascetical tradition has long devoted energies to interpreting the divine command to be fruitful and multiply in a variety of nonliteral ways.[17] Attempts to limit the command's meaning strictly to procreation ignore the rich interpretive tradition of the fathers.

Other Orthodox approaches are more nuanced. For example, Hopko argues against the use of reproductive technologies (e.g., sperm donation, surrogate mothers) as counter to Orthodox teaching, but he nonetheless acknowledges that same-sex couples are often parents. His approach here becomes pastoral, with an emphasis on the welfare of the family.[18]

In terms of the lives of contemporary Orthodox Christians, many families include both children from previous relationships as well as foster and adopted children. An overemphasis on the ideal of the young, virgin couple who marry and have children obscures the realities of actual human persons and their networks of relationships. Moreover, the narrow focus of the procreation argument precludes the marriage of couples who know one or more partner is infertile. This would include women who have entered menopause or individuals who lack the organs necessary for procreation, either through natural absence or surgical removal. As the ideal state for entering Orthodox marriage calls for the virginity of both spouses, there are no preexisting guarantees of procreative potential. Indeed, as we saw in chapter 4, in the presence of a typical external genital configuration, an individual may never seek confirmation of other sex-determining factors such as chromosomal makeup, internal gonadal and reproductive structures, hormonal balances, and so on. Deeper knowledge of the naturally occurring variations and complexities of human bodies further complicates the issue. While most people fall to one side of the sexual binary or the other, we are aware of many more factors now than we have been in the past. As with basic fertility, no Orthodox priest will ask about these various biological factors when assessing whether to fulfill a couple's request to wed. With all these factors in mind, procreative potential cannot be the deciding factor for deeming a relationship sacramental.

Ephesians 5: The Bridegroom and the Bride

In addition to objections raised based on readings of the creation account, the marital imagery in Eph 5 provides the basis for another argument in which marriage between a man and a woman is symbolic of the union between Christ and the Church. Opponents of same-sex marriage argue that a same-sex couple cannot properly image this mystical union of the Bridegroom with the Bride. As we saw previously, the Ephesian image is also used in arguments regarding women's ordination. The critique offered then also applies now. The essentialist claim fails again at the suggestion that a woman cannot image Christ and a man—whether priest or laïc—cannot image the feminine figure of the Bride, the Church, Body of Christ. The suggestion that a same-sex relationship can only parody the relationship between Christ and the Church assumes a gendered incommensurability between Bridegroom and Bride is essential to the relationship between spousal partners. However, as with a woman as presbyter or bishop, the problem is not with the persons who are imaging the great mystery of Christ and the Church, but rather with the failure on the part of the observer to look beyond concrete individuals with their anatomical features and gender roles to the spiritual realities their sacramental participation makes present.

Here I am not suggesting that every relationship symbolically participates in this union, but that the possibility is not predicated on the sexes of the partners—assigned, perceived, or subjectively experienced. As we saw in previous chapters, all humans, both male and female, are characterized as brides of Christ in both the imagery of Origen, as well as Aphrahat and Ephrem in the Syriac tradition.[19] The patristic tradition accommodates a great deal of gender fluidity both in the makeup of individual human persons and in its metaphors and allegorical formulations of transcendent spiritual realities. Returning to the Seventh Ecumenical Council, the elements of flesh and blood, like those of wood and paint, are created by God and

capable of conveying spiritual truths. Only an extra-traditional essentialism would attempt to limit participation in such a symbol of Christ *in toto*.
While it is nearly inconceivable that an Orthodox theologian would argue
that a man cannot image the Church, many reject out of hand a woman's
ability to image Christ the Bridegroom. However, as discussed above, aside
from unexamined beliefs, influenced by the two-sex body model of gender
complementarity, the only theological reasons that have been enlisted in the
debate have been borrowed from extra-Orthodox sources. These arguments,
while enjoying the authority associated with Vatican councils and papal encyclicals, have not been authoritative within the Orthodox tradition.

Thus, we come to the end of the typical arguments offered in the denial
of the sacramentality of same-sex relationships. Like the arguments deployed
against women's ordination in chapter 5, they rely on narrow interpretations of scripture, an overly restrictive use of symbols, and a denial of the
broader patristic tradition of allegorical interpretation, ensconced within an
uncritical acceptance of the two-sex model of human bodies. These readings, I argue, are not only overly narrow, but like their counterparts in the
arguments against women's ordination, assume a particular worldview as
normative, even as they seek to defend the status quo. But how might the
personalist anthropology presented in chapter 4 inform questions about
the sacrament of marriage and the value of same-sex relationships?

A Personalist View of Sacramental Relationality

As with all Orthodox sacraments, participation in marriage is a spiritual
practice, the goal of which is to foster divine-human communion. Like
other sacraments, it is not the wedding rite that conveys grace. The crown-
ing of the couple only sets the stage for the covenanted life together that
is to come. Within this relationship, both partners are presented with a multitude of daily opportunities to practice loving each other, mutually sub-
mitting to each other, building each other up, and practicing self-sacrificial
love. Over time, these practices work to dismantle the individual egos of
the spouses as they are transformed more fully into the likeness of Christ.

A gender essentialist argument presupposes male-female complementarity (generally coupled with the potential for procreation) as the basis for
such a union. However, it is not the biological sex, the culturally shaped
gender roles, or even the gender identity of the partners within a spousal
bond that serves as the basis of a relationship of self-sacrificial love. Rather,

the key to the spousal bond is the relationality nurtured between the partners. Their union commonly begins with an erotic attraction that springs from a desire based in a need for completion. In the Genesis account, Adam finds in Eve not an *opposite*, but an *apposite*, a human person who is like him, but also complements him.[20] What is crucial is not a complementarity of genders, but of persons with their unique combinations of needs and gifts. Each spousal pairing is unrepeatable, bringing together two persons in a complementarity of give and take that goes far beyond essentialist notions of male and female. By focusing on either Platonic principles or the application of natural law with its understanding of fitting particular body parts together with a *telos* of procreation, we risk obscuring unique persons, who always exceed the common human nature. As the relationship matures, this bond between partners is transformed.

In all the above, I am not suggesting that sex and gender are unimportant to the apposite dimensions of covenant partnerships. Rather, I am emphasizing the personal nature of each spousal relationship by focusing on the unique, free, and relational aspects of each coupling bond. The common experience of both heterosexual and homosexual individuals alike tells us that the sex of one's partner is an important factor in attraction and ongoing erotic relations. But it is not the only factor by far. Here perhaps the experience of some bisexuals may illuminate the issue. Bisexuals are often viewed with suspicion in our culture by gays and straights alike. Yet as a t-shirt slogan I recently saw proclaims: *When a bisexual settles down with someone they haven't chosen a side, they've chosen a person.* Another t-shirt drives the point home differently: *Bisexual and still not into you.*

A Personalist Interpretation of Ephesians 5

To see just how secondary the necessity of opposite-sexedness of a spousal pair can be, let us examine the sacramental vision of marriage offered by Christos Yannaras. Yannaras follows Vladimir Lossky in drawing a distinction between the individual and the human person. As we saw in chapter 4, individuals are described by the combination of characteristics that they embody from among potential possibilities in our common human nature. But no matter how long this list grows, it is always insufficient to the task of identifying a single, unique human being because the characteristics under consideration are part of the shared human nature. Lossky's human person is the *who* that cannot be reduced to the common nature.

This *who* is unique and unrepeatable. Building on Lossky's distinction, Yannaras suggests that "personal distinctiveness" is revealed only in relationship and communion with other persons,[21] and that knowledge of a person is experienced most fully in love. Love "does not project onto the other person individual preferences, demands, or desires," but accepts the other as they are, in the fullness of their uniqueness.[22] Within the marriage bond—itself held within the broader communion of the Church—*eros* progressively transforms into "true *eros*." This is facilitated by the ascetic practices of "reciprocal relinquishment of individual will and an acceptance of the other's will," which create a unity between the spousal pair. This unity is not based on "individual sexual impulse," but "self-transcendence and self-offering."[23]

Returning to Eph 5, Yannaras compares marriage to the twofold dynamic in the relationship between Christ and the Church. However, his reading does not depend on an essentialist paradigm. In the Incarnation, Christ assumes humanity. The Church, in turn, is accepted, despite its spots and wrinkles, taken up into the Trinitarian life, where it experiences transformation. The dynamics of assumption and acceptance are accomplished through the self-emptying of kenosis—"emptied of self-determination" and relinquishing "autonomous resistances." Yannaras transfers these dynamics to the spousal relationship with its progressive and "*personal* assumption" of the partner's nature, including its "autonomous resistance" and with it "the deadly consequences of its 'brutalized' existential self-sufficiency."[24] The "natural self-offering of sexual love" is transformed within sacramental marriage, becoming "a dynamic imitation of Christ's cross and the conformity to his voluntary assumption of our nature's death" whose fruits are incorruption and resurrection.[25] Appealing to Gregory of Nyssa and Maximus Confessor, Yannaras points out that sexual relations are not the problem. Rather, it is their incorrect orientation to sensual pleasure over communion and relationship.[26] Marriage as we know it occurs between two sinful people living within a fallen world. Each spouse, like all humans, is prone to selfish acts. A man (or a woman) may seek his own pleasure at the expense of his spouse. A woman (or a man) may fall short of loving acceptance of her partner. In our brokenness, we can—and do—hurt each other. The vulnerability of an intimate, spousal bond can magnify the pain a person experiences in relation to a spouse. And yet, united in this covenantal bond, the spousal couple are presented with opportunities to love despite the difficulties. Those who persevere are transformed.

Let us stop for a moment to appreciate a crucial moment easily obscured by reference to the Ephesian metaphor of Christ and Church as Bridegroom and Bride. While the biblical image is gendered, with Christ cast in a male role and humanity within the Church assuming a female role, the dynamics of self-emptying and acceptance (as well as being accepted with one's own shortcomings) are not gender specific in the human spousal relationship. In a spirit much more faithfully resembling the full Ephesian passage (as opposed to the smaller passage so often used to argue for the subordination of women), Yannaras's sacramental vision of marriage calls for mutual edification and reciprocal self-emptying. Beginning from v. 18, we find Paul's directive to sing to yourselves (*heautois*) "psalms and hymns and spiritual songs." This is coupled then with the command in v. 21 to be subjected *to one another* (*hypotassomenoi allēlois*) out of reverence for Christ. This vision calls for the acceptance of the other, with all their rough edges and selfish desires, continuing to love one's partner even when individual self-interest and ego-driven striving come to the surface. To love is to persevere, even in moments when the relationship is a source of pain or discomfort, as Christ emptied himself and took on flesh, entering personal relationship in which he displayed perfect love and suffered many rejections.[27] For Yannaras's human couple, none of these dynamics are gender specific. There is no division of tasks between masculine loving and feminine obeying. Rather, both spouses, regardless of their gender or biological sex, are called to the same twofold dynamic of accepting the other in self-sacrificial love and being accepted as they are, warts and all, in the open embrace of the other. Such a dynamic is in no way dependent on the biological sex of the partners.

At the same time, the true *eros* of sacramental marriage focuses not on biological reproduction, but on the freedom of personal relationship within the Church, freed from the constraint of "natural laws."[28] Yannaras further argues that marriage prefigures the Kingdom in which "the distinction between the sexes has been transcended" and with it the exclusive "*possession* of another," which refers to natural kinship.[29] Though Yannaras's description of the sacramental nature of marriage has promising points, problems remain. In his discussion of liturgical celebration, he describes a difference between the sexes. Yannaras affirms the shared priestly ethos, rank, and dignity of all the baptized within the Eucharist, and further denies an ontological distinction in the differentiation between the sexes. However, citing Gregory of Nyssa, Yannaras characterizes sexual differentiation as a difference in natural energies resulting from the fall. He then suggests that salvation within the Church transforms this difference without abolishing it. Thus, in discussing the ministerial priesthood, Yannaras appeals to an essential masculine activity, illustrated in biological procreation. The man, he tells us, must fertilize the body of the woman, whose role is to bring life to fruition. Yannaras then compares this to the liturgical setting in which the man, "who performs the ministry of endowing the world with meaning, making it 'word'" and the woman who "offers the natural flesh in which life is 'made word' and transfigured." Celebrating the sacraments is then interpreted as one of the ways that a man makes meaning in the world.[30] Yannaras's argument is neither scriptural nor biologically accurate. His idea of conception follows the Aristotelian pattern in which a male principle gives form to inchoate female materiality. In the division between the active, logical male and the passive female, he echoes the same Romantic paradigm that we explored in chapter 3. It is possible, though not concretely stated, that Yannaras holds this same Romantic essentialism as essential to the marital imagery of Eph 5 at least for its initial stage, even as he proclaims the goals of transcending biological sex and gender and freeing the spousal pair from the constraints of natural kinship. Yannaras, like Hopko, serves here as a cautionary example. Though he embraces a personalist anthropology, he does not follow it to its fully liberative conclusion. While grasping the difference between our common human nature and distinct human persons, he nonetheless falls back into essentialist tropes, subsuming personal uniqueness and unrepeatability under the broader categories of male and female.

In the holiest of marriages among the saints, Yannaras writes, the spouses cease their sexual activity, living together like siblings. In this they express the same spiritual virginity as espoused by celibate monastics.[31] Their relationship is characterized by *eros* "free from the natural constraint of lust and pleasures."[32] Here Yannaras is not alone. As we saw in chapter 2, patristic authors since Clement of Alexandria have described the dynamic in which sexual intercourse ceases when husband and wife live together as brother and sister after the birth of their children. But before reaching the illumined state of the great saints, marriage provides an outlet for sexual expression for the spousal couple.

Now we come to the greatest point of contention in the Orthodox conversation concerning same-sex relationships. Since sexual intercourse is reserved as an activity exclusive to the spousal couple and the sacrament of marriage extends only to the lifelong coupling of a man and a woman, all other sexual activity is characterized as illicit. Some readers may be surprised to hear that Hopko affirms that "same-sex love, when properly experienced and purely expressed, is always God's sacred gift."[33] The primary argument used to reject same-sex marriage comes from the long interpretive tradition of a handful of scriptural prohibitions, coupled with a broader appeal to avoiding all illicit sexual activity (*porneia*). Various lists of illicit sex acts, both scriptural and legal-canonical, include a variety of same-sex genital activities. This has led to the traditional view that all same-sex genital activity is inherently sinful. But is it possible to conceive of a sacramental same-sex relationship that includes a sexual component?

Sexual Activity

For Yannaras, knowledge of the distinctiveness of a person "achieves ultimate fullness" in the self-transcendence and offering of self that is sexual love."[34] This mystery of interpersonal communion becomes sacramental in relation to the Eucharist, celebrated within the broader community of the Church. It is not sexual love or the creation of family alone, but the couple's participation in the broader mysteries of the Body of Christ that constitute their "hypostasis," signified in the Eucharistic celebration of the Divine Liturgy in which the Orthodox wedding is situated. This sacramental understanding, Yannaras is quick to point out, does not make less of the "natural" relationship of the couple, but transforms "the natural sexual impulse into an event of *personal* communion" that is analogous to the communion of the Church. It is a "grace, a gift of personal distinctiveness and freedom."[35] The spousal relationship "does not deny or scorn its biological origin and fulfillment," but "merely refuses to confine itself" to the level of the bodily existence.[36] Rather, within the Eucharistic communion with Christ, the spouses are united in a way that transcends physical death.[37]

Yannaras's vision of the role of sex in the spousal relationship mirrors the broader ambiguity concerning sexual relations that has haunted Orthodoxy through the centuries. On the one hand, Yannaras sees sexual union as the avenue to the deepest knowledge of one another that two persons can share. Yet, at the same time, Orthodoxy has long prized consecrated virginity as a sign of the resurrected life in the eschaton. As far back as Paul, some Christians have foregone marriage and sexual activity for the sake of advancing the Kingdom of God. Yet Paul also notes that it is better for both the unmarried and the widowed to marry than to burn.[38]

While various controversies from encratism to Jovinian's argument with Jerome to Augustine's conflict with Julian of Eclanum have called for nuanced expositions regarding marriage and sexual activity, tension between sexual activity and celibacy remains for Orthodox even today.

Among Orthodox Christians, sexual continence is a complex subject. Even within the spousal relationship there are periods during which couples are encouraged to refrain from sexual intercourse. Further, many Orthodox worry about the effects of seeking sexual pleasure in ways that are not open to procreation.[39] At the same time, we should not lose sight of the reality that sexual activity, while often very important in a romantic relationship, nonetheless occupies a relatively minor portion of a couple's time together. Without diminishing the deep relational knowing of which Yannaras writes, most couples experience less sexual desire as they age, and their sexual activity tends to decrease. While many Orthodox thinkers tend to focus their discussion of same-sex relationships on what the partners do together sexually, the same decrease in sexual activity is also true of most same-sex couples. As such, while the next section explores the impediments to the recognition of homogenital activity as anything other than sinful, it is important to acknowledge the relative importance of sexual activity and the role it plays in the life of a long-term, committed relationship.

Unlike my previous appeals to a personalist anthropology that I argue clear the way for expanding sacramental practices of priesthood and recognizing marital relationships, the case for homogenital activity is more difficult. Orthodox condemnation of same-sex acts stems from a long interpretive tradition of a small collection of scriptural prooftexts, early church and patristic pronouncements, and a handful of legal canons. While I will explore each of these moments discretely, they do not exist in isolation from one another. Rather, these various sources reinforce one another through the formation of an interpretive matrix. In the following exploration, I will not attempt an in-depth critique of each of these impediments. I will only acknowledge their existence and offer some preliminary thoughts. Let us turn first to the common biblical references.

Homosexuality and Scripture

The standard collection of scriptural prooftexts used to condemn all same-sex genital acts includes Gn 19:1–11; Lv 18:22, 20:13; Rom 1:26–27; 1 Cor 6:9; and 1 Tm 1:9–11. To this collection some Orthodox commentators add

Jgs 19:22–25.[40] Others include 2 Pt 2:4 and Jude 7.[41] For centuries these passages have been taken from their original contexts and redeployed to condemn all homogenital acts. However, since the mid-twentieth century, historians, theologians, and biblical scholars have produced a wealth of essays, articles, and books questioning the traditional interpretations of these passages. For Orthodox thinkers, this work is often not enough. For example, in her own discussion of scriptural prooftexts, Moberly recognizes contemporary interpretative efforts, but remains unconvinced. "However much one may wish, quite legitimately, to qualify or contextualize these references," she writes, ". . . one may not avoid the conclusion that homosexual acts are always condemned and never approved."[42] While she acknowledges good faith on the part of those who seek more nuanced understandings of scripture that might open the possibility of specific forms of same-sex erotic activity, Moberly's own understanding of the passages she cites makes such an affirmation impossible. Indeed, this appears to be the nub of the argument for many people who might otherwise be accepting of other possibilities. But the very citation of these passages as prooftexts, with the expectation that their mention without any exegesis is sufficient to defend her point, is the result of a long history of taking these passages out of their original socio-historical contexts and reading them through the lens of a different interpretive framework. There is no need in this model to distinguish between various homogenital acts. Yet the prooftexts used to condemn homosexual acts describe many different things: gang rape, the purported cultic practices of ancient Near Eastern peoples, pederasty, and sexual encounters with prostitutes and household slaves. By ignoring context, these discrete phenomena are lumped together to form a blanket proscription against all same-sex acts.

Hopko also addresses the biblical prooftexts against same-sex genital acts. He begins on a broader note, warning that ignorance of scripture is the root of human spiritual enslavement of "theological, spiritual, and moral delusion." He further calls for critical readings of scripture, using intellectual and spiritual discernment, including "all available linguistic, literary, historical, and archaeological information to illumine the texts."[43] Hopko's willingness to employ the various exegetical tools used by biblical scholars opens a space for reexamining the ways in which this group of biblical texts has been historically interpreted. While a full examination and critique of the range of scholarly work now available falls beyond the scope of this book, I will, in light of the information presented in previous chapters, offer the following comments.[44]

Throughout the period covered by both testaments, the idea of a loving, reciprocal, sexual relationship between two persons of the same sex was an automatic non-starter. Both ancient Near Eastern and Greco-Roman cultural contexts envisioned sexual activity as embodying a hierarchy in which the penetrator in a sexual act subordinates a penetrated inferior. To be penetrated is to be feminine. This includes acts of mob violence with intention to sexually violate guests as portrayed in the account of Sodom in Gn 19 and the parallel account of the Gibeahites in Jgs 19. From the first century BCE, a period of intense Hellenization, Jewish exegetes linked the sin of Sodom with Greek pederasty, a connection that carries forward into the patristic corpus.[45] Also relevant to the ancient Near Eastern and Mediterranean contexts is the rape of foreign military rivals. Thus, when Saul falls in battle, he commands his armor bearer to kill him rather than face the fate of being captured and "abused" by the Philistines.[46] Another allusion to the practice is found in the abuse of David's emissaries by Hanun of the Ammonites. Suspecting David's men to be spies, Hanun seizes them, shaves half their beards, cuts off their clothing to reveal their buttocks (implying they have been penetrated), and sends them home.[47] These actions were intended to strip the men of their masculinity and honor.

Later, within the broader Mediterranean context, male citizens could licitly engage in sexual acts with a wife, concubine, or courtesan, but also with household slaves and prostitutes of both sexes. While sexual acts with freeborn youths were tolerable in Greek pederasty, Roman law prohibited sex with freeborn boys and youth under the laws against *stuprum*.[48] Irrespective of his partner's identity, the citizen male was expected to act as the penetrative partner, whether vaginally or anally. Fellatio was considered suspect in both Greek and Roman cultures.[49] In the Roman context, any freeborn man who allowed himself to be penetrated was punished through the confiscation of half his property and a declaration of *infamia*, stripping him of his citizen privileges such as the right to give testimony or participate in legal proceedings.[50] The use of household slaves and enslaved prostitutes was often brutal, with little recognition of a sexual object's personhood.[51]

It is in this environment of sexual domination, exploitation, and abuse that we find the intertestamental polemic of *geneseōs enallagē* (literally "changing of kind") in the Wisdom of Solomon that serves as the model for the speech presented by Paul in Romans 1.[52] In both texts, same-sex sexual behavior is characterized as a pagan practice, a result of a clouding of the mind due to idolatry.[53] Scholars agree that sexual exploitation is also the context of the vice lists offered in 1 Cor and 1 Tm that include the neologism *arsenokoitēs* and the more common ancient slur *malakos*, rendering problematic modern translations that substitute the word *homosexual* for these ancient figures.[54]

Within the scriptural context, there is no record of homosexual activity that is not immediately characterized as an activity engaged in by a social other: Sodomites or "sons of Belial" among the Gibeahites, various Canaanite nations, and pagans in the Greco-Roman context. Same-sex acts were not thought of as a part of loving relationships, but rather were characterized by the pursuit of self-seeking pleasures and the domination of others.[55]

The dynamics described above, while surely beyond the bounds of both Jewish and Christian sexual morality, cannot be used to characterize all homogenital acts in all times and in all places. What is missing from the prooftexts is any mention of sexual activity in a relationship that does not objectify or subordinate one of the participants. The biblical passages lack the specificity required to address the realities of sexual expression between two members of the same sex in a loving, committed relationship of equals in mutual submission to one another. This is a scenario unknown to the biblical authors. Neither the one-sex model of antiquity nor common hierarchical understandings of sex and gender of that time can accommodate such a coupling. For the ancients, penetration automatically implies femininity and subordination.

Early Church and Patristic References

While the sin of Sodom in both the Hebrew scriptures and the subsequent writings of the New Testament is commonly associated with inhospitality and the failure to receive foreign emissaries, both Philo and Josephus shift their interpretations to include polemics against pederasty.[56] This link between Sodom and pederasty carries over into texts from both the early church and patristic periods. Among the proscriptions of the *Didache* and the Epistle of Barnabas is a command against corrupting boys, while the Apocalypse of Peter gives a brief description of the punishments suffered in the afterlife by both men and women who engage in same-sex genital activity.[57] Commentaries also appear in the works of Tertullian, Clement of Alexandria, Gregory of Nyssa, and John Chrysostom.[58] Throughout these texts, the emphasis is placed nearly exclusively on the sexual use of adolescent boys for pleasure and casual sexual encounters with prostitutes. Very few references address female same-sex activity, and, when they do, the discussion centers on women usurping a man's role as penetrator. What is clear is that none of these scenarios envision same-sex genital activity as an expression of a loving, committed same-sex relationship. Such a relationship was simply inconceivable within the cultural contexts in which the patristic authors wrote.

Legal-Canonical Prohibitions

Finally, we turn to legal canons that are sometimes referenced in Orthodox debates over same-sex activity. Unlike civil legal codes or even the more developed canon law of other traditions, Orthodox legal canons often address *ad hoc* situations within localized contexts. Over time several compendia of canon laws have been assembled. Attempts to group the canons topically often obscure their situational nature under a false appearance of being systemically devised.[59] However, both the history of the discourses of sexuality and a broader understanding of the various historical framings of same-sex eroticism and sexual violence that predate contemporary categories call for caution in lumping canon laws together under a general category of "homosexuality" as, for example, modern translations of canonical collections are wont to do.[60] The role of canon law in contemporary Orthodoxy is often difficult to articulate. Some authors quote canons when they are conducive to their arguments, even as they note the difficulty in actually interpreting canons with any consistency.[61] Others note that canons are but attempts to apply the great dogmatic truths of the ecumenical councils to particular situations from the everyday life of the Church.[62] Many canons, while still "on the books," are completely ignored in modern Orthodox life.[63] Canons, unlike dogmas, may be redefined by a council. However, the common practice is to leave their interpretation to the local bishop. Depending on the situation, a bishop may choose to enforce a rule with strictness or exactness (*akribeia*). Likewise, the bishop also has the right to relax the rules (*oikonomia*) at his discretion. The ultimate criterion in the bishop's decision is discerning how best to foster spiritual growth towards divine-human communion for each person.

Conclusion

As this brief examination of the impediments to affirming same-sex genital activity makes clear, none of the traditional condemnations of homosexual acts address the modern phenomenon of a committed, loving, same-sex couple who are mutually submitted to one another. Such a relationship was inconceivable within the one-sex model of human bodies and the accompanying model of gendered subordination signified in acts of sexual penetration. In each case, what is required is a nuanced appraisal of the context of the passage in question. Each must be read through the socio-historical lens of its intended audience. Today's Orthodox Christians (and Christians more broadly) tend to read these texts instead through the lens of our contemporary cultural models, including our own ideas of gender roles and subordinationism, the two-sex model of human bodies, an overemphasis on procreative potential, and our own inflections of biblical texts.

The modern gender essentialist framework is also incapable of addressing the same-sex couple that I have described. In the essentialist model, metaphysical sexual polarities attract, while two members of the same gender repel one another.[64] For psychoanalytic models like Moberly's, same-sex love occurs only in a developmental stage leading to a mature heterosexual gender identity. Indeed, Moberly's reparative model has an undercurrent that suggests that eroticization of same-sex love dynamics moves from a natural stage of human development to something more closely resembling an exploitative relationship like pedophilia. Her model excludes, without providing any grounds, the possibility of a psychosexually mature relationship between same-sex partners. What might a personalist anthropology contribute to this conversation?

Returning to Yannaras, we recall his characterization of sexual union as a deep form of knowing. Sex becomes an avenue of relationality through which the elusive person within the human individual is at last knowable. Yannaras's description is independent of gendered roles, seeking transcendence of the divide between male and female. A personalist view, valuing both the unrepeatable *hypostasis* and the unique relationships that persons enter, focuses not on the genitals of the couple, but on the deep knowing, the acceptance of the other, the kenotic release of selfish desires, and a sacrificial, self-giving love for the other in mutual submission to one another. Such knowing is not excluded by traditional proscriptions against same-sex genital activity when these pronouncements are understood within their own contexts. However, much work is still required to reach a nuanced position. This is a task for further dialogue within the Church—true dialogue in which bishops listen and the entire Church discerns the paths to divine-human communion.

CHAPTER

8

SOME FINAL THOUGHTS ON PASTORAL CARE

All pastoral relationships are unique and personal, being subject to a multitude of individual personal factors. This makes generalization impossible, and the concept of an "open pastoral letter" about such things is a contradiction in terms, for it is not the case therefore that one size can fit all, or that such responses can be reduced to a blog post. . . . Pastoral care in such situations involves more listening than lecturing, and what a pastor says is conditioned by what he hears from the person he knows and loves.

—LAWRENCE FARLEY[1]

Introduction

This final chapter briefly addresses a set of pastoral care questions: definitions of family, adoption, and the care of intersex, transgender, and gender nonconforming parishioners. Before we proceed, I will point out that the epigraph above comes from a longer blog post with which I, in large part, disagree. Fr. Lawrence Farley and I differ in our conclusions about what the tradition has to offer parishioners who may come seeking advice about their sexual orientation or gender identity (the topic of his blog post). However, we strongly agree on this: there is no blanket advice that fits the unique circumstances of each human person. The first two topics explored in this chapter are only adjacent to Farley's original post, but they remain, nonetheless, within the constellation of theological concerns commonly informed by gender essentialism. May we, again, tread lightly as we proceed.

Defining the Family

Related to questions of same-sex relationships are Orthodox conceptions of the family. In 1992, the Holy Synod of the Orthodox Church in America released a document affirming several teachings of the Orthodox faith centered on "Marriage, Family, Sexuality, and the Sanctity of Life."[2] While emphasis is often placed on the "nuclear family" of a husband and wife together with their biological offspring, the affirmations emphasize the support and protection of the greater family structure that includes grandparents, aunts, uncles, and cousins. Single-parent families are also recognized, emphasizing the need to supplement children's relationships with "loving adults of the gender of the missing parent."[3] In light of these affirmations, how might we then approach families formed by same-sex couples? Responses among Orthodox thinkers are split.

John Breck characterizes same-sex and single-parent households as "ersatz families" because they do not fulfill the Orthodox understanding of the "one flesh" union between a man and a woman discussed above. In his judgment, same-sex relationships are inherently sinful and personally destructive. They must never be recognized by the Church.[4] However, as time passes and further legal recognitions are afforded to same-sex couples, this previous hardline position has begun to give way in some quarters to thoughtful pastoral responses. For example, even though Thomas Hopko is fully against recognizing same-sex relationships as sacramental and deems all homogenital activity sinful, he nonetheless advocates for full protection under the law, noting that legal protections are also beneficial for the children of same-sex couples. Christians cannot love everyone in word and deed while "at the same time denying basic human and civil rights to anyone."[5] Hopko's position, first articulated in 2006, but republished with his consent in 2015, has been received without controversy. However, another appeal written by Robert Arida has proven much more controversial. Arida takes the recognition of same-sex civil unions and marriages as a given, asking how Orthodox will respond to couples and their children when they come seeking Christ. He names a variety of responses: ignore them, turn them away, encourage them to divorce and dismantle their families as repentance, or offer pastoral care, love, and a spiritual home.[6] While unacknowledged within the academy, polemical responses to Arida's essay on the Internet hinge on his failure to characterize all same-sex relationships as sinful and to call for repentance that would, indeed, require the dismantling of the families in question.

Adoption

Like pronouncements about marriage and definitions of family, responses to the phenomenon of adoption by same-sex couples have also proven mixed. In her psychoanalytic volume, Moberly warns that adoption, fostering, or living in an orphanage all pose the possibility of trauma that may lead to a stunted gender identity, resulting in homosexuality.[7] Breck categorically rejects adoption by same-sex couples, citing the sinful nature of same-sex relationships and suggesting harmful effects on the children.[8] He further proposes that the only way a same-sex couple can raise a child without harm is by remaining celibate. However, as we saw above, other theologians such as Hopko and Arida have taken a more pragmatic approach, urging the church to move beyond theoretical constructs to prepare for encounters with actual couples and their children who might walk through the parish doors.

While working out appropriate responses, a great deal of pastoral *oikonomia* is afforded in the absence of explicit statements from bishops. However, pastoral letters from bishops carry broad consequences. For example, the statement released by Paul Gassios, former bishop of the Midwest for the Orthodox Church in America, places limits on access to communion for Orthodox Christians who enter state-sanctioned, same-sex relationships while they are "unrepentant." The text does not address the possibility of a same-sex, civil marriage that does not include sexual activity, nor does it spell out what repentance might look like.[9]

Regardless of the pastoral response to the civilly married couple, under no circumstances should the personal relationships of parents serve as a block to pastoral ministry to children. This includes unhindered access to Baptism and Chrismation, as well as the opportunities to participate in the Eucharist afforded other Orthodox children of the same developmental stage. Under no circumstances is it appropriate to withhold participation in the sacramental life of the Church from children in response to the perceived sins of their parents. Responses like those offered by Hopko and Arida provide clear models for prioritizing the fostering of spiritual growth and divine-human communion of individual persons over the demand that families conform to a particular model. They exemplify the exercise of pastoral *oikonomia* even as the Church continues to work through theological questions of the day. I suggest these responses can also provide models for ministry to intersex, transgender, and gender-nonconforming individuals within the parish.

Intersex, Transgender, and Gender-Nonconforming Persons

In the previous sections, the focus has been on two sexes: male and female. "Theologically, there are two clear-cut and definite genders," writes Lazar Puhalo, a Canadian abbot and retired archbishop of the Orthodox Church in America. "In reality, this is simply not the case."[10] In the general population, estimates for the frequency of intersex conditions range between one in every 59 to 268 people.[11] Roughly three in every 1,000 U.S. adults are transgender, while a recent study estimates more than one million nonbinary LGBTQ adults live in the United States.[12] Thus, there is some likelihood that many in ordained ministry will be called upon during their service to minister to people from one or more of these categories. From the Church's perspective, pastoral care for all people, regardless of biological sex, gender identity, and gender expression, is of primary concern. However, these are among the questions to which most parishes are least prepared to adequately respond. Exploring these topics before such an encounter occurs and staying abreast of new findings is important to providing the best possible pastoral care.

As an easy starting point, where it is feasible, parishes should consider maintaining at least one single-user bathroom that is not designated for a particular sex. Such accommodations in facilities provide neutral spaces for gender-nonconforming individuals to use the restroom in comfort and safety. A single-user space sidesteps the culture war trope of men who claim to be women in order to gain access to the women's restroom where they can observe and harass women. However, we should all be aware that the underlying fear in this scenario is of sexual predators rather than actual transgender and gender-nonconforming people.

Intersex Children

Because gender and sex are such fundamental elements of human identity, they tend to inflect all our relationships. This includes the interpersonal dynamics of parish life where, in the Orthodox tradition, a child's first communal participation in the sacraments often takes place shortly after birth with Baptism and Chrismation and continues in Eucharistic participation and eventually in other sacramental participation. Even before infants can tell us who they are, we begin to make assumptions about them based on their assigned sex. However, as we saw in chapter 4, determining the sex of a child is not always a straightforward process. Further, in some cases, the designation deemed best by medical professionals may turn out later to be in conflict either with further medical findings, the child's gender identity, or both. It is perfectly acceptable for clergy to admit when they are out of their depth and to aid in the search for qualified professionals (e.g., social workers, psychologists, and doctors) who can serve the needs of children and parents in distress.

In cases of intersex newborns, medical protocols followed since the 1950s have recommended a quick classification of the infant that considers genetic makeup as well as the possible outcomes of plastic surgeries that seek to "normalize" external genitalia. Because of the difficulties in fashioning a working penis, surgeons have historically considered the construction of a vagina to be the less complicated option. However, such corrective surgeries are not without their own risks. Among these is a potential mismatch between the genital configuration chosen for the child and the child's gender identity. While current neurobiological studies suggest that gender identity develops during fetal gestation, the preverbal infant is not able to reveal their subjectivity to parents and various health professionals. Thus, caution is warranted when determining a course of action. While sex correction protocols have traditionally called for early intervention to "normalize" the child's genitalia, debates over delaying noncritical surgical procedures are becoming more common. Critical surgical intervention includes creating a urethra for urination if the child is born without one. But other plastic surgeries such as vaginoplasty or clitoroplasty are difficult or impossible to reverse should the need arise later. Because of this, a growing movement suggests that such procedures should be delayed until the child's gender identity has been reasonably determined.

A growing number of countries recognize some form of nonbinary or third sex, several of which are intended to cover ambiguous situations in which a child's sexual designation is not immediately clear. At the writing of this chapter, a growing number of U.S. states recognize a nonbinary option for official documents. Parents may wish to avail themselves of these possibilities while they discern the best course of action. However, even if the parents choose a nonbinary designation for legal documents, they will most likely choose a gendered identity, based on the best possible gender assignment made in consultation with medical professionals.

The Intersex Society of North America (now closed) advocated for a transparency model to normalize intersex conditions and to replace shame-based models that choose to hide intersex individuals. However, the onus of educating the local parish should not fall on the intersex child or their family members. Bishops and broader administrative support bodies would do well to proactively prepare before such events arise by educating clergy and identifying resources that may be shared should the need arise.

Official Orthodox pronouncements on intersex phenomena are, thankfully, rare. I know of no official statements within the diaspora communities of the Paris School tradition. However, within the Russian Orthodox Church (ROC) context, the Holy Bishops' Council has adopted an official document containing positions on intersex and transgender conditions. The ROC's teaching makes an allowance for intersex conditions that result in "the wrong identification of the sex in one's infancy" resulting from "a pathological development of sexual characteristics." Surgical intervention in such cases is characterized as correction rather than sex-change.[13] The official declaration is terse, leaving room for medical practitioners to exercise broad discretion in evaluating the individual and offering recommendations. However, the underlying assumption of the document remains steadfastly rooted in a gender essentialist paradigm that suggests a person has but one "true" sex that can be determined through sufficient interrogation of the body. The ROC statement fails to consider a variety of physical conditions such as mixed-sex genetic chimerism, which cannot be recognized as strictly male or female.

Within parish life, it is common to baptize infants forty days after birth. The latitude of pastoral *oikonomia* should be freely observed during the actual baptism with regard to ambiguous genitalia. While infant baptisms are often performed with the child in the nude, a priest may choose to baptize the child in a diaper or symbolic baptismal garment. The family may wish to proceed with baptism based on the assigned gender. However, clergy should make clear their willingness to change a baptismal name and supporting documentation should the child's gender identity later change.

In 1985, a prayerbook appeared in Greece that included "A Prayer at the Giving of a New Name upon Change of Sex,"[14] written by Timotheos Matthaiakēs, then metropolitan of Nea Ionia and Philadelphia. An English version of the prayer made a splash in the Orthodox blogosphere in

2017 in a post claiming that the prayer was written to address name changes after sex reassignment surgeries.[15] Several online responses followed, discounting the blog post's claim and asserting the prayer was written for cases in which intersex children receive new names after corrective surgery. However, the translator of the prayer includes footnotes with his work, indicating that the original prayer was used for adults undergoing sex reassignment surgeries and that he modified the English version to make it more widely applicable for intersex children.[16] While the story of the prayer's initial purpose is disputed, both the original prayer and its modified English version offer examples of pastoral responses to the needs of the faithful.

Beginning with a doxology, the prayer praises God who created the human being with a "rational soul and dignified body" and who "made male and female and gave to each [sex] its own appearance and substance." The prayer continues, referencing name changes among the saints, specifically Cephas, son of Iona, who becomes Peter, and Saul of Tarsus, whom we better know as Paul. The English rendering then asks for grace for the person undergoing the "modification of gender" (literally the "change of sex" in the Greek), marveling at the "alteration" (literally "change") made possible by the technologies of modern medicine that the author attributes to God's hand and will.

Transgender Parishioners

Moving from intersex to transgender individuals, most clergy and laity are ill-prepared to formulate a theological, let alone therapeutic, response. This is not surprising, as transgender identity is an area in which research continues to develop.[17] In other Christian traditions, there have been a range of responses to transgender issues. On one end of the spectrum, a gender essentialist approach acknowledges gender dysphoria as a reality experienced by some people but rejects hormone replacement therapy and sex reassignment surgeries. A second approach sees transgender phenomena as an unfortunate cross to bear, drawing insights from disability studies to explore questions of theodicy and to offer hope for those who suffer in ways that may be difficult or impossible to remedy. A third approach suggests that advances in medical technologies can alleviate the suffering of trans people and should be embraced freely, while a fourth agrees with the good of transition for those who desire it while also pointing out the wonder of God's creation that exceeds the binaries that humanity attempts to impose.[18]

A personalist approach to transgender persons could embrace any of the latter three positions, based on the specifics of the situation.

It is worth noting that, in the case of intersex individuals with ambiguous genitalia, none of the four theological positions described above would strictly forbid corrective surgeries even if their justifications differ. For the essentialist, these surgeries are permissible as the correction of a defect. Such interventions are not seen as a transition from one God-given sex to another. The only concern that an adherent to any of these four viewpoints might express relates to the timing of corrective surgery and whether the child should be consulted in making the sex assignment. It would be an outlier who would stand on a principle of no corrective surgeries at all, though such an opinion does exist among some intersex advocates who suggest surgical interventions should be limited to extreme cases.

Accounts of the etiology of gender dysphoria and transgender identities are still a matter of much research. Elizabeth Moberly rejects biological causes for transgender phenomena. According to her one-size-fits-all psychoanalytic model, transgender identity is the most extreme form of homosexuality. She again returns to the hypothesis of early childhood trauma involving the same-sex parent. In this case, the trauma is so severe that the child not only defensively withdraws from the parent-child love relationship, but also radically dissociates from his or her own gender identity. For Moberly, transgender individuals do not so much identify with the opposite sex as simply reject their own, resulting in a complete lack of gender identity development. Her proposed cure then is the same as for homosexuality: reparative therapy with a therapist of the same anatomical sex. Because the disidentification with the same-sex parental love source is so profound, Moberly hypothesizes a longer treatment period. If normal human psychosocial development unfolds from birth through adolescence, then the therapeutic period could take several years to achieve success. Moberly does acknowledge intersex cases as a separate phenomenon. However, in recent years, earlier psychological theories have been characterized as outdated. Moberly's brief address is insufficient and based solely on the earliest findings by Money and his associates.[19]

Orthodox responses that consider biological data fall into two basic camps. Essentialists tend to point to either external genitalia or the twenty-third chromosomal pair as the basis for declaring an individual's sex. Once this "true sex" is established, any conflict between a person's gender identity and these biological markers is decided in favor of the latter.

An example of this essentialist approach appears in an essay by Robert Hart.[20] Anchored by the assertion that chromosomal makeup at the cellular level trumps gender identity, Hart argues that one cannot change sex, only become a masculinized woman or a feminized man through hormonal and surgical interventions that result in sterility. This argument has two parts. The first, which denies that actual biological sex change is impossible by an appeal to chromosomal makeup, is drawn from Paul McHugh, former psychiatrist-in-chief at Johns Hopkins University, who has disavowed the sexual reassignment surgeries that were pioneered by the hospital in which he worked.[21] The second element of his argument is based on the divine command of Gn 1:28 to be fruitful and multiply. Finally, Hart, like McHugh, misrepresents data from a Swedish study that found that the suicide rate for trans people who undergo gender reassignment surgery is twenty times higher than among cisgender people. Hart especially takes these findings out of context to suggest that reassignment surgery itself is somehow responsible for the increased risk of suicide.

As we saw in chapter 4, gender theorists have argued that the medical categories of sex are the products of discourses of gender. Yet our day-to-day approach to the categories male and female suggests a more metaphysical understanding of some sort of essential male or female nature. Advances in scientific knowledge have not done away with a strict sexual binary. Over time, essentialists have tended to move the goal posts. In the not-so-distant past, a penis was the signifier of the male sex. A bit more knowledge and the marker became a Y-chromosome. Still more research, and we find that a particular gene sequence, even in the absence of a Y-chromosome, will still masculinize an embryo. Each discovery redraws the boundary line, but the essentialists' fundamental conviction—that there are only two possibilities for the "true" sex of a human being—remains unchanged. Yet as the patristic survey reminds us, we all share a common human nature. We share in the same human traits and charisms, and we possess the same capacity for virtue. Biologically we all start with the same bodily structures that give rise to both male and female reproductive organs and genitalia. We are not so fundamentally different as any of the essentialist models would claim.

The second part of the argument above points to a Swedish study of a group of 324 sex-reassigned individuals that found the rate of suicide was nineteen times higher than in the general non-trans population. However, as the authors of the study were the first to point out, they did not establish a causal link between transition and suicide attempts. They went as far as to suggest the rates could have been higher had their subjects not transitioned.[22] What this study and others like it suggest is that transition alone is not a panacea for many trans people, who often suffer from additional problems such as depression, stigma, and lack of social support.

As we saw in chapter 4, a growing body of evidence points to the role of prenatal hormones in shaping the brain and gender identity. Based on these findings, Lazar Puhalo is a lone voice in North American Orthodoxy, suggesting that transgender identity is also an intersex condition in which the sex of the brain conflicts with other sexual characteristics of the body.[23] As a sexed organ, he argues, the brain should also be considered when establishing gender identity, choosing what brings greater relief to the dysphoric person.[24]

Not all essentialists come to the same conclusions. Returning to the prayer above, theologians from Greece have pointed out to me that if one believes that hormone replacement therapy and sex reassignment surgeries align the body with its "true" sex, it is, indeed, quite marvelous technology. However, decades later, after Matthaiakēs penned his prayer, the ROC teaching reflects a different response, also couched in essentialism. Here, the document referenced above glosses gender dysphoria as "the painful feeling of one's belonging to the opposite sex," further characterizing it as "perverted human sexuality." In such cases, the bishops forbid gender transition (with specific reference to hormone replacement therapy and sex reassignment surgeries) as being "rebellion against the Creator." The ROC allows persons who have already transitioned to be baptized on the condition that the rite is performed according to their "sex by birth."[25] While the document does not elaborate, baptism according to one's birth sex includes a set of gendered conventions such as the selection of a patronal saint whose name one takes on in baptism and what type of clothing might be worn during the rite. However, the bishops bar such persons' participation in the sacraments of holy orders and "marriage within the Church," raising questions about any civil marriage they enter and any sexual activity within the relationship.[26]

The best practices of qualified professionals should be given preference over both essentialist fundamentalism and unquestioning advocacy for transitioning, both of which may have preconceived notions of how particular cases must proceed. When working with children and adolescents, medical personnel, in consultation with trained mental healthcare providers, may recommend delaying pubertal changes by blocking hormones that trigger the development of secondary sex characteristics that alter the body in ways that are not easily reversed. With adults as well as children, there can be no blanket prescription for how clergy should respond. Deference to best professional practices should supersede well-intentioned advice informed by gender essentialist and trans advocacy paradigms.[27]

Those charged with pastoral care may worry about encouraging a delusion. Yet in so many cases, pastoral care involves meeting a person where they are, listening to their stories, asking clarifying questions, and loving the person amid uncertainty. One of the greatest gifts we can offer is a safe space for reflection and discernment for those who struggle to articulate their experience. Such acceptance is foundational to interpersonal communion. A pastor's responsibility is not to practice medical gatekeeping. Most clergy are simply not qualified to make such decisions. Instead, they should refer to specialists. While there are cases in which people who have begun or completed medical transition later regret their decision, these cases are a small number compared with the majority who experience relief. As the ones experiencing their own gender identities, dissonance, and incongruities, trans people are best positioned to make their own decisions regarding when and in what ways to transition with the following caveats. Hormone replacement therapy and sex reassignment surgeries both have effects that are difficult or impossible to reverse. As such, it behooves the person considering these procedures to learn about them before making any decisions. Likewise, attempts at self-administered hormone replacement therapy may signal inadequate discernment and planning.[28] Clergy may express concern over planning but ultimately should refer to qualified help.

Pronouns

Pronoun usage may also prove challenging. People often experience cognitive dissonance when shifting between *he* and *she* for a person with whom they have prior history. The same can be true when a person's gender identity does not conform to our perceptions. Likewise, some will balk at the use of *they* as a nonbinary pronoun on grammatical grounds. Yet English speakers have used *they* for hundreds of years when referring to a (usually unknown) individual. The novelty is in using *they* in reference to someone we perceive to be male or female or have previously known. In each of these cases, we are presented with a chance to grow past the discomfort of the unfamiliar to encounter the person who presents themselves before us. There may be mistakes along the way. We may use an incorrect pronoun or say the wrong name. Apologize and keep trying.

The continued use of pronouns in opposition to a parishioner's stated gender identity will almost certainly be interpreted negatively. The same is true of using a person's former name rather than the name they have requested to be called by—a practice known as *deadnaming* in transgender communities. Deliberate use of a person's former name and/or pronouns conveys personal rejection, disrespect, and even open hostility. None of these perceptions are conducive to building interpersonal relationships or fostering divine-human communion. As the prayer above illustrates, changes of name are a common occurrence within the biblical tradition. To Peter and Paul we may also add Abraham, Sarah, and Israel. Converts often take a new name in Baptism or Chrismation, while monastics may receive a new name at their tonsure as do some ordinands. Finally, within the Church's history, a number of women monastics have also taken masculine names and pronouns.[29] We are not without precedents.

Conclusion

In Part II of this book, we have explored various theological questions associated with biological sex and gender that have arisen within the Orthodox Church in response to broader cultural shifts. The gender essentialist paradigm espoused by many communities within the Paris School stream of Orthodoxy has shaped initial ecclesial responses. However, I have suggested alternative responses based in a personalist anthropology and a range of critiques offered from the biological sciences and gender and queer theorists. My approach allows us to move beyond the erroneous assumption that gender and biological sex are fixed, incommensurate ontological categories and that an individual's sex may be determined by an appeal to biological characteristics such as genitalia or chromosomal makeup. The essentialist paradigm suggests an ontological basis for gender-exclusive charisms, vocations, and access to sacraments. The personalist approach, in contrast, affirms a common nature shared by all human persons while also highlighting the freedom of each person that gestures beyond that nature through a variety of interpersonal relationships. These include relations between the various persons within the Body of Christ: the sacerdotal priesthood, spousal relationships, and familial structures.

The division between the essentialist and personalist responses is not always neat. For example, Thomas Hopko espouses many elements of personalism even as he posits an affinity between men and the Son and between women and the Holy Spirit. Likewise, Christos Yannaras is an avowed personalist, yet his model of marriage fails to account for the full freedom of human persons. Neither thinker pursues the full implications of the personalism they espouse. As with so many unsettled questions, we are on a journey, discerning as we go.

In approaching questions of ministerial priesthood, the personalist approach I have outlined denies that the charisms associated with the priesthood are limited by gender or biological sex. Rather, the focus is placed on personal vocation, acknowledging God's freedom to call what persons God will. Such persons, in turn, are free to respond. Each priest, regardless of sex or gender, is a unique person who participates in sacramental relationships of grace that open opportunities for divine-human communion, both for the priest as a unique person, but also for the communities that the priest serves. In exploring this model, I have responded to several arguments against women's ordination, most based in essentialist understandings of liturgical symbolism, scriptural metaphors, and spiritual authority. Beyond the appeal to tradition, the collection of arguments offered against women's participation in the ministerial priesthood is theologically novel and depends on an essentialist interpretation of several scriptural metaphors in ways that are foreign to the broader Orthodox tradition.

In approaching the array of questions associated with homosexuality, I have offered theological justifications for a reexamination of current teaching and practices. While an increasing number of Orthodox draw a distinction between an immutable sexual orientation and the choice to engage in genital same-sex activity, I have sought to reframe the discussion. Moving away from essentialist vs. non-essentialist debates, I have focused on the personal nature of each relationship, arguing that labels such as hetero- and homosexual, like the labels male and female, tend to obscure unique human persons and their unique interpersonal relationships. I have further argued for sacramental recognition of the grace that may be found in same-sex, erotic relationships that leads the couple into divine-human communion in a manner analogous to an opposite-sex, sacramental marriage. Such sacramentality is not dependent on procreative potential, but on a life of accepting one another, even in difficult times, and the practice of self-emptying love. Recognizing that questions of sexual activity complicate the question of same-sex relationships, I have briefly explored the impediments that must be addressed to draw a distinction between sexual relations within a committed, loving, same-sex relationship and the acts proscribed in scripture, patristic texts, and canon law. Finally, I have argued that Orthodox must pay attention to the experiences of intersex, transgender, and gender-nonconforming individuals. Rather than continuing to entertain outmoded psychoanalytic theories that reinforce essentialist paradigms, a sound pastoral approach will consider biological data, professional mental health standards, and the subjectivity of individual parishioners. As with each of the questions I have explored, the emphasis remains on deepening divine-human communion, a task that is unique to the particularities of each human person.

The roles of teacher and shepherd include a sacred responsibility for the spiritual health of the people whom ministerial clergy are called to serve. With this responsibility comes the need for professional expertise and a humble heart. Bishops, as the teachers in the Orthodox tradition, bear a great responsibility to educate themselves, to listen to the reports of the faithful (and, as I suggested in chapter 1, those outside of the Church who engage in good-faith conversation), and to prepare the clergy they oversee for the realities they may face in today's ministry contexts.

I offer these arguments to the broader theological and ecclesiastical discussion that has, as Orthodox measure time, only just begun. While further theological discernment continues, pastoral *oikonomia* has wide latitude for the care of intersex and gender-nonconforming individuals, as well as LGBT parishioners and their families in the sacramental life of the Church. In the Church's ongoing deliberation, the ultimate goal of divine-human communion must not only set the theological standard, but also provide the measure of pastoral responses. This includes honest dialogue and communal discernment to reach unity within the Body of Christ.

NOTES

1. Setting the Stage

1. Kallistos Ware, "The Witness of the Orthodox Church," *Ecumenical Review* 52, no. 1 (2000): 55.

2. The obvious exception is the Christian celebration of consecrated virginity and the monastic vocation.

3. In using the phrase *divine-human communion* as a contemporary formulation for the meaning of theosis, I follow Aristotle Papanikolaou. See Aristotle Papanikolaou, "Divine Energies or Divine Personhood: Vladimir Lossky and John Zizioulas on Conceiving the Transcendent and Immanent God," *Modern Theology* 19, no. 3 (2003): 358–59; *The Mystical as Political: Democracy and Non-Radical Orthodoxy* (Notre Dame: University of Notre Dame Press, 2012), 1–2. Other accounts of theosis are offered in Timothy Ware, *The Orthodox Church*, New ed. (New York: Penguin Books, 1993), 231–38; John Breck, *The Sacred Gift of Life: Orthodox Christianity and Bioethics* (Crestwood: St Vladimir's Seminary Press, 1998), 38–42.

4. For a schematization of theologians of the Paris School into five streams of thought and emphasis, see Hilarion Alfeev, "Orthodox Theology on the Threshold of the 21st Century: Will There Be a Renaissance of Russian Theological Scholarship?," *Ecumenical Review* 52, no. 3 (2000). Other proposed names include "Russian theology in exile" and "theology in the Russian Diaspora." See Paul L. Gavrilyuk, *Georges Florovsky and the Russian Religious Renaissance*, Changing Paradigms in Historical and Systematic Theology (Oxford: Oxford University Press, 2013), 133–37. I have used the older name "Paris School" for its broader name recognition with my audience.

5. Theologians and religious philosophers such as Kallistos Ware, Andrew Louth, Dumitru Stăniloae, Christos Yannaras, and John Zizioulas are among the later wave of scholars influenced by the patristic revival. Their works will also appear as my exploration unfolds.

6. This section draws its title from Vladimir Lossky's essay "La Tradition et les traditions," *Messager de l'Exarchat du patriarche russe en Europe occidentale*, no. 30–31 (1959). Further citations are from the commonly available English translation.

7. Vladimir Lossky, "Tradition and Traditions," in *In the Image and Likeness*, ed. John H. Erickson and Thomas E. Bird (Crestwood: St Vladimir's Seminary Press, 1974), 154–55.

8. Gn 32:30.

9. Lazarus Moore writes that human traditions "try to perpetuate things that are transient. They cling to things that time destroys: acting, clothing, customs, dancing, eating, building, education, painting, soldiering, entertainment, politics, and etiquette. Such things are all subject to change or dissolution." See Lazarus Moore, *Sacred Tradition in the Orthodox Church* (Minneapolis: Light and Life Publishing Company, 1984), 24. Moore's essay draws heavily on the sensibilities of Georges Florovsky.

10. Vasily Bolotov, "Thesen über das "Filioque" von einem russischen Theologen," *Revue internationale de théologie* 6, no. 24 (1898): 681–85.

11. Georges Florovsky, "Bogoslovskie otryvki" [Theological Fragments] *Put'*, no. 31 (1931): 13; John Meyendorff, *Living Tradition: Orthodox Witness in the Contemporary World* (Crestwood: St Vladimir's Seminary Press, 1975), 20.

12. Lossky, "Tradition and Traditions," 165.

13. Andrew Blane, Mark Raeff, and George H. Williams, *Georges Florovsky: Russian Intellectual and Orthodox Churchman* (Crestwood: St Vladimir's Seminary Press, 1993), 154.

14. Kallistos Ware, *Orthodox Theology in the Twenty-First Century*, ed. Pantelis Kalaitzidis, Doxa & Praxis (Geneva: Word Council of Churches, 2012), 31.

15. Thomas Hopko, *Christian Faith and Same-Sex Attraction: Eastern Orthodox Reflections* (Chesterton: Ancient Faith Publishing, 2015), 93.

16. Alexei V. Nesteruk, "Patristic Theology and the Natural Sciences (Part II)," *Sourozh*, no. 85 (2001): 34–35.

17. For an overview of the idea the *Logos* and *logoi* from Philo and Maximus, see Lars Thunberg, *Man and the Cosmos: The Vision of St. Maximus the Confessor* (Crestwood: St. Vladimir's Seminary Press, 1985), 132–37. Nesteruk provides citations for references to the *logoi* in the works of Gregory of Nazianzus, Gregory of Nyssa, Basil of Cappadocia, Pseudo-Dionysius, and Evagrius of Pontus in "Patristic Theology and the Natural Sciences (Part I)," *Sourozh*, no. 84 (2001): 24, n.25.

18. See Nesteruk, "Patristic Theology I," 32.

19. Cf. "Patristic Theology II," 34.

20. Georges Florovsky, "'As the Truth is in Jesus' (Ephes. 4:21)," *Christian Century* 68, no. 51 (1951): 1458.

21. Lossky, "Tradition and Traditions," 145.

22. *Incarnatione* 57.1.

23. *Incarnatione* 57.3. For further information, see John Anthony McGuckin, "Recent Biblical Hermeneutics in Patristic Perspective: The Tradition of Orthodoxy," *Greek Orthodox Theological Review* 47, no. 1–4 (2002): 312.

24. See Andrew Louth, *Maximus the Confessor*, The Early Church Fathers (New York: Routledge, 1996), 57–58.

25. Here, I must add a note of caution. While the fruits of the Spirit are the general outcome of the cultivation of divine-human communion, the Orthodox tradition teaches that judgment is the purview of Christ alone. No one in this life can make definitive judgments about the relation of any soul, including one's own, to God.

26. Kathleen Stein, "Interview [with] John Money," *Omni* 8, no. 7 (1986): 80. Money worked with a team whose pioneering research was published in a series of four journal articles. John Money, Joan G. Hampson, and John L. Hampson, "An Examination of Some Basic Sexual Concepts: The Evidence of Human Hermaphroditism," *Bulletin of The Johns Hopkins Hospital* 97, no. 4 (1955); "Hermaphroditism: Recommendations Concerning Assignment of Sex, Change of Sex and Psychologic Management," *Bulletin of The Johns Hopkins Hospital* 97, no. 4 (1955); "Sexual Incongruities and Psychopathology: The Evidence of Human Hermaphroditism," *Bulletin of The Johns Hopkins Hospital* 98, no. 1 (1956); "Imprinting and the Establishment of Gender Role," *Archives of Neurology and Psychiatry* 77 (1957).

27. For an analysis of the trends in the usage of sex and gender in scholarly literature, see David Haig, "The Inexorable Rise of Gender and the Decline of Sex: Social Change in Academic Titles, 1945–2001," Archives of Sexual Behavior 33, no. 2 (2004).

28. Thomas Walter Laqueur, *Making Sex: Body and Gender from the Greeks to Freud* (Cambridge: Harvard University Press, 1990), viii, 8.

29. Laqueur builds his case using texts from the Hippocratic corpus (spanning the mid-fifth to early fourth centuries BCE), Plato (429/423–348/347 BCE), Aristotle (394/322 BCE), and Galen of Pergamum (130–210 CE). These texts appear in discussions in later periods.

30. Cf. Galen, *Us. part.* 2.629, Aristotle *Hist. an.* 1.9.491b26ff and 4.8.533a1–13. See Laqueur, *Making Sex*, 28, 252 n.8.

31. In Greek texts of the period, both testes and ovaries are referred to as ὄρχεις.

32. Cf. Laqueur, *Making Sex*, 149; "Sex in the Flesh," *Isis* 94, no. 2 (2003): 306. In opposition to Laqueur, see Helen King, "The Mathematics of Sex: One to Two, or Two to One?," *Studies in Medieval and Renaissance History* 17, no. 2 (2005): 48. For conflicting evidence in the 13th to 16th centuries in Europe, see Katharine Park and Robert A. Nye, "Destiny Is Anatomy," *New Republic* 204, no. 7 (1991): 54.

33. See King, "Mathematics of Sex," 50–51; *The One-Sex Body on Trial: The Classical and Early Modern Evidence* (Farnham: Ashgate Publishing Limited, 2013).

34. For an accessible summary of the various models of sexual reproduction, see Michael Boylan, "The Galenic and Hippocratic Challenges to Aristotle's Conception Theory," *Journal of the History of Biology* 17, no. 1 (1984). For an in-depth view of Galen's model, see Sophia M. Connell, "Aristotle and Galen on Sex Difference and Reproduction: A New Approach to an Ancient Rivalry," *Studies in History and Philosophy of Science* 31, no. 2 (2000).

35. Susan Wessel, "The Reception of Greek Science in Gregory of Nyssa's 'De hominis opificio'" *Vigiliae Christianae: A Review of Early Christian Life and Language* 63, no. 1 (2009).

36. Teresa M. Shaw, "Creation, Virginity and Diet in Fourth-Century Christianity: Basil of Ancyra's *On the True Purity of Virginity*," *Gender & History* 9, no. 3 (1997).

37. *Nat. hom.* 25. For an English translation, see Nemesius of Emesa, "On the Nature of Man," in *Cyril of Jerusalem and Nemesius of Emesa*, ed. William Tefler (Philadelphia: Westminster Press, 1955), 369–70.

38. Laqueur, *Making Sex*, 49.

39. See Paul A. Anthony, "Sex, Sin and the Soul: How Galen's Philosophical Speculation Became Augustine's Theological Assumptions," *Conversations: A Graduate Journal of the Humanities, Social Sciences, and Theology* 1, no. 1 (2013), http://ojs.acu.edu/ojs/index.php/conversations/article/view/5.

2. (No) Male and Female: Recapitulating Patristic Reflections on Gender

1. Georges Florovsky, "Eastern Orthodox Church and the Ecumenical Movement," *Theology Today* 7, no. 1 (1950): 78–79.

2. See Michel Foucault, "Nietzsche, Genealogy, History," in *Language, Counter-Memory, Practice*, ed. Donald F. Bouchard (Ithaca: Cornell University Press, 1977).

3. For the critical edition of the Platonic corpus, see Plato, *Platonis opera*, 5 vols., Oxford Classical Texts (New York: Oxford University Press, 1902–1906).

4. *Symp.* 189d–193e.

5. While Plato describes the ἀνδρόγυνος in positive terms, the word was commonly used to refer to an effeminate or cowardly man. See n.25, Plato,

M. C. Howatson, and Frisbee C. C. Sheffield, *The Symposium*, trans. M. C. Howatson, Cambridge Texts in the History of Philosophy (New York: Cambridge University Press, 2008), 22.

6. *Symp.* 190d–e. Ibid., 23.

7. *Symp.* 191d. Ibid., 24.

8. *Tim.* 41d–42e; 90e; 91d–92c.

9. Plato and Donald J. Zeyl, *Timaeus* (Indianapolis: Hackett Publishing Company, 2000), 87.

10. *Tim.* 90e–91d.

11. Plato and Zeyl, *Timaeus*, lxxxix.

12. See Donald Zeyl's commentary. Ibid., lxxxviii.

13. *Tim.* 91c–d. Ibid., 87.

14. For example, Tertullian's *Anima*. An example of the shift in understandings of reproduction among the patristic sources is Gregory of Nazianzus, who follows the idea of a male and female seed that join. See Verna E. F. Harrison, "Male and Female in Cappadocian Theology," *Journal of Theological Studies* 41, no. 2 (1990): 442, n.6.

15. *Phaedrus* 246a–254e.

16. *Phaedrus* 253d–e. Plato and Stephen Scully, *Plato's Phaedrus* (Newburyport: Focus Publishing, 2003), 35.

17. καὶ ἐποίησεν ὁ θεὸς τὸν ἄνθρωπον κατ᾽ εἰκόνα θεοῦ ἐποίησεν αὐτόν ἄρσεν καὶ θῆλυ ἐποίησεν αὐτούς·

18. For more information on the mythopoetic adaptation of *Enuma Elish* for use in the biblical narrative see Bernard Frank Batto, *Slaying the Dragon: Mythmaking in the Biblical Tradition* (Louisville: Westminster John Knox Press, 1992), 33–40, 73–101.

19. The use of the neuter pronoun in English denotes the sexless nature of the human before the fashioning of the woman. The Greek word ἄνθρωπος is grammatically masculine, and it performs double duty as the word for both "man" and for all of humanity regardless of sex. An ancient Greek speaker wishing to explicitly denote the male sex/gender would use the words ἀνήρ ("man") and ἄρρην/ἄρσην ("masculine"). The corresponding forms γυνή ("woman") and θῆλυ ("female") are used to explicitly denote the female sex/gender.

20. The distinction between ἀνήρ and ἄνθρωπος is not always strictly observed in the Greek translation of the Hebrew Bible. For example, the combination ἄνθρωπος/γυνή is used to describe a husband and wife three times in Num 5:31 and 1 Sam 35:3. The same combination is used more generically of men and wives (either future wives or another's wife) three times in Dt 22:29, 25:7, and 25:11. The combination ἄνθρωπος/γυνή is used in Est 4:11 to refer to men and women generically. Finally, the expression

"man of God" is commonly rendered as ἄνθρωπος (τοῦ) θεοῦ throughout the Greek text.

21. See Batto, *Slaying the Dragon*, 203–04, n.31.

22. In her seminal essay, Phyllis Trible also notes that the word *'ēzer* taken alone does not imply a relational inferiority. Her discovery in the Hebrew is analogous to the work I have done here with the LXX translation. See Phyllis Trible, "Eve and Adam: Genesis 2–3 Reread," *Andover Newton Quarterly* 13, no. 4 (1973). Hebrew scholar Richard Elliott Friedman, following R. D. Freedman, translates the phrase *'ēzer kənegdô* (עזר כנגדו) as "corresponding strength" in his *Commentary on the Torah: With a New English Translation* (New York: HarperSanFrancisco, 2001), 19.

23. Strength: Ex 15:2; Ps 27:7, 58:18; Is 25:4. Help: Ex 18:4; Dt 33:7; Ps 26:9, 32:20, 45:2. Rock: Ps 17:3, 78:35. Other passages use stronghold (Ps 9:10), refuge (Ps 61:9, 70:7), or hiding place (Ps 119:114).

24. The connection between Plato and Philo in the minds of early Christian exegetes is a complex one. See David T. Runia, *Philo in Early Christian Literature: A Survey*, Compendia Rerum Iudaicarum ad Novum Testamentum Section 3, Jewish Traditions in Early Christian Literature (Minneapolis: Fortress Press, 1993), 4; n.5, 4–5; 313–14.

25. For an exhaustive list of references, see ibid., 4–6.

26. For an exploration of the use of allegory in Hellenic Judaism and early Christianity, see Jon Whitman, *Interpretation and Allegory: Antiquity to the Modern Period* (Leiden: Brill, 2000). For Philo's knowledge of *Timaeus*, see David T. Runia, *Philo of Alexandria and the Timaeus of Plato*, ed. W. J. Verdenius and J. C. M. Van Winden, Philosophia Antiqua (Leiden: Brill, 1986), 365–71.

27. Modern biblical scholars generally attribute the two creation stories of Genesis (1:3–2:3a and 2:3b–24) to different sources. But Philo, unaware of this redaction process, stands instead in the tradition that attributes lone authorship of the Pentateuch to Moses. Philo's sole task then is one of navigating the points of tension in what reads as a single, complex narrative.

28. *Opif.* §76.

29. *Opif.* §135. Philo of Alexandria and David T. Runia, *On the Creation of the Cosmos according to Moses: Introduction, Translation and Commentary*, trans. David T. Runia, vol. 1, Philo of Alexandria Commentary Series (Leiden: Brill, 2001), 82.

30. *Opif.* §134. Ibid.

31. Though Philo uses Plato's story to his own ends in *Opif.*, Runia notes that the exegete is less friendly in his evaluation offered in *Vit. contempl.* §63. Here "he is scathing about 'mythical fictions concerning double-bodied persons who originally attached to each other by unifying forces,' and states that the

disciples of Moses have nothing but contempt for such presentations." See ibid., 358. While Runia's translation of διασσομάτους as the non-gender-specific "double-bodied persons" is grammatically valid, the older translation "double-bodied men" is more apropos. Philo's disgust in the context of the *Vita* is connected to his critique of Plato's *Symposium* and its allusion to the ancient Greek practice of pederasty.

32. *Opif.* §151–152.

33. *Opif.* §165. The masculine intellect/feminine perception dichotomy also characterizes much of Philo's *Leg. allegor.* and forms the basis for his interpretation for the entire Genesis narrative of creation and the fall. See Philo of Alexandria and Runia, *On the Creation of the Cosmos*, 1, 381.

34. *Opif.* §69.

35. *Phaedrus* 246e. Philo of Alexandria and Runia, *On the Creation of the Cosmos*, 1, 227.

36. *Phaedrus* 246d–249d. Ibid., 229.

37. *Agr.* §73. Philo of Alexandria, Albert C. Geljon, and David T. Runia, *Philo of Alexandria, On Cultivation*, ibid. (2013), 59, emphasis added.

38. *Leg. allegor.* I.70.

39. *Migratione* §67. Lars Thunberg and A. M. Allchin, *Microcosm and Mediator: The Theological Anthropology of Maximus the Confessor*, 2nd ed. (Chicago: Open Court, 1995), 185, n.86. Also 374.

40. Though the theologians of our survey often misquote the passage as "neither male nor female," Paul uses the conjunction *and*, which suggests that the formula is not simply juxtaposing the sexes in parallel with the pairs Jew/Greek and slave/free, but rather alludes to the LXX rendering of Gn 1:27.

41. See Wayne A. Meeks, "The Image of the Androgyne: Some Uses of a Symbol in Earliest Christianity," *History of Religions* 13, no. 3 (1974); Hans Dieter Betz, *Galatians: A Commentary on Paul's Letter to the Churches in Galatia*, Hermeneia (Philadelphia: Fortress Press, 1979), 181–201; J. Louis Martyn, *Galatians: A New Translation with Introduction and Commentary*, The Anchor Bible (New York: Doubleday, 1998), 373–83. In addition to this reading, Carolyn Osiek offers four other possible interpretations for this passage: (1) an emancipation proclamation ahead of its time; (2) a reference to the order of creation but not to the order of the fall; (3) the time of salvation anticipated in the present; and (4) a glimpse of the still-distant future. See Carolyn Osiek, "Galatians," in *Women's Bible Commentary*, ed. Carol A. Newsom and Sharon H. Ringe (Louisville: Westminster John Knox, 1992), 335.

42. Gal 2:20.

43. Cf. 1 Cor 15:20–23, 45–49 and Rom 5:12–21.

44. Mt 22:28; cf. Mk 12:23, Lk 20:33.

45. Lk 20:36.

46. Biblical examples include references to the virtuous woman (γυναῖκα ἀνδρείαν) of Prv 31:10 and Paul's admonition to the women of Corinth to be brave like men (ἀνδρίζεσθε) in 1 Cor 16:13. Extra-canonical references include many brave deeds (πολλά ἀνδρεῖα) performed by women mentioned in 1 Clement 55:3, and the virgins of the *Herm. pas.* 9.2[79].5 who stood up like men (οὖσαι ἀνδρείως εἰστήκεισαν).

47. Gospel of Thomas, *Logion* 114. For an English translation and commentary see Petr Pokorný, *A Commentary on the Gospel of Thomas: From Interpretations to the Interpreted*, Jewish and Christian Texts in Contexts and Related Studies (New York: T & T Clark, 2009), 154–56.

48. *Strom.* 6.12.100.3. See Clement of Alexandria et al., *Les Stromates*, 7 vols., Sources chrétiennes (Paris: Les Éditions du Cerf, 1981), VI:260, 62.

49. *Pas. SS. Perp.* X.7. For an English translation and commentary see Thomas J. Heffernan, *The Passion of Perpetua and Felicity* (New York: Oxford University Press, 2012), 130, 262.

50. See Harrison, "Male and Female in Cappadocian Theology."

51. *Hom. mart. Jul.*, PG 31.237a–c, as quoted in ibid., 446.

52. *Vit. sua*, 1.60. English translation from Gregory of Nazianzus, *Gregory of Nazianzus: Autobiographical Poems*, trans. Carolinne White, Cambridge Medieval Classics (Cambridge: Cambridge University Press, 1996), 15.

53. *Vit. Moy.* II.3, English translation from Gregory of Nyssa, *The Life of Moses*, trans. Abraham J. Malherbe and Everett Ferguson, Classics of Western Spirituality (New York: Paulist Press, 1978), 55–56.

54. *Vit. Mac.* §1, as translated in Harrison, "Male and Female in Cappadocian Theology," 446.

55. *Vit. Mac.* §16.

56. *Vit. Mac.* §26. Note that while Gregory gives himself over to lamentation in the moment of Macrina's death, he is also the first to recover his composure. Assuming Macrina's role as instructor, he then shouts down the cries of the virgins and reminds them of how Macrina would wish to see them go on. In this way, while he does not embody the full "manliness" of Macrina's self-control, he does paint himself in a better light than the virgins of the convent.

57. *Hom. Pel. II* (*PG* 50:585). See Elizabeth A. Clark, *Jerome, Chrysostom, and Friends: Essays and Translations*, 2nd ed., vol. 2, Studies in Women and Religion (New York: E. Mellen Press, 1982), 15. The Latin reads ". . . *genere quidem et sex feminam, animo autem ipso marem!*"

58. *S. Dros.*, 3 (*PG* 50:688) as translated in ibid.

59. *SS. Bern. et Pros.*, 4 (*PG* 50:635) as translated in ibid. The Greek reads "καὶ γὰρ ἐν γυνακείῳ σόματι ἀνδρῶν ἐπεδείξαντο φρόνημα μόνον."

60. *Homiliae* 281.1. See Augustine of Hippo, *The Works of Saint Augustine: A Translation for the 21st Century*, ed. Edmund Hill, John E. Rotelle, and Boniface Ramsey (Brooklyn: New City Press, 1990), III/8, 78.

61. *Homiliae* 280.1. See ibid., III/8, 72.

62. From Aphrahat's *Demonstratio* VI.6 as translated in Sebastian P. Brock, *The Luminous Eye: The Spiritual World Vision of Saint Ephrem*, Cistercian Studies Series (Kalamazoo: Cistercian Publications, 1992), 138. For a broader discussion of baptism as (1) betrothal to Christ, (2) return to paradise, and (3) entrance into the angelic (or sexless) life, ibid., 136–41. The medieval Western monastic tradition also echoes the imagery of monks betrothed to Christ.

63. For a discussion of virginity in Syriac Christianity, see ibid., 137–41.

64. The Gospel according to the Egyptians is a no longer extant text, quotations from which are found in Clement, as well as Hippolytus and Epiphanius. Surviving quotations promote "sexual asceticism as the means of breaking the lethal cycle of birth and of overcoming the alleged sinful differences between male and female, enabling all persons to return to what was understood to be their primordial and androgynous state." See Ron Cameron, *The Other Gospels: Non-Canonical Gospel Texts* (Philadelphia: Westminster Press, 1982), 49.

65. *Strom.* 3.13.93.1.

66. *Hom. in Gen.* I.15. For an English translation of the text, see Origen, *Homilies on Genesis and Exodus*, trans. Ronald E. Heine, Fathers of the Church (Washington: Catholic University of America Press, 1982). The oldest extant text of this particular homily is a Latin translation by Rufinus. As such I am unable to determine whether his translation "spirit" corresponds to the neuter Greek πνεῦμα or the masculine νοῦς. However, the male-female generative bond holds in the production of children.

67. *Hom. in Gen.* I.15. See ibid., 68.

68. Stephen Thomas, "Anthropology," in *The Westminster Handbook to Origen*, ed. John Anthony McGuckin (Louisville: Westminster John Knox Press, 2004), 55.

69. For the Latin, see *PL* 14. English translations are quoted from Ambrose of Milan, *Hexameron, Paradise, and Cain and Abel*, trans. John J. Savage (New York: Catholic University of America Press, 1961).

70. *Paradiso* 11.15.

71. *Paradiso* 51.73. Quote from Ambrose of Milan, *Hexameron, Paradise, and Cain and Abel*, 351–52.

72. *An. et res.* §3. *PG* 46:49c. Gregory of Nyssa, *On the Soul and the Resurrection*, trans. Catharine P. Roth (Crestwood: St Vladimir's Seminary Press, 1993), 50.

73. Dn 9:23; 10:11; 10:19; "man of desires" (ἀνὴρ ἐπιθυμιῶν) as the alternate reading in the LXX, per ibid., 54, n.12.

74. Nm 25:6–15. *Hom. in Gen.* 1.17. Origen, *Homilies on Genesis and Exodus*, 70. While Macrina portrays Phineas's anger as a positive thing, modern sensibilities have made zeal that leads to the execution of one's enemies much less morally clear cut.

75. *Mal. cog.* 3. English quotation from Evagrius of Pontus and Robert E. Sinkewicz, *Evagrius of Pontus: The Greek Ascetic Corpus*, Oxford Early Christian Studies (Oxford: Oxford University Press, 2006), 154–55, emphasis added.

76. See Thunberg and Allchin, *Microcosm and Mediator*, 375.

77. *Gen. c. Man.* II.11.15. Augustine wrote this work in 388–389 CE leading up to his ordination to the priesthood.

78. Gn 2:23. *Gen. c. Man.* II.13.18.

79. *Confes.* XIII.xxxiv(49). It is commonly accepted that Augustine wrote *Confessiones* in 397–401 CE. For dating see Augustine of Hippo, *Works of Saint Augustine*, I/1, 10; Peter Brown, *Augustine of Hippo: A Biography* (Berkeley: University of California Press, 2000), 178.

80. Augustine generally uses the feminine *anima* to describe the breath or soul that enlivens the body. He sometimes also uses the masculine *animus* to describe the rational element of the soul. Both terms map back to meanings of the Greek ψυχή. In this comment, Augustine uses the most generic term. However, in this passage, as well as the subsequent passages examined below, he uses the word *mens* to refer to the mind that he has subdivided into masculine and feminine parts. For a discussion of Augustine's use of *anima*, *animus*, and *mens* to describe variously "soul" and "mind," see Gerard J. P. O'Daly, *Augustine's Philosophy of Mind* (Berkeley: University of California Press, 1987), 7; Gareth B. Matthews, *The Augustinian Tradition* (Berkeley: University of California Press, 1999), 224–25.

81. Augustine began work *Gen. ad lit.* between in 399 and 404 CE. The section in question was revised in about 410 CE, while the whole work was finally published in 416 CE. See Augustine of Hippo, *Works of Saint Augustine*, I/13, 164.

82. This was the view of Origen, who saw in Gn 1:27 the creation of human souls, while the second creation was the result of the souls' cooling and falling away from God and into matter in the lower physical realm.

83. *Gen. ad lit.* III.22.34. A misreading of this passage by some feminist scholars insists that Augustine is suggesting that women are not created in the image of God separately from men. However, Augustine directly refutes this idea. Both women and men possess the complete human mind, consisting of the portions that contemplate Truth and handle rational action in day-to-day affairs. For an example of the misreading, see Rosemary Radford Reuther,

"Augustine: Sexuality, Gender, and Women," in *Feminist Interpretations of Augustine*, ed. Judith Chelius Stark (University Park: The Pennsylvania State University Press, 2007), 55–56.

84. Here the NRSV reads "image and reflection." However, the Greek δόξα is commonly translated as "glory."

85. *Gen. ad lit.* VI.7.12. For an argument that the unnamed author is the Donatist Tychonius, see Augustine of Hippo, Works of Saint Augustine, I/13, 307, n.6.

86. Specifically, in *Trin.* XII.1.1–4.

87. *Trin.* XII.1.3. Quotations from Augustine of Hippo, *Works of Saint Augustine*, I/5, 323.

88. *Trin.* XII.3.12. Quotation from ibid., I/5, 329.

89. For three different though not mutually exclusive explanations of Augustine's move away from an Origenian reading of the divine command to be fruitful and multiply, see Elizabeth A. Clark, "Heresy, Asceticism, Adam, and Eve: Interpretations of Genesis 1–3 in the Later Latin Fathers," in *Ascetic Piety and Women's Faith: Essays on Late Ancient Christianity* (Lewiston: Edwin Mellen Press, 1986); Willemien Otten, "The Long Shadow of Human Sin: Augustine on Adam, Eve, and the Fall," in *Out of Paradise: Eve and Adam and Their Interpreters*, ed. Bob Becking and Susan Hennecke (Sheffield: Sheffield Phoenix Press, 2010); Ilaria L. E. Ramelli, "Origen in Augustine: A Paradoxical Reception," *Numen: International Review for the History of Religions* 60 (2013).

90. *Paed.* 4.10.2–4.11.2. My translation.

91. Kari Vogt, "'Becoming Male': One Aspect of an Early Christian Anthropology," in *Women: Invisible in Theology and Church* (Edinburgh: T & T Clark, 1985), 73–74.

92. *Strom.* 6.12.100.3.

93. Michel Spanneut, *Le Stoïcisme des Pères de l'Église, de Clément de Rome à Clément d'Alexandrie* (Paris: Éditions du Seuil, 1957), 166, 254, as referenced in Vogt, "'Becoming Male': One Aspect of an Early Christian Anthropology," 81, n.7.

94. For more on Clement's views of sexuality, see Kyle Harper, *From Shame to Sin: The Christian Transformation of Sexual Morality in Late Antiquity* (Cambridge: Harvard University Press, 2013), 105–17.

95. *Ep.* 207, 2. English translation found in Philip Schaff and Henry Wace, *A Select Library of Nicene and Post-Nicene Fathers of the Christian Church: Second Series*, 14 vols. (New York: The Christian Literature Company, 1890), 8:247.

96. See Fredrik Ivarsson, "Vice Lists and Deviant Masculinity: The Rhetorical Function of 1 Corinthians 5:10–11 and 6:9–10," in *Mapping Gender in Ancient Religious Discourses*, ed. Todd Penner and Caroline Vander Stichele, Biblical Interpretation Series (Leiden: Brill, 2007), 165–66.

97. Burrus discusses this particular dynamic as part of chapter 1 on Athanasius and his anti-Arian works in *Begotten, Not Made: Conceiving Manhood in Late Antiquity* (Stanford: Stanford University Press, 2000).

98. Harrison, "Male and Female in Cappadocian Theology," 444.

99. See chapter 2 of Burrus, *Begotten, Not Made*, especially 100, 03.

100. See Mathew Kuefler, *The Manly Eunuch: Masculinity, Gender Ambiguity, and Christian Ideology in Late Antiquity* (Chicago: University of Chicago Press, 2001).

101. Gn 3:21.

102. *An. et res.* §10. *PG* 46:148c–149a. *Gregory of Nyssa, On the Soul and the Resurrection*, 114.

103. See Édouard Jeauneau, "La division des sexes chez Grégoire de Nysse et chez Jean Scot Érigène," in *Études érigéniennes* (Paris: Études augustiniennes, 1987), beginning at 36; Peter Dronke, "Eriugena's Earthly Paradise," in *Begriff und Metapher: Sprachform des Denkens bei Eriugena: Vorträge des VII. Internationalen Eriugena-Colloquiums, Werner-Reimers-Stiftung Bad Homburg, 26.–29. Juli 1989*, ed. Werner Beierwaltes (Heidelberg: Winter, 1990), 215.

104. *Hom. op.* XVI.7, *PG* 44:181a. Schaff and Wace, *Nicene and Post-Nicene Fathers, 2*, 5:64.

105. Gregory is among those who misquote Gal 3:28 as οὔτε ἄρρεν οὔτε θῆλύ ἐστιν ("is neither male nor female") rather than using the καὶ construction. However, it is interesting to note that he correctly quotes the LXX rendering of Genesis only a few lines prior to this as ἄρσεν καὶ θῆλυ ἐποίησεν αὐτούς (*PG* 44:181a), complete with the alternate spelling for male.

106. *Hom. op.* XVI.14, *PG* 44:185a.

107. *Hom. op.* XXII.4, *PG* 44:204d–205a. Schaff and Wace, *Nicene and Post-Nicene Fathers, 2*, 411–12.

108. *Hom. op.* XXII.4, *PG* 44:205d.

109. *Hom. op.* XVII.2, *PG* 44:189b–d.

110. *Hom. op.* XXII.6, *PG* 208a; XVIII.9, *PG* 196a–b.

111. John Behr, "The Rational Animal: A Rereading of Gregory of Nyssa's *De hominis opificio*," *Journal of Early Christian Studies* 7, no. 2 (1999): 240–41.

112. Valerie A. Karras, "Patristic Views on the Ontology of Gender," in *Personhood: Orthodox Christianity and the Connection between Body, Mind, and Soul*, ed. John T. Chirban (Westport: Bergin & Garvey, 1996).

113. *Virg.* XIV.3, *PG* 48:543. John Chrysostom, *On Virginity, Against Remarriage*, trans. Sally Rieger Shore, Studies in Women and Religion (Lewiston: The Edwin Mellen Press, 1983), 21.

114. *Virg.* XIV.6, *PG* 48:544. Ibid., 22.

115. *Virg.* XIX.1, *PG* 48:547. Ibid., 27.

116. *Amb.* 41. *PG* 91:1305c. Andrew Louth, *Maximus the Confessor*, The Early Church Fathers (New York: Routledge, 1996), 157.

117. An allusion to *Orationes* 39, 13 by Gregory of Nazianzus. See *PG* 36:348d.

118. 1308d–1309a. See Louth, *Maximus the Confessor*, 159. Emphasis in the original. Maximus also uses the languages of neither/nor (οὔτε ἄρρεν οὔτε θῆλυ), in lieu of the οὐκ ἔνι ἄρσεν καὶ θῆλυ of Gal 3:28.

119. Thunberg and Allchin, *Microcosm and Mediator*, 374–75.

120. *PG* 91:1039b. Louth, *Maximus the Confessor*, 159.

121. Karras, "Patristic Views on the Ontology of Gender," 116–17.

122. *Exposit.* I.8.89–94. Quotation from John of Damascus, *Writings*, trans. Frederic Hathaway Chase, Jr., The Fathers of the Church: A New Translation (Washington, D.C.: Catholic University of America Press, 1958), 180.

123. *Exposit.* II.30.21–22, 28–30.

124. *Exposit.* IV.24.16–23. Quotation from John of Damascus, *Writings*, 394.

125. For Eriugena's dependence on the Cappadocians and Maximus Confessor, see Édouard Jeauneau, "Pseudo-Dionysius, Gregory of Nyssa, and Maximus the Confessor in the Works of John Scottus Eriugena," in *Carolingian Essays: Andrew W. Mellon Lectures in Early Christian Studies*, ed. Uta-Renate Blumenthal (Washington, D.C.: Catholic University of America Press, 1983).

126. For Eriugena following Gregory, see Dronke, "Eriugena's Earthly Paradise," 215. *Periphys.* IV-833A. Quotation from Johannes Scottus Eriugena, *Periphyseon: The Division of Nature*, trans. I. P. Sheldon-Williams and John J. O'Meara (Washington, D.C.: Dumbarton Oaks, 1987), 491.

127. *Amb.* 41, 1309A. For an exploration of Eriugena's methodology for the further development and deepening of patristic texts with which he engaged, see Giulio d'Onofrio, "The *Concordia* of Augustine and Dionysius: Toward a Hermeneutic of the Disagreement of Patristic Sources in John the Scot's *Periphyseon*," in *Eriugena: East and West*, ed. Bernard McGinn and Willemien Otten (Notre Dame: University of Notre Dame Press, 1994), 126.

128. *Periphys.* II, 537D–538A. Eriugena, *Periphyseon*, 138. Emphasis in the original.

129. Donald Duclow, "The Sleep of Adam, the Making of Eve: Sin and Creation in Eriugena," (2011).

130. *Periphys.* II, 543A. Eriugena, *Periphyseon*, 143. Emphasis in the original.

131. For a discussion of how Eriugena negotiated this topic after Augustine's claims of sexual division in original humanity had shifted the Latin trajectory, see Dronke, "Eriugena's Earthly Paradise," 215; d'Onofrio, "The *Concordia* of Augustine and Dionysius."

132. Ephrem the Syrian, *Selected Prose Works*, trans. Edward G. Matthews, Jr. and Joseph P. Amar, Fathers of the Church (Washington, D.C.: Catholic University of America Press, 1994), 30.

133. Tryggve Kronholm, *Motifs from Genesis 1–11 in the Genuine Hymns of Ephrem the Syrian with Particular Reference to the Influence of Jewish Exegetical Tradition* (Lund: CWK Gleerup, 1978).

134. David Bundy, "Language and the Knowledge of God in Ephrem Syrus," *The Patristic and Byzantine Review* 5, no. 2 (1986): 94–97.

135. See Ephrem the Syrian, *Selected Prose Works*, 10–13.

136. For a list of citations from rabbinic literature see Kronholm, *Motifs from Genesis*, 81, n.106.

137. *Com. Gen.* I.29.2. English translation found in Ephrem the Syrian, *Selected Prose Works*, 94. Kronholm notes the unitary human is found in the broader Syriac tradition, citing a passage from Išoʿdad. See Kronholm, *Motifs from Genesis*, 106, n.81.

138. *Com. Gen.* II.12.1. Ephrem the Syrian, *Selected Prose Works*, 105.

139. *Hymn. eccl.* XLV.2. For the Syriac text of this hymn see *Hymnen de ecclesia*, ed. Edmund Beck, vol. 198, Corpus scriptorum Christianorum Orientalium (Louvain: Secrétariat du CorpusSCO, 1960), 113–17. The English translation used here can be found in Kronholm, *Motifs from Genesis*, 81.

140. *Car. Nis.* XLVIII.10.1–4. See *Motifs from Genesis*, 81.

141. Like the Greek πλευρά and the Hebrew *selaʿ*, the Syriac *ʾelʿā* can also be translated as both "rib" and "side." It can additionally be translated as "wife." See R. Payne Smith, *A Compendious Syriac Dictionary: Founded upon the Thesaurus Syriacus of R. Payne Smith* (Oxford: Clarendon Press, 1979), 18.

142. Gn 3:20. See Kronholm, *Motifs from Genesis*, 84.

143. For Greek usage of *hypostasis* and *ousia*, see chapter 4.

144. Gn 1:28. Augustine's dependence on Origen for his *Gen. c. Man.* is well attested in Roland J. Teske, "Origen and St Augustine's First Commentary on Genesis," in *Origeniana Quinta: Historica, Text and Method, Biblica, Philosophica, Theologica, Origenism and Later Developments: Papers of the 5th International Origen Congress, Boston College, 14–18 August 1989* (Leuven: Peeters, 1992). Cf. György Heidl, "Did the Young Augustine Read Origen's 'Homily on Paradise'?" in *Origeniana Septima: Origenes in den Auseinandersetzungen des 4. Jahrhunderts* (1999), 604.

145. Composed in the period 412–418 CE.

146. *Civ. Dei* XIV.23–24. English quotation from Augustine of Hippo, *Works of Saint Augustine*, I/7, 131–32.

147. Ephesians 4:13, "εἰς ἄνδρα τέλειον" in the Greek and "*in virum perfectum*" in the Latin Vulgate.

148. This appears to be a paraphrase from Rom 8:29, which reads "conformed to the image of his Son."

149. See Augustine of Hippo, *Works of Saint Augustine*, I/7, 526, n.83. Cf. Ronald E. Heine, Origen, and Jerome, *The Commentaries of Origen and Jerome on St. Paul's Epistle to the Ephesians*, Oxford Early Christian Studies (New York: Oxford University Press, 2002), 237–38.

150. *Civ. Dei* XXII.17. Rosemary Radford Reuther charges, in an argument from silence, that male bodies will not require the same sort of renewal. See Reuther, "Augustine: Sexuality, Gender, and Women," 63–64. However, this is unwarranted. The text in question is a defense of female sexual embodiment. Neither male nor female reproductive organs will any longer be used for procreation in Augustine's theology.

151. While the Greek of Mt 22:29 reads οὔτε γαμοῦσιν οὔτε γαμίζονται, and the Latin Vulgate *neque nubent neque nubentur*, Augustine's paraphrase reads *neque nubent neque uxores ducent*.

152. *Civ. Dei* XXII.17 Augustine of Hippo, *Works of Saint Augustine*, I/7, 527.

153. 1 Cor 12:27.

154. *Civ. Dei* XXII.18 Augustine of Hippo, *Works of Saint Augustine*, I/7, 528.

155. *Retractationes* I.10.2.

156. *C. Faust. man.* XXIX.4, Augustine of Hippo, *Works of Saint Augustine*, I/20, 399.

157. *Civ. Dei* XXII.19. *Retractationes* II.7(34).3. See ibid., I/2, 117.

158. See *Princip.* II.8.3.

159. *Hom. op.* XXIX.11.

160. *An. et res.* §9. *PG* 46:125a. Gregory of Nyssa, *On the Soul and the Resurrection*, 99.

161. *An. et res.* §9. *PG* 46:125c. Ibid., 100.

162. *An. et res.* §9. *PG* 46:128b. Ibid., 100–01.

163. *Homiliae* 7, "On the Soul" as quoted in Michael Pomazansky, *Orthodox Dogmatic Theology: A Concise Exposition*, ed. Seraphim Rose (Platina: St. Herman of Alaska Brotherhood, 2005), 130–31.

164. *Hom. mart. Jul.* 2.44. *PG* 31:204d–241a. Translated by Harrison in "Male and Female in Cappadocian Theology," 449–50.

165. Macarius the Egyptian, *Fifty Spiritual Homilies of St. Macarius the Egyptian*, trans. Arthur James Mason (London: Society for Promoting Christian Knowledge, 1921), 223.

166. *Hexaemeron* 9.VI.2. English translation from Anastasius of Sinai, *Hexaemeron*, trans. Clement A. Kuehn and John D. Baggarly, vol. 278, Orientalia Christiana analecta, 1590–7449 (Roma: Pontificio istituto orientale, 2007), 345.

167. *Anima* §27. William Patrick O'Connor, "The Concept of the Human Soul according to Saint Augustine" (Ph.D., Catholic University of America, 1921), 73. For a discussion of Aristotelian, Stoic, and other frameworks for the generation of the human body and soul, see Tertullian, *De anima*, ed. J. H. Waszink (Amsterdam: J. M. Meulenhoff, 1947), 342–48.

168. Alexander Roberts et al., *The Ante-Nicene Fathers: Translations of the Writings of the Fathers Down to A.D. 325*, 10 vols. (Grand Rapids, Mich.: William B. Eerdmans Publishing Company, 1980), 207.

169. *Gen. ad lit.* X.24.40–26.45.

170. *Ep.* 166.9; 164.7, as cited in O'Connor, "The Concept of the Human Soul according to Saint Augustine," 72, n.249. Matthew Drever, *Image, Identity, and the Forming of the Augustinian Soul* (New York: Oxford University Press, 2013), 26. These three models are discussed at length in *Gen. ad lit.*, Book X.

171. Drever notes that the *rationes* are a key feature of *Gen. ad lit.* However, they fade during the discussion of post-Adamic souls in both chapters VII and X of Book XI. See *Image, Identity, and the Forming of the Augustinian Soul*, 27.

172. *Ep.* CLXVI.

173. For a fuller discussion, see chapter 6 of O'Connor, "The Concept of the Human Soul according to Saint Augustine," esp. 70–75. Cf. Drever, *Image, Identity, and the Forming of the Augustinian Soul*, 26. Augustine's indecision lasted through the very end of his life, as witnessed in both his *Retractationes* I.1 and his *Opus imperfectum contra Julianum*, left incomplete in the year of his death (430 CE).

174. For an example of the use of patristic attitudes toward women as the authority on "the proper role of women and men in the life of the Church," see Patrick Mitchell, *The Scandal of Gender: Early Christian Teaching on the Man and the Woman* (Salisbury: Regina Orthodox Press, 1998).

175. In the same letter, Florovsky continues: "So many in our time are still looking for authoritative answers, even before they have encountered any problem. I am fortunate to have in my seminars students who are studying Fathers because they are interested in creative theology, and not just in history or archaeology." Anastassy Brandon Gallaher, "Georges Florovsky on Reading the Life of St Seraphim," *Sobornost* 27, no. 1 (2005): 62. Emphasis in the original.

176. From the epigraph of the chapter, Florovsky, "Eastern Orthodox Church and the Ecumenical Movement," 79.

177. A good example is found in the sarcasm of Gregory of Nazianzus as he discusses those who would take the generative Father and his generated Son as literal propositions rather than pointing to spiritual truths in *Orationes* 31 (*Theologica V, De Spiritu sancto*) §7. "For it does not follow that because the Son is the Son in some higher relation (inasmuch as we could not in any other way than this point out that he is of God and consubstantial), it would also be necessary to think that all of the names of this lower world and of our kindred should be transferred to the Godhead. Or maybe you would consider our God to be a male, according to the same arguments, because he is called God and Father, and that deity is feminine, from the gender of the word, and Spirit neuter, because it has nothing to do with generation. . . ." English translation from *Christology of the Later Fathers*, ed. John Baillie, John T. McNeill, and Henry P. Van Dusen, Library of Christian Classics (London: SCM Press, 1954), 198.

178. Philo of Alexandria, Geljon, and Runia, *Philo of Alexandria, On Cultivation*, 59.

179. The work of Mary Daly comes to mind.

180. See Harrison, "Male and Female in Cappadocian Theology."; Dronke, "Eriugena's Earthly Paradise," 217.

181. Gn 2:7.

182. As we will see in chapter 3, Orthodox use of allegory is not always clearly delineated from other interpretive strategies more accurately labeled as typology, anagogy, and exegesis. The term *allegory* is used in Orthodox theological reflection in a variable and non-technical sense. It includes not only the formal literary device (e.g., Plato's chariot metaphor), but also the spiritual senses of scripture (e.g., Origen's spiritual readings at the level of the flesh, the soul, and the spirit as found in *Princip.* IV.II.4).

3. Gender Essentialism in Contemporary Orthodox Thought

1. Thomas Hopko, "On the Male Character of Christian Priesthood," *St Vladimir's Theological Quarterly* 19, no. 3 (1975): 149.

2. Ibid., 150; Thomas Hopko, "On the Male Character of the Christian Priesthood: A Reply to Criticism," *St Vladimir's Theological Quarterly* 21, no. 3 (1977): 167.

3. God and Gender, p. 142, 144.

4. See Hopko, "On the Male Character of the Christian Priesthood: A Reply to Criticism," 164.

5. See Deborah Belonick, *Feminism in Christianity: An Orthodox Christian Response*, 2nd ed., Contemporary Life Series (Yonkers: St Vladimir's Seminary Press, 2012), 31; Verna E. F. Harrison, "Male and Female in Cappadocian Theology," *Journal of Theological Studies* 41, no. 2 (1990): 442, n.6.

6. Hopko, "On the Male Character of Christian Priesthood," 148.

7. Ibid.

8. Among Hopko's conversation partners, the monarchy of the Father is embraced by Verkhovskoy and Lossky. See Serge S. Verkhovskoy, "Procession of the Holy Spirit According to Orthodox Doctrine of the Trinity," *St Vladimir's Seminary Quarterly* 2, no. 1 (1953): 16–17, 19, 26; Vladimir Lossky, "La procession du Saint-Esprit dans la doctrine trinitaire orthodoxe," in *À l'image et à la ressemblance de Dieu* (Paris: Aubier-Montaigne, 1967), 77–79; "The Procession of the Holy Spirit in Orthodox Trinitarian Doctrine," in *In the Image and Likeness of God*, ed. John H. Erickson and Thomas E. Bird (Crestwood: St Vladimir's Seminary Press, 1974), 81–83.

9. Hopko, "On the Male Character of Christian Priesthood," 153–54. The kernel of Hopko's economic Trinity is a passage by Irenaeus of Lyons in which the bishop describes the Son and the Spirit as the two hands of God [the

Father] acting in the world. See *Ad. haer.* iv.praef.4. Cf. *Ad. haer.* iv.20.1; v.6.1; v.28.4. This reference is also found in Joan P. Schaupp, *Woman: Image of the Holy Spirit* (Bethesda: International Scholars Publications, 1996), 64, 66–68. Schaupp takes her inspiration from Henry Barclay Swete, *The Holy Spirit in the Ancient Church: A Study of Christian Teaching in the Age of the Fathers* (London: Macmillan and Company, Limited, 1912), 87–88.

10. Hopko, "On the Male Character of the Christian Priesthood: A Reply to Criticism," 165. Cf. Verkhovskoy, "Procession of the Holy Spirit," 24.

11. See "On the Male Character of Christian Priesthood," 156.

12. *Women and the Priesthood*, ed. Thomas Hopko (Crestwood: St Vladimir's Seminary Press, 1983), 181–82.

13. *Orationes* 40 (*In sanctum baptisma*) §41. See Thomas Hopko, "Apophatic Theology and the Naming of God in Eastern Orthodox Theology," in *Speaking the Christian God: The Holy Trinity and the Challenge of Feminism*, ed. Alvin F. Kimel, Jr. (Grand Rapids: William B. Eerdmans Publishing Company, 1992), 147, 49.

Note that Gregory's use of *monarchia* in the two cited passages cannot be interpreted as referring to the Father alone without first resorting to question begging. For much more fully developed analysis, identifying a movement between the two meanings of *monarchia* in Cappadocian writings see chapter 3 of John D. Zizioulas, *Communion and Otherness: Further Studies in Personhood and the Church* (London: T & T Clark, 2006).

14. *Women and the Priesthood*, 182.

15. Cf. Zizioulas, *Communion and Otherness: Further Studies in Personhood and the Church*, 137ff. See also chapter I.II of Sergey Nikolayevich Bulgakov, *Uteshitel' - O bogochelovechestve - Chast' II* [The Comforter: On God-Manhood, Part II] ([Tallinn]: YMCA Press, 1936), 81–92. An abridged English translation is found in *The Comforter*, trans. Boris Jakim (Grand Rapids: William B. Eerdmans Publishing Company, 2004), 68–73.

16. Hopko, "On the Male Character of Christian Priesthood," 170.

17. "Women and the Priesthood: Reflections on the Debate," in *Women and the Priesthood* (Crestwood: St Vladimir's Seminary Press, 1983), 182–83. Cf. Zizioulas, *Communion and Otherness: Further Studies in Personhood and the Church*, 138, n.78.

18. Cf. Verkhovskoy, "Procession of the Holy Spirit," 24.

19. Hopko, "On the Male Character of Christian Priesthood," 149. See also Vladimir Lossky, "Catholic Consciousness: Anthropological Implications of the Dogma of the Church," in *In the Image and Likeness of God*, ed. John H. Erickson and Thomas E. Bird (Crestwood: St Vladimir's Seminary Press, 1974), 185; Serge S. Verkhovskoy, "Creation of Man and the Establishment of the Family

in the Light of the Book of Genesis," *St Vladimir's Seminary Quarterly* 8, no. 1 (1964): 7.

20. Hopko, "On the Male Character of Christian Priesthood," 149, n.4. On Gregory, see also "Galatians 3:28: An Orthodox Interpretation," *St Vladimir's Theological Quarterly* 35, no. 2–3 (1991): 184, n.17; "God and Gender: Articulating the Orthodox View," *St Vladimir's Theological Quarterly* 37, no. 2–3 (1993): 161. On Maximus, see "On the Male Character of Christian Priesthood," 149, n.4; "Galatians 3:28," 184, n.17.

21. *Hom. op.* XVII.2. See "On the Male Character of Christian Priesthood," 152.

22. Ibid.

23. See Orthodox Church in America. Ecumenical Task Force, *Women and Men in the Church: A Study of the Community of Women and Men in the Church* (Syosset: Department of Religious Education, Orthodox Church in America, 1980), 33.

24. Hopko, "Galatians 3:28." Written in 1991, Orthodox theologian Elisabeth Behr-Sigel had already argued against an analogy between men and the Logos and women and the Holy Spirit (a central theme of Hopko's work that we will explore directly) using Gal 3:27–28. See Elisabeth Behr-Sigel, "La place de la femme dans l'église," *Irénikon* 58, no. 1, 2 (1983): 48. For an English translation see "The Place of Women in the Church," in *The Ministry of Women in the Church* (Redondo Beach: Oakwood Publications, 1991), 175. Verna Harrison had also explored the Cappadocians' use of this passage in "Male and Female in Cappadocian Theology," 442, 51, 59, 67, 70, 71.

25. Hopko, "Galatians 3:28," 169, n.1.

26. Ibid., 173.

27. Ibid., 175–76.

28. See also Hopko, "God and Gender," 181.

29. "On the Male Character of Christian Priesthood," 172; *The Spirit of God* (Wilton: Morehouse-Barlow Company, Inc., 1976), 42. See also Orthodox Church in America, Ecumenical Task Force, *Women and Men in the Church*, 29, 33. Cf. David Ford, review of *Eros and Transformation: Sexuality and Marriage: An Eastern Orthodox Perspective*, *Sobornost* 16, no. 1 (1994): 83. Contrast Sergey Nikolayevich Bulgakov, "Muzhskoe i zhenskoe v bozhestve," in *S. N. Bulgakov: Religiozno-filosofskiy put'*, ed. A. P. Kozyrev (Moscow: Russkiy Put', 2003), 354.

30. Hopko, "On the Male Character of Christian Priesthood," 155.

31. Ibid., 155–56, reformatted for ease of reading. All emphases in original.

32. The word *sexuality* has many meanings in contemporary usage. Hopko does not offer a definition for his usage. However, he comes closest when he suggests sexuality differs from other human conditions in that "being male

and female is an ontological reality in the order of creation." Subsequently he briefly discusses "human di-sexuality" and suggests that its purpose cannot be limited to a merely procreative function. See ibid., 151, n.6; 52. In an unattributed educational resource of the Orthodox Church in America, Hopko defines a person's sexuality as "his or her being a man or a woman." See Orthodox Church in America, Ecumenical Task Force, *Women and Men in the Church*, 21. Cf. Deborah Belonick, "The Spirit of the Female Priesthood," in *Women and the Priesthood*, ed. Thomas Hopko (Crestwood: St Vladimir's Seminary Press, 1983), 142, n.15.

33. Hopko, "On the Male Character of Christian Priesthood," 152.

34. Ibid., 155.

35. At this point several authors also establish an analogy between the consubstantiality of divine Persons and the consubstantiality of human persons, comparing the procession of the Holy Spirit with the "procession" of Eve from Adam. Vladimir Lossky, *Orthodox Theology: An Introduction* (Crestwood: St Vladimir's Seminary Press, 1978), 69–70. Lossky is quoted by Deborah Belonick, "Women in the Church," in *Orthodox Perspectives on Pastoral Praxis: Papers of the Intra-Orthodox Conference on Pastoral Praxis (24–25 September 1986) Celebrating the 50th Anniversary of Holy Cross Greek Orthodox School of Theology (1937–1987)*, ed. Theodore Stylianopoulos (Brookline: Holy Cross Orthodox Press, 1988).

As a precursor to the later metaphysical discussions, Methodius of Olympus (third century) refers to the Holy Spirit as the "rib of the Word." *Symp. dec. virg.* 3.8.34–36. An English translation is found in Swete, *The Holy Spirit in the Ancient Church*, 147. Cf. Schaupp, *Woman*, 87–88. Schaupp cites Matthias Joseph Scheeben, *The Mysteries of Christianity*, trans. Cyril O. Vollert (St. Louis: B. Herder Book Company, 1946), 182–85.

Other patristic references include Gregory of Nazianzus, *Orationes* 31 (*Theologica* V, *De Spiritu sancto*) §11 and Anastasius of Sinai, *Const. hom.* I.1.89. Cf. Deborah Belonick, "Father, Son, and Spirit—So What's in a Name?," in *The Politics of Prayer: Feminist Language and the Worship of God*, ed. Helen Hull Hitchcock (San Francisco: Ignatius Press, 1992), 305.

36. "On the Male Character of Christian Priesthood," 155–56, n.13. Hopko does not provide citations for these assertions. However, the texts in question are *Symp. dec. virg.* 3.9.15–16, *Dial. Tryph.* §100, and *Ad. haer.* 3.22.4.

37. For example, see *Ad. haer.* 3.22.1–4.

38. For an example of this hint see Hopko, "On the Male Character of Christian Priesthood," 150–51, 52, 72; "On the Male Character of the Christian Priesthood: A Reply to Criticism," 165; "Apophatic Theology and the Naming of God in Eastern Orthodox Theology," 160; "God and Gender," 145, 59, 60, 62, 83.

39. Cf. Verkhovskoy, "Creation of Man and the Establishment of the Family in the Light of the Book of Genesis," 23.

40. Cf. Deborah Belonick, "The Spirit of the Female Priesthood" (M.Div. thesis, St Vladimir's Orthodox Theological Seminary, 1979), 47.

One other potential (and unacknowledged) source for Hopko's terminology is found in the work of Paul Jewett. See Paul King Jewett, *Man as Male and Female: A Study in Sexual Relationships from a Theological Point of View* (Grand Rapids: William B. Eerdmans Publishing Company, 1975), 45, 174.

41. Hopko, "On the Male Character of Christian Priesthood," 156. Cf. Lossky, "La Procession du Saint-Esprit," 80; "Procession of the Holy Spirit," 84. For the move from non-interchangeable Trinitarian Persons to the revealed nature and names of the Trinity, see Belonick, "Father, Son, and Spirit — So What's in a Name?," 305–06; Kenneth Paul Wesche, "God: Beyond Gender—Reflections on the Patristic Doctrine of God and Feminist Theology," *St Vladimir's Theological Quarterly* 30, no. 4 (1986).

42. For thoughts by other named conversation partners, see C. S. Lewis, "Priestesses in the Church?," in *God in the Dock: Essays on Theology and Ethics*, ed. Walter Hooper (Grand Rapids: William B. Eerdmans Publishing Company, 1970), 237–38. See also Verkhovskoy, "The Orthodox Understanding of the Relationship between Man and Woman and the Christian Family" (unpublished) as quoted in Belonick, "Spirit of the Female Priesthood," 151, n.39.

43. Hopko, "On the Male Character of Christian Priesthood," 157. By "existential" he refers not to the philosophy, but rather to observable cases in the created order.

44. Ibid., 158. This theme is repeated in Hopko, *The Spirit of God*, 44.

45. "On the Male Character of Christian Priesthood," 158. To support this list of associations, Hopko draws a variety of sources. In comparing the feminine, the Church, and the Holy Spirit, cf. *The Spirit of God*, 48; Vladimir Lossky, *Essai sur la théologie mystique de l'Eglise d'Orient* (Aubier: Éditions Montaigne, 1944), 157, 65, 243; *The Mystical Theology of the Eastern Church* (London: J. Clarke, 1957), 160, 68, 244; "La Procession du Saint-Esprit," 92; "Procession of the Holy Spirit," 88. Much more support for the remaining list of cascading associations between the Holy Spirit, Wisdom, Eve, woman in general, motherhood, and the Church appears in the works of Stein, Schaupp, and Schmemann. See Edith Stein, "Problems of Women's Education," in *Writings of Edith Stein* (Westminster: The Newman Press, 1956), 154–55; Schaupp, *Woman*, 22–22; Alexander Schmemann, "On Mariology in Orthodoxy," *Marian Library Studies* 2, no. 1 (1971): 27–28, 30–31; "Our Lady and the Holy Spirit," *Marian Studies* 23, no. 1 (1972): 70, 72. The trope of recapitulation is found first in Justin Martyr, *Dial. Tryph.* §100, and in Irenaeus, *Ad. haer.* 3.22.4. See also "On Mariology in Orthodoxy," 28.

46. Hopko, "On the Male Character of Christian Priesthood," 159. See also *The Spirit of God*, 43–44.

47. Cf. Gn 2:18.

48. Hopko, "On the Male Character of Christian Priesthood," 159.

49. Ibid., 159–60.

50. Ibid., 160.

51. An allusion to John Chrysostom's *Hom. in Eph.* XX.

52. Hopko, "On the Male Character of Christian Priesthood," 160.

53. "On the Male Character of the Christian Priesthood: A Reply to Criticism," 164.

54. Hopko does not reveal the identities of those who responded to his works.

55. Hopko, "On the Male Character of Christian Priesthood," 157, n.14. This follows Gregory of Nazianzus's *Orationes* 31 (*Theologica* V, *De Spiritu sancto*).

56. "On the Male Character of the Christian Priesthood: A Reply to Criticism," 164.

57. "On the Male Character of Christian Priesthood," 157–58.

58. "On the Male Character of the Christian Priesthood: A Reply to Criticism," 165.

59. Ibid. I have been unable to identify any other passages in Hopko's body of work that return to address this question.

60. Ibid.

61. Ibid., 165–66.

62. Ibid., 165.

63. Hopko, "On the Male Character of Christian Priesthood," 157.

64. *The Spirit of God*, 49–50.

65. Ibid., 50.

66. See Hopko, "God and Gender," 150.

67. With this pair, Hopko suggests that sexual differentiation remains a characteristic of resurrected bodies in the eschaton. Early in his first essay on gender, he is quick to distance himself from sophiology and the eternal feminine as expressed in Russian religious philosophy. See "On the Male Character of Christian Priesthood," 157, n.14.

68. Orthodox Church in America, Ecumenical Task Force., *Women and Men in the Church*, 21–22.

69. Cf Hopko, "God and Gender," 168, 72, 74; "Presbyter/Priest: A Masculine Ministry," in *Women and the Priesthood*, ed. Thomas Hopko (Crestwood: St Vladimir's Seminary Press, 1999), 158. Note that in the latter source, Hopko characterizes Jesus as the "personal" image of God "the Father" rather than the *visible* image as found in Col 1:15.

70. Schaupp, *Woman*, 58–59.

71. See also Stein, "The Vocation of Man and Woman according to Nature and Grace," 103. Note that the formulation of Stein's analogy is problematic for Hopko in two ways. First, in her model, the mode of existence of Eve is no longer analogous with that of the Holy Spirit, but rather with that of the Son. Procession here is predicated of the "prosperity" (in Nazianzen's example as Seth) and follows the Roman Catholic doctrine of the *filioque*, with the Third Person of the Trinity proceeding from both the First and the Second.

72. Schaupp, *Woman*, 90. Schaupp attributes this find to George H. Tavard, *Woman in Christian Tradition* (Notre Dame: University of Notre Dame Press, 1973). Further research reveals the passage is from *Hymn. par.* XI, discussed at ibid., 154–55.

73. *Autolycum* i.7, ii.18. Cf. Vladimir Lossky, *The Vision of God* (London: Faith Press Ltd., 1964), 28–29; Schaupp, *Woman*, 30, 63–64, 115; Belonick, "Women in the Church," 96. These passages are discussed in Swete, *The Holy Spirit in the Ancient Church*, 46.

74. *Ad. haer.* iv.praef.4. Cf. iv.20.1; v.6.1; v.28.4. Cf. Schaupp, *Woman*, 64, 66–68.

75. Ibid., 25–26, 32; Belonick, "Women in the Church," 97.

76. Schaupp, *Woman*, 29, 32.

77. See Hopko, "Apophatic Theology and the Naming of God in Eastern Orthodox Theology," 160, n.29; "God and Gender," 157–59.

78. Schaupp, *Woman*, 18. Cf. *Trin.* XV.17–19.

79. Ibid. Here she alludes to *Trin.* XV.3.5; 7.11–13; 20.39; 23.43. Cf. Hopko, "On the Male Character of Christian Priesthood," 150, n.5.

80. See chapter 4 of Schaupp, *Woman*, 18.

81. Hopko is clear in his own work that he does not advocate the view of the eternal feminine. See Hopko, "On the Male Character of Christian Priesthood," 157, n.14.

82. *The Great Mother: An Analysis of the Archetype* (London: Routledge & K. Paul, 1955).

83. Schaupp, *Woman*, 43.

84. The usage here of *anima* and *animus* should not be confused with the Augustinian usage of these terms as explained in chapter 2, endnote 80.

85. Schaupp, *Woman*, 100–01. Schaupp's argument here closely mirrors the thought of Paul Evdokimov. While she makes no direct attribution to Evdokimov's work, she does cite the work of Tavard, whose book *Woman in the Christian Tradition* includes a summary of Evdokimov's work. See Tavard, *Woman in Christian Tradition*, 167–69.

86. Schaupp, *Woman*, 73, 90.

87. Ford (1928–2015) was a Catholic theologian and professor of theology at the University of Notre Dame. Ford quotes rabbinic sources in *The Spirit and the Human Person* (Dayton: Pflaum Press, 1969), 87–89.

88. Schaupp, *Woman*, 73.

89. Ford, *The Spirit and the Human Person*, 6, 9, 88.

90. Jewett bases his argument on *CD* III/1 §41, pts. 2,3; III/2 §45, pts. 2, 3; and III/4 §54. See Jewett, *Man as Male and Female*, 35, n.16.

91. Cf. Stein, "The Vocation of Man and Woman according to Nature and Grace," 112, 25. In her latter passage, the idiom "son of man" (Hebrew *ben-'ādām* (בן אדם), Aramaic *bar ʾĕnāš* (בר אנש), Greek υἱὸς τοῦ ἀνθρώπου) is taken to literally point to biological sex rather than the meaning of "mortal" that the phrase traditionally connotes.

92. Lk 2:21.

93. Rom 5:12–19.

94. Hopko does allude to some of these authors in later work. See Hopko, "Apophatic Theology and the Naming of God in Eastern Orthodox Theology," 161, n.30.

95. For example, Elisabeth Behr-Sigel, review of *Women and the Priesthood*, *Contacts: Revue française de l'orthodoxie* 36 (1984): 210; "The Ordination of Women: A Point of Contention in Ecumenical Dialogue," *St Vladimir's Theological Quarterly* 48, no. 1 (2004): 54–56; "The Ordination of Women: An Ecumenical Problem," *Sobornost* 13, no. 1 (1991): 30–32; Elisabeth Behr-Sigel and Kallistos Ware, *The Ordination of Women in the Orthodox Church*, Risk Book Series (Geneva: WCC Publications, 2000), 25; Karras, "Patristic Views on the Ontology of Gender," 114, 17–18; Sarah Hinlicky Wilson, "Tradition, Priesthood, and Personhood in the Trinitarian Theology of Elisabeth Behr-Sigel," *Pro Ecclesia* 19, no. 2 (2010): 142, 49.

96. Evdokimov first explores this idea in *Le mariage. Sacrement de l'amour* (Paris: Éditions du livre français, 1945), 142.

97. Ibid. In this earliest work, Evdokimov, like Schaupp, references Matthias Joseph Scheeben as his inspiration for this insight.

98. Peter Phan suggests that since "the Logos is called Son, a male figure," the link between the Logos and the male sex may have seemed obvious to Evdokimov. See Peter C. Phan, "Gender Roles in the History of Salvation: Man and Woman in the Thought of Paul Evdokimov," *Heythrop Journal* 31 (1990): 57.

99. While Evdokimov is the first person presented in this chapter to make this argument, he is not the originator. The first use of the icon of Theotokos and Christ Child for this sort of argument is found in the work of Sergius Bulgakov. See Bulgakov, "Muzhskoe i zhenskoe v bozhestve," 353. He repeats this idea in *Agnets Bozhiy - O bogochelovechestve - Chast' I* [The Lamb of God: On God-Manhood, Part I] (Paris: YMCA Press, 1933), 227–28. For an English

translation, see *The Lamb of God*, trans. Boris Jakim (Grand Rapids: William B. Eerdmans Publishing Company, 2008), 202.

100. Evdokimov, *Le mariage*, 209. See also *La femme et le salut du monde. Étude d'anthropologie chrétienne sur les charismes de la femme* (Tournai: Casterman, 1958), 15. An English translation for the latter can be found in *Woman and the Salvation of the World: A Christian Anthropology on the Charisms of Women* (Crestwood: St Vladimir's Seminary Press, 1994), 17.

101. *Le mariage*, 209.

102. *Sacrement de l'amour: Le mystère conjugal à la lumière de la tradition orthodoxe* (Paris: Éditions de l'ÉPI, 1962), 76; *The Sacrament of Love: The Nuptial Mystery in the Light of the Orthodox Tradition* (Crestwood: St Vladimir's Seminary Press, 1985), 57. "La femme et la parole," *Catéchèse*, no. 16 (1964): 270–71; "Les charismes de la femme," in *La nouveauté de l'Esprit: Études de spiritualité* (Bégrolles: Abbaye de Bellefontaine, 1977), 245–46; "The Charisms of Woman," in *In the World, of the Church*, ed. Michael Plekon and Alexis Vinogradov (Crestwood: St Vladimir's Seminary Press, 2001), 237. See also "Panagion and Panagia," *Bulletin de la Société français d'études mariales* 29 (1970); "Le Saint Esprit et la Mère de Dieu"; "Panagion and Panagia: The Holy Spirit and the Mother of God," in *In the Word, of the Church*, ed. Michael Plekon and Alexis Vinogradov (Crestwood: St Vladimir's Seminary Press, 2001).

103. *Le mariage*, 210–11.

104. Ibid.

105. Evdokimov, *La femme et le salut du monde*, 15; *Woman and the Salvation of the World*, 17.

106. *La femme et le salut du monde*, 15; *Woman and the Salvation of the World*, 17.

107. *La femme et le salut du monde*, 16; *Woman and the Salvation of the World*, 17.

108. See *Sacrement de l'amour*. This is a substantially revised work based on his previous work, Evdokimov, *Le mariage*. The revised work is translated into English as *The Sacrament of Love: The Nuptial Mystery in the Light of the Orthodox Tradition*.

109. In a footnote, Hopko lists Evdokimov among a group of Orthodox theologians who find a connection between the feminine, Mary, the Church, Israel, and the Holy Spirit and its role in creation, though he characterizes Evdokimov's description as "tentative." See Hopko, "Apophatic Theology and the Naming of God in Eastern Orthodox Theology," 161, n.30. In a subsequent essay, Hopko mentions Evdokimov in a list of church fathers (Gregory of Nyssa, Augustine, Maximus Confessor) and "modern thinkers" (Vladimir Solovyov, Pavel Florensky, and Sergius Bulgakov) whose teachings on gender and sexuality

have "not found a place within the Church's holy tradition." He goes on to characterize their teachings as "at best questionable and confusing, and, at worst, mistaken and misleading," influenced by extra-biblical worldviews including Hellenism and idealism. See "God and Gender," 161.

110. For Evdokimov's use of Jung, see especially part 3, chapter 2, "Les Archétypes" of *La femme et le salut du monde*. In English, chapter 12 of *Woman and the Salvation of the World*. For more details on how Bachofen functions in Evdokimov's thought, see Phan, "Gender Roles in the History of Salvation: Man and Woman in the Thought of Paul Evdokimov," 54–57.

111. For background see the volume of essays entitled Bernice Glatzer Rosenthal, ed. *The Occult in Russian and Soviet Culture* (Ithaca: Cornell University Press, 1997).

112. While our exploration of Russian religious and philosophical thought of this period is limited to providing background for the thought of Sergius Bulgakov and Paul Evdokimov, it is worth noting the influence these authors have had more broadly. Anglican theologian D. Sherwin Bailey, in addition to reading Martin Buber, C. S. Lewis, and Charles Williams, was also influenced by the works of Solovyov and Berdyaev. I owe this insight to Mark D. Jordan. In the Roman Catholic sphere, Hans Urs von Balthasar makes use of themes he garnered from Solovyov, Berdyaev, and Bulgakov. For an in-depth study, see Jennifer Newsome Martin, *Hans Urs von Balthasar and the Critical Appropriation of Russian Religious Thought* (Notre Dame: University of Notre Dame Press, 2015).

113. For more on the *sefirot*, see Gershom Scholem, *Kabbalah* (New York: Quadrangle/The New York Times Book Company, 1974), 106–07. For their adaptation by Christian Kabbalists, see Konstantin Burmistrov, "Christian Orthodoxy and Jewish Kabbalah: Russian Mystics in the Search for Perennial Wisdom," in *Polemical Encounters: Esoteric Discourse and Its Others*, ed. Olav Hammer and Kocku von Stuckrad (Leiden: Brill, 2007), 33, n.30.

114. For more on *Adam Kadmon*, see Scholem, *Kabbalah*, 100, 36.
For associations between *Ḥokmah*, *Shekhinah*, and the Holy Spirit, see ibid., 136.

115. See Burmistrov, "Christian Orthodoxy and Jewish Kabbalah: Russian Mystics in the Search for Perennial Wisdom," 39.

116. Cf. Isodore Singer, *Jewish Encyclopedia*, 12 vols. (New York: Funk and Wagnalls, 1901), I:181; Scholem, *Kabbalah*, 9.

117. *Zohar* I, 85b, 91b. See *Sepher ha-Zohar (Le livre de la splendeur): Doctrine ésotérique des Israélites*, trans. Jean de Pauly (Paris: Leroux, 1906), 493, 520.

118. Jakob Böhme (1575–1624) was a German Lutheran mystic and theologian. For a historical overview of the popularity of Böhme's work in Russia and Ukraine, see Zdenek V. David, "The Influence of Jacob Boehme on Russian Religious Thought," *Slavic Review* 21, no. 1 (1962).

119. Raymond Furness, "The Androgynous Ideal: Its Significance in German Literature," *The Modern Language Review* 60, no. 1 (1965): 59.

120. For a full exposition of Böhme's androgyne, see Nikolay Berdyaev, "Iz etyudov o Ya. Beme. Etyud II. Uchenie o Sofii i androgine. Ya. Beme i russkiy sofiologicheskiy techeniya" [From Studies concerning J. Böhme. Etude II. The Teaching on Sophia and the Androgyne. J. Böhme and the Russian Sophiological Current.] *Put'*, no. 21 (1930). An English translation is available at "Etude II. The Teaching about Sophia and the Androgyne," frsj Publications, http://berdyaev.com/berdiaev/berd_lib/1930_351.html.

121. See Adrian Daub, *Uncivil Unions: The Metaphysics of Marriage in German Idealism and Romanticism* (Chicago: University of Chicago Press, 2012), 168–69. For an overview of Schelling's views, see Alison Stone, "Sexual Polarity in Schelling and Hegel," in *Reproduction, Race, and Gender in Philosophy and the Early Life Sciences*, ed. Susanne Lettow (Albany: State University of New York Press, 2014), 260–66.

122. Vladimir Sergeyevich Solovyov, "Zhiznennaya drama Platona," in *Sobranie sochineniy Vladimira Sergeevicha Solov'eva*, ed. M.S. Solovyov and E. L. Radlov (St. Petersburg: Knigoizdatel'skoe Tovarishchestvo "Prosveshchenie," 1913), IX:234–35; "Plato's Life-Drama," in *Politics, Law, and Morality: Essays by V. S. Soloviev*, ed. Vladimir Wozniuk (New Haven: Yale University Press, 2000), 248–49.

123. Baader's influence on the Russian adoption of androgyny is documented in Nikolay Berdyaev, *Smysl tvorchestva: Opyt opravdaniya cheloveka* [Meaning of the Creative Act: An Attempt of Justification of the Human Being] (Moscow: Izdanie G A Lemana i S I Sakharova, 1916), 188–89; *The Meaning of the Creative Act*, trans. Donald A. Lowrie (New York: Harper, 1954), 182–83.

124. Vladimir Sergeyevich Solovyov, "Smysl' lyubvi," in *Sobranie sochineniy Vladimira Sergeevicha Solov'eva*, ed. M.S. Solovyov and E. L. Radlov (St. Petersburg: Knigoizdatel'skoe Tovarishchestvo "Prosveshchenie", 1913), 9; "The Meaning of Love," in *The Heart of Reality: Essays on Beauty, Love, and Ethics by V. S. Soloviev*, ed. Vladimir Wozniuk (Notre Dame: University of Notre Dame Press, 2003), 89.

125. Solovyov has paraphrased the text. Most curious is his use of the forms мужа and жену for the two gendered human beings. Cf. "Zhiznennaya drama Platona," 234; Vladimir Sergeyevich Solovyov and Judith Deutsch Kornblatt, *Divine Sophia: The Wisdom Writings of Vladimir Solovyov* (Ithaca: Cornell University Press, 2009), 71; Solovyov, "Plato's Life-Drama," 248.

126. Ibid. The passage contains untranslatable wordplay between половина ("half") and пол (either "sex" or "half").

127. Solovyov, "Smysl' lyubvi," 21; "The Meaning of Love," 100.

128. "Smysl' lyubvi," III:22 n.6; "The Meaning of Love," 100 n.1.

129. "Smysl' lyubvi," III:24; "The Meaning of Love," 102.

130. Cf. Verkhovskoy, "Creation of Man and the Establishment of the Family in the Light of the Book of Genesis," 23.

131. Solovyov, "Smysl' lyubvi," 41; "The Meaning of Love," 117–18.

132. Nikolay Berdyaev, *O naznachenii cheloveka: Opyt paradoksal'noi etiki* [The Destiny of Man: An Experiment in Paradoxical Ethics] (Paris: Izdatel'stvo "Sovremenye zapiski", 1931), 70; *The Destiny of Man*, trans. Natalie Duddington (New York: Charles Scribner's Sons, 1937), 64. See also his essay devoted to Böhme's androgyne: "Iz etyudov o Ya. Beme. Etyud II." For an English translation see "Etude II."

133. *O naznachenii cheloveka*, 70; *The Destiny of Man*, 64.

134. *Smysl' tvorchestva*, 186; *Meaning of the Creative Act*, 192.

135. Here he claims inspiration from Freud. *O naznachenii cheloveka*, 67–68; *The Destiny of Man*, 61–62.

136. *Smysl' tvorchestva*, 211; *Meaning of the Creative Act*, 217.

137. *The End of Our Time: Together with an Essay on the General Line of Soviet Philosophy*, trans. Donald Atwater (New York: Sheed & Ward, 1933), 118.

138. Sergey Nikolayevich Bulgakov, "Pol v cheloveke: (Fragment iz antropologii)," [Sex in the Human: (A Fragment from Anthropology)], *Khristiyanskaya mysl' ezhemesyachniy zhurnal*, no. 11 (1916). A reprint is available as "Pol v cheloveke: (Fragment iz antropologii)," in *Trudy po sotsiologii i teologii: Stat'i i raboty raznykh let 1902–1942* (Moscow: Nauka, 1997).

139. *Svet nevecherniy: Sozertsaniya i umozreniya* [Unfading Light: Contemplations and Speculations] (Moscow: n.p., 1917), 287–91; *Unfading Light: Contemplations and Speculations*, trans. Thomas Allan Smith (Grand Rapids: William B. Eerdmans Publishing Company, 2012), 295–99.

140. *Svet nevecherniy*, 292–93; *Unfading Light*, 300.

141. *Svet nevecherniy*, 291; *Unfading Light*, 299.

142. Lk 2:22–24. *Svet nevecherniy*, 291; *Unfading Light*, 299. These particular themes are repeated in other works, supported by references to Lk 11:27, Gal 4:4 and Lk 2:23. See *Drug zhenika: O pravoslavnom pochitaniy Predtechi* [*Friend of the Bridegroom: On the Orthodox Veneration of the Forerunner*] (Paris: Imprimerie de Navarre, 1927), 59; *The Friend of the Bridegroom: On the Orthodox Veneration of the Forerunner*, trans. Boris Jakim (Grand Rapids: William B. Eerdmans Publishing Company, 2003), 38.

143. "Muzhskoe i zhenskoe v bozhestve," 344. Also in *Nevesta Agntsa— O bogochelovechestve—Chast' III* [Bride of the Lamb: On God-Manhood, Part III] (Paris: [YMCA Press], 1945), 100; *The Bride of the Lamb*, trans. Boris Jakim (Grand Rapids: William B. Eerdmans Publishing Company, 2002), 90–91.

144. "Muzhskoe i zhenskoe v bozhestve," 346.

145. Ibid.

146. Ibid., 350.

147. For potential reasons, see Anton Pavlovich Kozyrev, "Androgin "na piru bogov": Publikatsiya rabot o. Sergeya Bulgakova "Muzhskoe i zhenskoe," "Muzhskoe i zhenskoe v Bozhestve" (1921)," in *S. N. Bulgakov: Religiozno-filosofskiy put': Mezhdunarodnaya nauchnaya konferentsiya, posvyashchennaya 130-letiyu so dnya rozhdeniya, 5–7 marta 2001 g.*, ed. Anton Pavlovich Kozyrev (Moscow: Russkiy put', 2003), 338.

148. The minor trilogy begins with Bulgakov's Mariology, *Kupina neopalimaya: Opyt dogmaticheskago istolkovaniya nekotorykh chert v pravoslavnom pochitanii Bogomateri* [The Burning Bush: On the Orthodox Veneration of the Mother of God] (Paris: YMCA Press, 1927); *The Burning Bush: On the Orthodox Veneration of the Mother of God*, trans. Thomas Allan Smith (Grand Rapids: William B. Eerdmans Publishing Company, 2009). In the same year he published a study on John the Forerunner, Bulgakov, *Drug zhenika; Friend of the Bridegroom*. In the final volume, Bulgakov develops his angelology, *Lestvitsa Iakovlya: Ob angelakh* [Jacob's Ladder: On Angels] (Paris: [Imp. de Navarre], 1929); *Jacob's Ladder: On Angels*, trans. Thomas Allan Smith (Grand Rapids: William B. Eerdmans Publishing Company, 2010). None of the English translations were yet available when Hopko wrote his essays on gender.

149. "Ipostas' i ipostasnost' (*Scholia* k *Svetu neverchernemu*)," in *Sbornik statey posvyashchennyx Petru Berngardovichu Struve ko dnyu tridtsatipyatiletiya ego nauchno-publitsisticheskoy deyatel'nosti, 1890 30 yanvarya 1925* (Prague: Legiografie, 1925), 363, n.1. An English translation of the full essay can be found in Anastassy Brandon Gallaher and Irina Kukota, "Protopresbyter Sergii Bulgakov: Hypostasis and Hypostaticity: Scholia to *The Unfading Light*," *St Vladimir's Theological Quarterly* 49, no. 1–2 (2005).

As the Russian philosopher Pyotr Savitsky noted in response to Bulgakov's attempt, the words for femininity (женственность), womanliness (женскость), and woman (женщина) are all derived from the same root in Russian. As such, he suggested that talk of a femininity with no relation to womanliness or woman is comparable to the search for a fire that does not burn. See the excerpts from correspondence appended to Sergey Nikolayevich Bulgakov, "Ipostas' i ipostasnost' (*Scholia* k *Svetu neverchernemu*)," in *Trudy o Troichnosti*, ed. Anna Reznichenko, Issledovaniya po istorii russkoy mysli (Moscow: OGI, 2001), 39.

150. "Muzhskoe i zhenskoe v bozhestve," 346.

151. Ibid., 354–55.

152. Bulgakov, *Uteshitel'*, 369; *Comforter*, 324.

153. *Drug zhenika*, 59–60; *Friend of the Bridegroom*, 38–39.

154. *Kupina neopalimaya*, 142–43; *Burning Bush*, 82. I have modified the English translation. In the last sentence of the quotation, Bulgakov further

develops Solovyov's untranslatable wordplay, offering a series of contrasts between biological sex (пол) halfness (половинчатность), unfullness (неполнота), and fullness (полнота).

155. See the discussion of Platonic and Philonic allegory in chapter 2.

156. Bulgakov, *Kupina neopalimaya*, 167; *Burning Bush*, 94–95. Bulgakov later offers a fuller explanation in *Agnets Bozhiy*, 329–30; *Lamb of God*, 299.

157. *Kupina neopalimaya*, 167; *Burning Bush*, 95.

158. *Drug zhenika*, 59; *Friend of the Bridegroom*, 38.

159. *Drug zhenika*, 59; *Friend of the Bridegroom*, 38–39.

160. *Lestvitsa Iakovlya*, 123–24; *Jacob's Ladder*, 87.

161. *Lestvitsa Iakovlya*, 124; *Jacob's Ladder*, 88.

162. Bulgakov repeats this idea later in *Agnets Bozhiy*, 227–28; *Lamb of God*, 202.

163. *Kupina neopalimaya*, 141; *Burning Bush*, 81–82. I have modified the English translation to reflect the Russian more accurately.

164. Cf. Evdokimov, *La femme et le salut du monde*, 15; *Woman and the Salvation of the World*, 17; *Sacrement de l'amour*, 47; *The Sacrament of Love: The Nuptial Mystery in the Light of the Orthodox Tradition*, 38.

165. Cf. *La femme et le salut du monde*, 257; *Woman and the Salvation of the World*, 261.

166. As previously noted, Bulgakov elsewhere has claimed that, within the Godhead, the *taxis* of the Trinity confirms the Father as First Person; however, all that can be said of the Son and the Spirit is that both are not the First. Bulgakov, *Uteshitel'*, 90–91; *Comforter*, 71–72.

167. *Nevesta Agntsa*, 100; *Bride of the Lamb*, 90.

168. *Nevesta Agntsa*, 100; *Bride of the Lamb*, 90–91.

169. For details about the origins of Behr-Sigel's participation, see Olga Lossky, *Vers le jour sans déclin: Une vie d'Élisabeth Behr-Sigel (1907–2005)* (Paris: Les Éditions du Cerf, 2007), 296–97; *Toward the Endless Day: The Life of Elisabeth Behr-Sigel*, trans. Jerry Ryan (Notre Dame: University of Notre Dame Press, 2010), 205–06; Leonie B. Liveris, *Ancient Taboos and Gender Prejudice: Challenges for Orthodox Women and the Church*, Ashgate New Critical Thinking in Religion, Theology, and Biblical Studies (Burlington: Ashgate Publishing, 2005), 66.

170. Elisabeth Behr-Sigel, "The Meaning of the Participation of Women in the Life of the Church," in *Orthodox Women: Their Role and Participation in the Orthodox Church. Report on the Consultation of Orthodox Women, September 11–17, 1976, Agapia, Roumania*, ed. Constance J. Tarasar and Irina Kirillova (Geneva: WCC Publications, 1977), 19.

171. Ibid., 22.

172. Ibid., 25.

173. Ibid., 28.

174. Elisabeth Behr-Sigel, "La femme dans l'église orthodoxe: Vision céleste et histoire," *Contacts: Revue française de l'orthodoxie* 29, no. 4 (1977). Translated into English as "Women in the Orthodox Church: Heavenly Vision and Historical Realities."

175. "La femme dans l'église orthodoxe," 309; "Women in the Orthodox Church," 130.

176. "L'église orthodoxe: Est-elle patriarcaliste!," *Contacts: Revue française de l'orthodoxie* 38, no. 3 (1986): 236. (The exclamation mark was a typographical mistake. Behr-Sigel intended a question mark.)

177. "Woman Is Also Made in the Image of God," in *The Ministry of Women* (Redondo Beach: Oakwood Publications, 1991), 87.

178. Cf. Hopko, "On the Male Character of Christian Priesthood," 149 n.4; Elisabeth Behr-Sigel, "The Otherness of Men and Women in the Context of a Christian Civilization," in *The Ministry of Women in the Church* (Redondo Beach: Oakwood Publications, 1987), 41; Hopko, "God and Gender," 91.

179. Behr-Sigel, "Woman Is Also Made in the Image of God," 89.

180. "Otherness of Men and Women," 41.

181. "The Meaning of the Participation of Women in the Life of the Church," 19; 28, n.3. Unattributed moments also appear, as for example her reference to women who seek to compete with men in the fallen image of Adam. Cf. Hopko, "On the Male Character of Christian Priesthood," 58; Behr-Sigel, "The Meaning of the Participation of Women in the Life of the Church," 20.

182. *Women and the Priesthood.* The volume includes reprints of both Hopko's first academic essay and his initial response to criticism, as well as a new closing reflection.

183. Behr-Sigel, "Otherness of Men and Women," 47–48.

184. "Review," 212. The translation is mine.

185. Ibid.

186. Ibid., 213.

187. Ibid., 212.

188. Behr-Sigel, "The Meaning of the Participation of Women in the Life of the Church," 20. Cf. "La femme dans l'église orthodoxe," 299; "Women in the Orthodox Church," 119.

189. "La femme aussi est à l'image de Dieu," *Supplément au Service Orthodoxe de Presse*, no. 64 (1982): 17; "Woman Is Also Made in the Image of God," 84–85.

190. "L'ordination des femmes: Un problème œcuménique," *Contacts: Revue française de l'orthodoxie* 42, no. 2 (1990): 122; "The Ordination of Women: An Ecumenical Problem," 38. Here the English translation is abridged. However, Behr-Sigel's description of Lossky's anthropology and her subsequent takeaway serve as the epigraph for the next chapter of this book.

4. Person, Gender, Sex, Sexuality

1. "L'ordination des femmes: Un problème œcuménique," *Contacts: Revue française de l'orthodoxie* 42, no. 2 (1990): 122. The translation is my own.

2. Initially offered by Thomas Hopko (whose thought is explored in the previous chapter) and Deborah Belonick, these arguments were also championed at the 1988 Rhodes Consultation by Chrysostomos (Konstantinidis), bishop of Myra. See Chrysostomos Konstantinidis, "Priesthood and Women in Ecclesiological Perspective," in *The Place of the Woman in the Orthodox Church and the Question of the Ordination of Women*, ed. Gennadios Limouris (Katerini: Tertios Publications, 1992).

3. Vladimir Lossky, *The Mystical Theology of the Eastern Church* (London: J. Clarke, 1957), 122.

4. Other Orthodox personalists include Christos Yannaras, John Zizioulas, and Sergey Horujy. While Yannaras clearly attributes inspiration for his work to Lossky, Zizioulas is more reticent, admitting only the potential for indirect influence. See Aristotle Papanikolaou, "Divine Energies or Divine Personhood: Vladimir Lossky and John Zizioulas on Conceiving the Transcendent and Immanent God," *Modern Theology* 19, no. 3 (2003): 383, n.85. See also "Personhood and Its Exponents," in *The Cambridge Companion to Orthodox Christian Theology*, ed. Mary B. Cunningham and Elizabeth Theokritoff (Cambridge: Cambridge University Press, 2008), 243, n.3; 44, n.22.

5. Lossky, *The Mystical Theology of the Eastern Church*, 23–43.

6. Kallistos Ware, noting an increased interest in Orthodox theological anthropology, suggests that such interest must lead to an apophatic anthropology that reflects the undefinable mystery of human personhood. See Kallistos Ware, *Orthodox Theology in the Twenty-First Century*, ed. Pantelis Kalaitzidis, Doxa & Praxis (Geneva: Word Council of Churches, 2012), 33.

7. Sergey Nikolayevich Bulgakov, *Agnets Bozhiy—O Bogochelovechestve— Chast' I* [*The Lamb of God: On GodManhood, Part I*], 138; The *Lamb of God*, trans. Boris Jakim (Grand Rapids: William B. Eerdmans Publishing Company, 2008), 115.

8. *Agnets Bozhiy*, 138; *Lamb of God*, 115.

9. The gnostics that Sergius refers to are Sethian and Valentinian Christians. The "spiritual Christians" are sects in Russia that had rejected Orthodox liturgy and hierarchy while embracing folk traditions.

10. Vladimir Lossky, "Spor o Sofii [Controversy about Sophia]," in *Bogovidenie [Vision of God]* (Moscow: ACT, 2006), 98, my translation.

11. *Spor" o Sofii [Controversy concerning Sophia]* (Paris: E.I.R.P., 1936).

12. "Spor," 38, 39.

13. Ibid., 38.

14. Lossky mentions that this analogy appears in *Mystagogy of the Holy Spirit* by St. Photius. See ibid. However, as we saw in the previous chapter, later

Orthodox authors will allude to Methodius of Olympus's *Symp. dec. virg.* 3.8.34–36. An English translation is found in Henry Barclay Swete, *The Holy Spirit in the Ancient Church: A Study of Christian Teaching in the Age of the Fathers* (London: Macmillan and Company, Limited, 1912), 147.

15. For example, see Gregory of Nazianzus's usage in *Orationes 31 (Theologica V, De Spiritu sancto)* 11.

16. Lossky, "Spor," 38.

17. Bulgakov would agree with this assessment. See Sergey Nikolayevich Bulgakov, "Muzhskoe i zhenskoe v bozhestve," in *S. N. Bulgakov: Religiozno-filosofskiy put'*, ed. A. P. Kozyrev (Moscow: Russkiy Put', 2003), 346.

18. Lossky, "Spor," 39.

19. Speaking specifically of the Russian context, Paul Gavrilyuk includes populism, socialism, Marxism, positivism, utilitarianism, and economic materialism among the collectivist philosophies that shaped Russian philosophical and theological discourses. Paul L. Gavrilyuk, *Georges Florovsky and the Russian Religious Renaissance*, Changing Paradigms in Historical and Systematic Theology (Oxford: Oxford University Press, 2013), 83.

20. For a more detailed description of the origins of European personalism, see chapter 1 of Juan Manuel Burgos, *An Introduction to Personalism*, trans. R. T. Allen (Washington, D.C.: The Catholic University of America Press, 2018). For personalist schools in the United States, see Rufus Burrow, Jr., *Personalism: A Critical Introduction* (St. Louis: Chalice Press, 1999).

21. Gavrilyuk, *Georges Florovsky and the Russian Religious Renaissance*, 83–84.

22. For a more detailed discussion of the various personalist systems among Russian religious thinkers, see chapter 8 of Rowan Williams, "The Theology of Vladimir Nikolaievich Lossky: An Exposition and Critique" (Oxford University, 1975).

23. For an in-depth description of Vladimir Lossky's intellectual context and influences, see chapter 1 of Ekaterina Ivanovna Grishaeva, "Uchenie o lichnosti v filosofii V. N. Losskogo: Istoriko-filosofskiy analiz [Study on Personhood in the Philosophy of V. N. Lossky: A Historico-Philosophical Analysis]" (PhD diss., Ural Federal University, 2011).

24. Vladimir Lossky, "The Theological Notion of the Human Person," in *In the Image and Likeness of God*, ed. John H. Erickson and Thomas E. Bird (Crestwood: St Vladimir's Seminary Press, 1974), 123. Of course, the explicit outworking of Trinitarian terminology of *homoousion* in a Triad of divine Persons or *hypostaseis* was not fully articulated until the fourth century CE, well after the Genesis account of God's deliberations during creation were recorded.

25. *The Mystical Theology of the Eastern Church*, 124, modified. Cf. *Essai sur la théologie mystique de l'Eglise d'Orient*, 119.

26. "The Theology of the Image," 129.

27. "Theological Notion," 112.

28. "Catholic Consciousness: Anthropological Implications of the Dogma of the Church," in *In the Image and Likeness of God*, ed. John H. Erickson and Thomas E. Bird (Crestwood: St Vladimir's Seminary Press, 1974), 185.

29. Ibid.

30. It would take the later work of Gregory of Nazianzus and a subsequent gathering in Constantinople to declare the full deity of the Holy Spirit along with the Father and the Son. However, the Nicene Creed uses biblical references to demonstrate the divinity of the Holy Spirit rather than also using the term *homoousios*.

31. Lossky, "Theological Notion," 113.

32. For example, *The Mystical Theology of the Eastern Church*, 122.

33. Russian personalists had used the word личность, commonly translated into English as "personality," to describe this new concept of the human person. While the English *personality* carries the archaic meaning of "possessing the quality of being a person," the modern reader is more likely to hear something along the lines of a collection of characteristics that distinguishes a particular individual or group from others. While some translators choose to use the older *personality*, many use *person*, echoing the philosophical personalist discourse. For a discussion of the difficulties in translating personalist terminology from Russian to English, see Dominic Rubin, *The Life and Thought of Lev Karsavin: "Strength Made Perfect in Weakness . . .",* On the Boundary of Two Worlds: Identity, Freedom, and Moral Imagination in the Baltics (New York: Rodopi, 2013), 251, n.38.

34. *Persona est substantia individua rationalis naturae. Lib. c. Eut.*, III.

35. Lossky, "Theological Notion," 116.

36. This same tendency is true of the French *personne* and *individu*, which were the original words used by Lossky.

37. Lossky, *The Mystical Theology of the Eastern Church*, 121.

38. Ibid.

39. Lossky, "Theological Notion," 118.

40. This attribution of the one *hypostasis* to the preexistent Logos (rather than to the union of divine and human natures) occurs quickly after Chalcedon. See Aloys Grillmeier, *Christ in Christian Tradition* (Atlanta: John Knox Press, 1975), II/1, 166–72; 233–35.

41. Lossky, "Theological Notion," 118.

42. Ibid. The reference is to *Trin.* IV.7. *Persona divina est divinae naturae incommunicabilis existentia.*

43. Ibid., 119. Also Lossky, "Theology of the Image," 138–39.

44. Note: Gregory of Nyssa wrote before the Chalcedonian Definition was adopted at the Fourth Ecumenical Council in 451 CE.

45. The phrase ψυχή λογική is equivalent to *nous* within the definition, standing in opposition to Apollinaris's teaching that Christ was composed of an animal soul (ψυχὴ ἄλογος) and a body (σῶμα). See John Norman Davidson Kelly, *Early Christian Doctrines*, 5th ed. (San Francisco: HarperSanFrancisco, 1978), 289–95.

46. "Theological Notion," 120.

47. *Ep.* 101.

48. "Theological Notion," 120, modified. Emphasis in the original.

49. In the earlier reference, Lossky correctly reflects the usage of *enhypostasized* (ἐνυπόστατος) in the sixth-century theologian's work. However, Lossky here goes a step further, creating an active verbal form, *enhypostasize*, that does not appear in Leontius's work. Lossky's usage echoes a reading, first offered by nineteenth-century German theologian Friedrich Loofs, that suggests that Christ's human nature somehow insubsists within the *hypostasis* of the Son. This reading has been repeated by a variety of thinkers up to the present, including Orthodox personalists such as Stelios Ramfos. However, it is based on a misunderstanding of Leontius's terminology. The *en-* (ἐν-) prefix in this instance is not a suggestion of existing "within," but rather functions as an antonymic pairing with the alpha-privative prefix (ἀ- or ἀν-) that denotes the absence of a property. Thus, ἐνυπόστατος is the opposite of ἀνυπόστατος. The former denotes the property of being real or concretely instantiated, whereas the latter describes the absence of such an instantiation. In his own use of ἐνυπόστατος, Leontius makes no metaphysical argument regarding the way in which human nature exists *within* the hypostasis of the Logos. Rather, he makes only the more modest Chalcedonian claim that Jesus Christ has a real human nature. See Grillmeier, *Christ in Christian Tradition*, II/2, 193–98; Leontius of Byzantium and Brian E. Daley, *Complete Works*, Oxford Early Christian Texts (Oxford: Oxford University Press, 2017), 73–75. While this misreading does not undermine Lossky's intuition about the human person explored here, it does move him into territory beyond earlier patristic arguments. It also causes complications for his understanding of the union of Christ and humanity in the Church, a related topic beyond the scope of the argument currently under discussion.

50. Cf. John of Damascus, who uses Aristotle's definition in his *Cap. phil.* § 66.

51. Lossky, "Catholic Consciousness," 185.

52. Kallistos Ware, "'In the Image and Likeness': The Uniqueness of the Human Person," in *Personhood: Orthodox Christianity and the Connection between Body, Mind, and Soul*, ed. John T. Chirban (Westport: Bergin & Garvey, 1996), 2.

53. Originally published in "La théologie orthodoxe au vingt-et-unième siècle," *Irénikon* 77, no. 2–3 (2004): 28. An English translation is found in *Orthodox Theology in the Twenty-First Century*, 32.

54. Kathleen Stein, "Interview [with] John Money," *Omni* 8, no. 7 (1986): 80.

55. For references to Galenic and Hippocratic texts on the subject, see Maud W. Gleason, *Making Men: Sophists and Self-Presentation in Ancient Rome* (Princeton: Princeton University Press, 1995), 59, n.16.

56. Ibid., 66–67.

57. Note that the pursuit of male sexual partners was not the deciding issue, but rather the giving up of masculine appearance or the overindulgence in pleasures that resulted in charges of softness.

Gleason warns about the overgeneralization of all grooming to be indicative of gender deviance. A person aspiring to some elegance might also risk the use of fragrances, trim his hair, and speak with ingratiating inflections. Each of these traits is associated with the youthful beauty of the ephebe. See ibid., 74. For a discussion of the Roman categories of *mollitia* and *mollis*, see Craig A. Williams, *Roman Homosexuality*, 2nd ed. (Oxford: Oxford University Press, 2010), 139–48.

58. In addition, within Greek society an older man could penetrate a freeborn youth with whom he had entered a patronage relationship (pederasty). However, in the Roman context, the use of a freeborn boy as a sexual partner was also forbidden under the laws concerning *stuprum*, or illicit sexual activity, and carried severe penalties. As such, the use of boys as sexual objects was limited to slaves, both within one's own household and those forced into brothels, known as *pueri meritorii* ("professional boys") and *pueri lenonii* ("pimps' boys"). See Harper, *From Shame to Sin: The Christian Transformation of Sexual Morality in Late Antiquity* (Cambridge: Harvard University Press, 2013), 90.

59. See John J. Winkler, *The Constraints of Desire: The Anthropology of Sex and Gender in Ancient Greece* (New York: Routledge, 1990), 46; David M. Halperin, *One Hundred Years of Homosexuality: And Other Essays on Greek Love*, The New Ancient World (New York: Routledge, 1990), 33–34.

60. Candace West and Don H. Zimmerman, "Doing Gender," *Gender and Society* 1, no. 2 (1987). Also the discussion of gender performativity in Judith Butler, *Gender Trouble: Feminism and the Subversion of Identity* (New York: Routledge, 1990).

61. To the examples from Solovyov, Berdyaev, Bulgakov, and Evdokimov previously discussed, we can add contemporary Orthodox such as Deborah Belonick, "Women in the Church," in *Orthodox Perspectives on Pastoral Praxis: Papers of the Intra-Orthodox Conference on Pastoral Praxis (24–25 September 1986) Celebrating the 50th Anniversary of Holy Cross Greek Orthodox School of Theology (1937–1987)*, ed. Theodore Stylianopoulos (Brookline: Holy Cross Orthodox Press, 1988), 84; Thomas Hopko, "On the Male Character of Christian Priesthood," *St Vladimir's Theological Quarterly* 19, no. 3 (1975); Kenneth Paul

Wesche, "God: Beyond Gender—Reflections on the Patristic Doctrine of God and Feminist Theology," Ibid. 30, no. 4 (1986).

62. See Paul Evdokimov, *La femme et le salut du monde: Étude d'anthropologie chrétienne sur les charismes de la femme* (Tournai: Casterman, 1958), 210–11; *Woman and the Salvation of the World: A Christian Anthropology on the Charisms of Women* (Crestwood: St Vladimir's Seminary Press, 1994), 214–15; Thomas Hopko, "God and Gender: Articulating the Orthodox View," *St Vladimir's Theological Quarterly* 37, no. 2–3 (1993): 173–74.

63. See Orthodox Church in America, Ecumenical Task Force, *Women and Men in the Church: A Study of the Community of Women and Men in the Church* (Syosset: Department of Religious Education, Orthodox Church in America, 1980).

64. Halperin, *One Hundred Years of Homosexuality*, 133.

65. Even among binary trans people, non-binary trans people are often misunderstood. A good resource for further information is CN Lester, *Trans Like Me: Conversations for All of Us* (New York: Seal Press, 2017).

66. Though critiques of the construction of biological categories of sex began earlier, the publication of Judith Butler's *Gender Trouble* is often marked as a popularizing moment for the idea that the determination of biological sex is a cultural production informed by gender norms. See Butler, *Gender Trouble: Feminism and the Subversion of Identity*. For an intellectual history of how gender roles and expectations have effected understandings of biological sex, see Anne Fausto-Sterling, *Sexing the Body: Gender Politics and the Construction of Sexuality* (New York: Basic Books, 2000).

67. Biological indicators include brain morphology, fetal hormones, pubertal differentiation (e.g., facial hair, deepening of the voice, development of breasts), chromosomes, gonads, internal reproductive structures, and external genital morphology. Categories that make up the matrix of an adult gender identity include adult responses to an infant's gender, body image, juvenile gender identity, pubertal eroticism, and adult gender identity. See *Sexing the Body*, 257–58, n.11.

68. For the discussion of these estimates, see Melanie Blackless et al., "How Sexually Dimorphic Are We? Review and Synthesis," *American Journal of Human Biology* 12, no. 2 (2000); Carrie L. Hull, "Letter to the Editor," ibid., 15, no. 1 (2003); Leonard Sax, "How Common is Intersex? A Response to Anne Fausto-Sterling," *Journal of Sex Research* 39, no. 3 (2002).

69. In the most highly polarized version of these rubrics, bisexuality falls under deep suspicion or is dismissed out of hand. Infrequent same-sex erotic activity is chalked up to "experimentation," while at other times, especially within the gay community, bisexuality is attributed to a reticence to commit

to one's "true" orientation (assumed homosexual) in the face of social stigma or cultural expectations.

70. Sexologist Alfred Kinsey suggested that the word *homosexual* should not be used to describe a person or an orientation, but rather to characterize individual sexual acts and responses in a person's history. See Alfred Charles Kinsey, Wardell Baxter Pomeroy, and Clyde Eugene Martin, *Sexual Behavior in the Human Male* (Philadelphia: W. B. Saunders Company, 1948), 610–66.

71. See Michel Foucault, *The History of Sexuality*, trans. Robert Hurley, 1st American ed., Social Theory (New York: Pantheon Books, 1978), I:105. A common yet incorrect reading of Foucault's *History of Sexuality* is that before the rise of the medical and psychiatric discourses of the nineteenth century, there were sexual *acts*, but these acts did not constitute sexual *identities*. See ibid., I:43. However, in the passage in question, the emphasis is on the movement from a legal and canonical identity to a psychological subjectivity.

72. Ibid.

73. Mark D. Jordan, *The Invention of Sodomy in Christian Theology* (Chicago: University of Chicago Press, 1997), 123, 63. Jordan returns to the misreading of Foucault as a distinction between acts and identities in chapter 4 of *Convulsing Bodies: Religion and Resistance in Foucault* (Stanford: Stanford University Press, 2015), 93–118.

74. Jordan, *Invention of Sodomy*, 163–64.

75. Eve Kosofsky Sedgwick, *Epistemology of the Closet*, 2nd ed. (Berkeley: University of California Press, 2008), 44–48, especially 46.

76. Halperin, *One Hundred Years of Homosexuality*. See also *How to Do the History of Homosexuality* (Chicago: University of Chicago Press, 2002).

77. The most popular example is the pseudonymous Sambia of New Guinea. Anthropologist Gilbert Herdt provides an account of their secret male initiation rituals that include prolonged periods during which boys perform fellatio on older youths and ingest their semen. The Sambia believe that this insemination is necessary for boys to develop into men. Elaborate rituals and taboos regulate the practice. See Gilbert H. Herdt, *Guardians of the Flutes: Idioms of Masculinity* (New York: McGraw-Hill, 1981). Anthropologist Deborah Elliston has critiqued references to the practice of the Sambia as homosexual as the term "imputes Western model of sexuality . . . that relies on Western ideas about gender, erotics and personhood. . . ." See Deborah A. Elliston, "Erotic Anthropology: 'Ritualized Homosexuality' in Melanesia and Beyond," *American Ethnologist* 22, no. 4 (1995). Quoted in Fausto-Sterling, *Sexing the Body*, 18.

78. See Lisa M. Diamond, *Sexual Fluidity: Understanding Women's Love and Desire* (Cambridge: Harvard University Press, 2008); Elizabeth Jane Ward, *Not Gay: Sex between Straight White Men*, Sexual Cultures (New York: New York University Press, 2015); Tony Silva, "Bud-Sex: Constructing Normative

Masculinity among Rural Straight Men That Have Sex with Men," *Gender & Society* 0 (2016).

79. bell hooks, *Feminist Theory: From Margin to Center*, 2nd ed. (Cambridge: South End Press, 2000), 157.

80. Ibid.

81. Elisabeth Behr-Sigel, "La consultation interorthodoxe de Rhodes: La femme dans l'église," *Contacts: Revue française de l'orthodoxie* 41, no. 2 (1989): 91. The allusion is from Mt 11:12.

82. Note that while essentialist arguments for gender and biological sex are often used within Orthodoxy, essentialist arguments for sexualities, while gaining some ground, are often not the focus of Orthodox discussions. Rather, they are often used by advocates of legal rights and protections for lesbians and gays or in response to civil and ecclesial calls for change in sexual orientation. I will explore the full ramifications of my argument against an ontological or essentialized sexual orientation in chapter 6.

83. It would be easy enough to read Lossky this way. See Lossky, "Catholic Consciousness," 185.

84. See Georges Canguilhem, *On the Normal and the Pathological*, trans. Carolyn R. Fawcett (Boston: D. Reidel Publishing Company, 1978), 90.

85. See chapter 2.

5. Women and the Priesthood

1. Elisabeth Behr-Sigel, *The Ministry of Women in the Church* (Crestwood: St Vladimir's Seminary Press, 1990), xiv.

2. Paul Evdokimov, *La femme et le salut du monde: Étude d'anthropologie chrétienne sur les charismes de la femme* (Tournai: Casterman, 1958), 211; *Woman and the Salvation of the World: A Christian Anthropology on the Charisms of Women* (Crestwood: St Vladimir's Seminary Press, 1994), 215.

3. The question became real with women's ordination in the Episcopal Church. See *Anglican-Orthodox Dialogue: The Dublin Agreed Statement 1984* (Crestwood: St Vladimir's Seminary Press, 1985), 2–3.

4. Elisabeth Behr-Sigel, "The Meaning of the Participation of Women in the Life of the Church," in *Orthodox Women: Their Role and Participation in the Orthodox Church. Report on the Consultation of Orthodox Women, September 11–17, 1976, Agapia, Roumania*, ed. Constance J. Tarasar and Irina Kirillova (Geneva: WCC Publications, 1977), 28.

5. Some Orthodox are also actively discussing the ordination of women to the diaconate. I have limited the discussion in this chapter to the priesthood, and with it the episcopacy, because the arguments used to reject women in these roles are often supported by essentialist assumptions. The historical existence of deaconesses is not contested. Rather, contemporary arguments

tend to focus on whether there is a current need to reinstitute the practice. A secondary argument attempts to shut down discussion, suggesting that reinstituting the women's diaconate is a slippery slope that could lead to the acceptance of women as priests.

6. See "'The Ordination of Women: An Ecumenical Problem': A Reply to a Reply," *Sobornost* 15, no. 1 (1993): 25; Behr-Sigel and Ware, *The Ordination of Women in the Orthodox Church, in the Orthodox Church*, Risk Book Series (Geneva: WCC Publications, 2000), 8.

7. For examples, see Thomas Hopko, "Galatians 3:28: An Orthodox Interpretation," *St Vladimir's Theological Quarterly* 35, no. 2–3 (1991): 185; Lawrence R. Farley, *Feminism and Tradition: Quiet Reflections on Ordination and Communion* (Yonkers: St Vladimir's Seminary Press, 2012), 55, 105.

8. Thomas Hopko, "On the Male Character of Christian Priesthood," *St Vladimir's Theological Quarterly* 19, no. 3 (1975): 159, n.16; *The Spirit of God* (Wilton: Morehouse-Barlow Company, Inc., 1976), 44.

9. Behr-Sigel, "The Ordination of Women: A Point of Contention in Ecumenical Dialogue," *St Vladimir's Theological Quarterly* 48, no. 1 (2004): 480; "The Participation of Women in the Life of the Church," *Sobornost* 7, no. 6 (1978): 66. Cf. Maria Gwyn McDowell, "The Iconicity of Priesthood: Male Bodies or Embodied Virtue?," *Studies in Christian Ethics* 26, no. 3 (2013): 364.

10. Thomas Hopko, "Presbyter/Priest: A Masculine Ministry," in *Women and the Priesthood*, ed. Thomas Hopko (Crestwood: St Vladimir's Seminary Press, 1999), 162. Cf. Ti 1:5–9. Note that the requirements for deacons in 1 Tm 3:7–12 also dictate that a deacon must be the husband of one wife (v. 12). However, this passage did not prevent women from serving as deaconesses.

11. Canon 3 of the Quinisext Council. There are rare exceptions to this rule. See John Matusiak, "Divorce and Ordination," Orthodox Church in America, https://oca.org/questions/priesthoodmonasticism/divorce-and-ordination.

12. Apostolic Cannon 26 makes allowances for those who have entered the orders of cantors and lectors to marry, but no other orders. This is repeated in Canon 6 of the Quinisext Council. In the contemporary practice of some jurisdictions, subdeacons are also allowed to marry without surrendering their liturgical rank despite canon law.

13. Quinisext Council, Canon 6.

14. Quinisext Council, Canon 12.

15. See chapter 3.

16. Authors in this line include Justin Martyr, Cyprian of Carthage, Ignatius of Antioch, Antiochus the Monk, and Theodore the Studite. For passage citations see Kallistos Ware, "Man, Woman and the Priesthood of Christ," in *Man, Woman, Priesthood*, ed. Peter Moore (London: Fletcher and Son, 1978), 79–80.

17. See Pius XII's *Mediator Dei* 40, 68–69. This thought was expanded by Vatican II in *Lumen gentium* 28.

18. Hopko, "On the Male Character of Christian Priesthood," 168, n.25.

19. *Inter Insigniores* 5, published in 1976.

20. Alexander Schmemann, "Concerning Women's Ordination: A Letter to an Episcopal Friend," *St Vladimir's Theological Quarterly* 17, no. 3 (1973): 242. Emphasis in the original.

21. *Hom. in Joan.* LXXVII.4.

22. For a more detailed discussion, see the revised essay Kallistos Ware, "Man, Woman and the Priesthood of Christ," in *Women and the Priesthood*, ed. Thomas Hopko (Crestwood: St Vladimir's Seminary Press, 1999), 47–49.

23. See Elisabeth Behr-Sigel, "The Ordination of Women: An Ecumenical Problem," *Sobornost* 13, no. 1 (1991): 10; "'The Ordination of Women: An Ecumenical Problem': A Reply to a Reply," 25; Behr-Sigel and Ware, *The Ordination of Women in the Orthodox Church*, 23; Behr-Sigel, "The Ordination of Women: A Point of Contention in Ecumenical Dialogue," 65; Ware, "Man, Woman and the Priesthood (1999)," 49.

24. "Man, Woman and the Priesthood (1978)," 80. Cf. G. A. Ostrogorsky, "Gnoseologicheskiya osnovy vizantiyskago spora o sv. ikonakh," in *Seminarium Kondakovianum II* (Prague: Seminarium Kondakovianum, 1928), 48.

25. Ware, "Man, Woman and the Priesthood (1978)," 80.

26. Cf. Theodore the Studite, *Antirrhetici* III.C.5. For an English translation, see Theodore the Studite, *St. Theodore the Studite on the Holy Icons*, trans. Catharine P. Roth (Crestwood: St Vladimir's Seminary Press, 1981), 104.

27. Ware, "Man, Woman and the Priesthood (1978)," 81. The reference is to Basil's *Spir.* 18:45.

28. For the text of the *horos* of Nicaea II, see *Decrees of the Ecumenical Councils*, ed. Norman P. Tanner (London: Sheed & Ward, 1990), 133–38.

29. A custom deriving from Mt 9:20–22.

30. Ware, "Man, Woman and the Priesthood (1978)," 81.

31. Ibid.

32. For example, Behr-Sigel, "'The Ordination of Women: An Ecumenical Problem': A Reply to a Reply," 20–26; McDowell, "The Iconicity of Priesthood: Male Bodies or Embodied Virtue?," 365.

33. Verna E. F. Harrison, "Orthodox Arguments against the Ordination of Women as Priests," *Sobornost (incorporating Eastern Churches Review)* 14, no. 1 (1992): 14. Harrison cites Basil of Caesarea and Umberto Neri, *Il Battesimo* (Brescia: Paideia, 1976), 604–06.

34. Thomas Hopko, *The Orthodox Faith*, ed. Constance J. Tarasar, 2nd ed., 4 vols. (Yonkers: Orthodox Church in America and St Vladimir's Seminary Press, 1981), II.23.

35. See Theodore the Studite's *Antirrhetici* III.A.34, Theodore the Studite, *St. Theodore the Studite on the Holy Icons*, 90.

36. *Decrees of the Ecumenical Councils*, 136.

37. Again, turning to the Nicene Creed, the Son was made flesh by the Holy Spirit and the Virgin Mary. In addition to the confession of the virgin birth in the Nicene Creed, see the troparion for the Sunday of the Forefathers, the kathisma hymn for matins on the Feast of the Nativity, and the Theotokion of Lord I Cry at Great Vespers for Sunday in Tone 4.

38. Ware, "Man, Woman and the Priesthood (1978)," 81. See also chapter 3, endnote 69.

39. Maximos Aghiorgoussis, *Women Priests?* (Brookline: Holy Cross Orthodox Press, 1976), 3.

40. Ibid., 5.

41. Ware, "Man, Woman and the Priesthood (1999)," 51.

42. Cf. Ibid.

43. Farley, *Feminism and Tradition*, 101.

44. Ibid.

45. Ibid., 101–02.

46. Ibid., 102. For a follow-up to this argument, based on a juxtaposition between Christ the Bridegroom and his Church the Bride in Eph 5, "the authority of scripture," and "equal rights," see ibid., 102–03.

47. Jn 13:1–17.

48. 1 Th 2:7, Gal 4:19.

49. Hopko, "Presbyter/Priest," 162.

50. For another personalist approach to ordained ministry, see chapter 6 of John D. Zizioulas, *Being as Communion: Studies in Personhood and the Church*, Contemporary Greek theologians no. 4 (Crestwood: St Vladimir's Seminary Press, 1985).

6. Homosexuality

1. Thomas Hopko, *Christian Faith and Same-Sex Attraction: Eastern Orthodox Reflections* (Chesterton: Ancient Faith Publishing, 2015), 18.

2. As examples, see Orthodox Church in America Holy Synod of Bishops, "Synodal Affirmations on Marriage, Family, Sexuality, and the Sanctity of Life," news release, July 1992, https://oca.org/holy-synod/statements/holy-synod /synodal-affirmations-on-marriage-family-sexuality-and-the-sanctity-of-life; Michael Dahulich, "Archpastoral Letter of His Grace, Bishop Michael, Re-Affirming the Sanctity of Marriage," news release, June 24, 2011, http:// www.nynjoca.org/files/2011/Release-2011.27.1.pdf; Jonah Paffhausen, "Archpastoral Letter Regarding Marriage to the Faithful of the Archdiocese of Washington," news release, July 28, 2011, http://wdcoca.org/files/met_jonah

/To-Faithful-re-marriage.pdf; Matthias Moriak, "Archpastoral Letter of His Grace, Bishop Matthias," news release, August 2, 2011, http://www.domoca.org /news_110802_1.html; Assembly of Canonical Orthodox Bishops of the United States of America, "2013 Assembly Statement on Marriage and Sexuality," news release, 2013, http://assemblyofbishops.org/about/documents/2013-assembly -statement-on-marriage-and-sexuality.

3. Elizabeth R. Moberly, "Can Homosexuals *Really* Change?," *Journal of Christian Nursing* 9, no. 4 (1992): 15.

4. "Homosexuality: Restating The Conservative Case," *Salmagundi*, no. 58–59 (1982).

5. *Psychogenesis: The Early Development of Gender Identity* (London: Routledge & Kegan Paul, 1983); *Homosexuality: A New Christian Ethic* (Cambridge [Cambridgeshire]: James Clarke, 1983).

6. "New Perspectives on Homosexuality," *Journal of the Royal Society of Health* 105, no. 6 (1985): 206. In her exclusive emphasis on relationship problems between the child and their same-sex parent, Moberly differs from the other major exponent of reparative therapy, Joseph Nicolosi. Nicolosi (1947–2017) was a psychologist, founder of the Thomas Aquinas Psychological Clinic, and a founding member of the National Association for Research and Therapy of Homosexuality (NARTH). His seminal work is Joseph Nicolosi, *Reparative Therapy of Male Homosexuality: A New Clinical Approach* (Northvale: Jason Aronson Inc., 1997).

7. Moberly, *Psychogenesis*, 37.

8. *Homosexuality: A New Christian Ethic*, 6.

9. *Psychogenesis*, 36–37.

10. Cf. "Homosexuality: Restating the Conservative Case," 283; *Homosexuality: A New Christian Ethic*, 19–20.

11. *Psychogenesis*, 84–85.

12. *Homosexuality: A New Christian Ethic*, 32.

13. Moberly cites Anglican theologians Michael Green and David Watson as her sources. Ibid., 28. See Michael Green, David Holloway, and David Watson, *The Church and Homosexuality: A Positive Answer to Current Questions* (London: Hodder and Stoughton, 1980), 19, 136. Cf. ibid., 74–75, which Moberly does not reference. The line of thought is borrowed from Don Williams, *The Bond That Breaks: Will Homosexuality Split the Church?*, The New Ancient World (Los Angeles: BIM, 1978), 53, 90–95. Williams takes the idea from Paul Jewett (who was mentioned in chapter 3 as Hopko's evangelical interlocutor). Jewett's inspiration, covered in detail in Williams's book, was Karl Barth. For references to Barth, see also chapter 3, endnote 90.

14. Moberly, *Homosexuality: A New Christian Ethic*, 29.

15. Ibid., 31.

16. See chapter 5, endnote 37.

17. See Maximus Confessor, *Amb. 41*, §7. For a translation see Maximus Confessor, *On Difficulties in the Church Fathers: The Ambigua*, trans. Nicholas Constas, Dumbarton Oaks Medieval Library (Cambridge: Harvard University Press, 2014), II:111.

18. See Gregory of Nazianzus, *Orationes* 31 (*Theologica* V, *De Spiritu sancto*) §7.

19. For Pseudo-Dionysius's discussion of the threefold path see *The Mystical Theology*, translated in Pseudo-Dionysius and Paul Rorem, *Pseudo-Dionysius: The Complete Works*, trans. Colm Luibhéid, Classics of Western Spirituality (New York: Paulist Press, 1987), 133–41.

20. See Elizabeth R. Moberly, "Homosexuality and Truth," *First Things* 71 (1997); "Can Homosexuals *Really* Change?" 17.

21. *Psychogenesis*, 75; *Homosexuality: A New Christian Ethic*, 42.

22. *Homosexuality: A New Christian Ethic*, 41.

23. Ibid., 42.

24. Gn 2:18; Rom 1:26. See ibid., 41, 42.

25. Moberly, "Homosexuality: Restating The Conservative Case," 296. This theme is more fully developed, including a list of scriptural citations addressing the care of orphans, in *Homosexuality: A New Christian Ethic*, 35.

26. *Homosexuality: A New Christian Ethic*, 40, 43.

27. Ibid., 44.

28. Ibid., 48.

29. Ibid., 49. Cf. Gal 4:19.

30. In his book on same-sex attraction, Hopko makes several references to receiving healing for childhood developmental deficiencies, though he only mentions Moberly by name once. See Thomas Hopko, *Christian Faith and Same-Sex Attraction: Eastern Orthodox Reflections* (Ben Lomond: Conciliar Press, 2006), 19, 41, 48, 51, 69, 70, n.2. Cf. William Basil Zion, "Elizabeth Moberly: Orthodox Theologian," *St Vladimir's Theological Quarterly* 32, no. 1 (1988): 54–60; *Eros and Transformation: Sexuality and Marriage: An Eastern Orthodox Perspective* (Lanham: University Press of America, 1992), 311–17, 320–21.

31. John Breck, *The Sacred Gift of Life: Orthodox Christianity and Bioethics* (Crestwood: St Vladimir's Seminary Press, 1998), 109, 15. Breck's mention of Moberly in a sentence mixed with his own descriptions may lead a reader unfamiliar with Moberly's work to conclude that she characterizes homosexuals as "inherently promiscuous." Ibid., 115. However, this is Breck's own erroneous characterization of Moberly's ideas.

32. Moberly's own list includes the illness of a parent, birth of a sibling, temporary absence of a parent, and even a succession of people responsible for childcare. See Moberly, *Psychogenesis*, 78.

33. Wendy VanderWal-Gritter, *Generous Spaciousness: Responding to Gay Christians in the Church* (Grand Rapids: Baker Publishing Group, 2014), 36–37.

34. Moberly's ideas and the damage caused by ministries trying to incorporate them is briefly explored in ibid., 34–38.

35. This is the premise, for example, in Joseph Nicolosi and Linda Ames Nicolosi, *A Parent's Guide to Preventing Homosexuality* (Downers Grove: InterVarsity Press, 2002).

36. Sigmund Freud, "Leonardo da Vinci and a Memory of His Childhood," in *The Standard Edition of the Complete Works of Sigmund Freud*, ed. James Strachey (London: The Hogarth Press and the Institute of Psycho-Analysis, 1957), 99. For an overview of Freud's four etiologies for homosexuality, see Jack Drescher, "I'm Your Handyman: A History of Reparative Therapies," *Journal of Homosexuality* 36, no. 1 (1998): 22.

37. Sigmund Freud, "Three Essays on the Theory of Sexuality," in *The Standard Edition of the Complete Psychological Works of Sigmund Freud* (London: The Hogarth Press and the Institute of Psycho-Analysis, 1953), 145n. Emphasis in the original.

38. "On Narcissism: An Introduction," in *The Standard Edition of the Complete Psychological Works of Sigmund Freud*, ed. James Strachey (London: The Hogarth Press and the Institute of Psycho-Analysis, 1957), 87.

39. "Leonardo da Vinci," 100.

40. Breck, *The Sacred Gift of Life*, 116; Clark Carlton, "Sexual Reorientation Therapy: An Orthodox Perspective," *Christian Bioethics: Non-Ecumenical Studies in Medical Morality* 10, no. 2–3 (2004): 152, n.5; Zion, *Eros and Transformation*, 321.

41. Grigorios D. Papathomas, "Homosexualité, *nature contre-nature?,*" *Academia* (2000), https://www.academia.edu/19580826/43._The_existential _centrifugal_situation_between_endo-hypostatic_narcissism_Rm_1_23_and _intra-creationnal_orientation_Rm_1_25_in_French_.

7. Marriage: The Sacrament of Love

1. Paul Evdokimov, *The Sacrament of Love: The Nuptial Mystery in the Light of the Orthodox Tradition* (Crestwood: St Vladimir's Seminary Press, 1985), 19.

2. Michael Dahulich, "Archpastoral Letter of His Grace, Bishop Michael, Re-Affirming the Sanctity of Marriage," news release, June 24, 2011, http://www .nynjoca.org/files/2011/Release-2011.27.1.pdf; Jonah Paffhausen, "Archpastoral Letter Regarding Marriage to the Faithful of the Archdiocese of Washington," news release, July 28, 2011, http://wdcoca.org/files/met_jonah/To-Faithful-re -marriage.pdf; Matthias Moriak, "Archpastoral Letter of His Grace, Bishop Matthias," news release, August 2, 2011, http://www.domoca.org/news_110802 _1.html; Assembly of Canonical Orthodox Bishops of the United States of

America, "2013 Assembly Statement on Marriage and Sexuality," news release, 2013, http://assemblyofbishops.org/about/documents/2013-assembly-statement -on-marriage-and-sexuality; Paul Gassios, "To All Clergy, Monastics, and Faithful of the Diocese of the Midwest," news release, 2015, http://domoca.org/files/news /2015/2015-0626-same-sex-marriage.pdf.

3. There are exceptions. See Paffhausen, "Archpastoral Letter Regarding Marriage to the Faithful of the Archdiocese of Washington"; Assembly of Canonical Orthodox Bishops of the United States of America, "2013 Assembly Statement on Marriage and Sexuality. "

4. See David J. Dunn to The Huffington Post, July 13, 2011, http://www .huffingtonpost.com/david-j-dunn-phd/eastern-orthodox-gay-marriage_b _894982.html.

5. Thomas Hopko, *Christian Faith and Same-Sex Attraction: Eastern Orthodox Reflections* (Ben Lomond: Conciliar Press, 2006), 83.

6. Ibid., 85.

7. See Basil Zion, *Eros and Transformation: Sexuality and Marriage: An Eastern Orthodox Perspective* (Lanham: University Press of America, 1992), 309, 18; John Breck, *The Sacred Gift of Life: Orthodox Christianity and Bioethics* (Crestwood: St Vladimir's Seminary Press, 1998), 110. The scriptural passages in question are Gn 2:24, Mk 10:8, Mt 19:5, 1 Cor 6:16, and Eph 5:31.

8. See Eph 5:31. Cf. Hopko, "On the Male Character of Christian Priesthood," *St Vladimir's Theological Quarterly* 19, no. 3 (1975): 163; Zion, *Eros and Transformation*, 38; Breck, *The Sacred Gift of Life*, 115; Lawrence R. Farley, *Feminism and Tradition: Quiet Reflections on Ordination and Communion* (Yonkers: St Vladimir's Seminary Press, 2012), 86.

9. Gn 2:20. For more on the translation of the Hebrew *ʿēzer kənegdô*, see chapter 2, endnote 22.

10. James V. Brownson, *Bible, Gender, Sexuality: Reframing the Church's Debate on Same-Sex Relationships* (Grand Rapids: William B. Eerdmans Publishing Company, 2013), 32–35, 85–109.

11. Gn 29:14; 37:27. The Hebrew *bāśār* (בשר) translated in the LXX as σάρξ, has a denotative meaning of "flesh."

12. 1 Cor 6:16.

13. Breck, *The Sacred Gift of Life*, 115; John Edgar Parker, III, "The Sanctity of Chastity: An Orthodox Approach to Homosexuality" (St Vladimir's Orthodox Theological Seminary, 2004), 30–31.

14. Gn 1:28.

15. See chapter 2, endnote 115.

16. See *Bon. conj.* 16.18, 22.27. Cf. *Coni. ad.* II.12.12.

17. Elizabeth A. Clark, *Reading Renunciation: Asceticism and Scripture in Early Christianity* (Princeton: Princeton University Press, 1999), 80–81, 88, 120, 49–51, 65, 80–81, 309–10, 40, 60.

18. Hopko, *Christian Faith and Same-Sex Attraction*, 81–82, 83.

19. The idea of Christians as brides of Christ also appears in the *Pas. SS. Serg.* 7. For a Greek version of the text see I. Van den Gehn, ed., "Passio antiquior SS. Sergii et Bacchi graece nunc primum edita," *Analecta bollandiana* 14 (1895). An English translation is found in John Boswell, *Same-Sex Unions in Premodern Europe* (New York: Villiard Books, 1994), 375–90, with the passage in question at 79.

20. I am indebted to Eugene Rogers for the opposite/apposite distinction as it relates to complementarity. See Eugene F. Rogers, Jr., "Same-Sex Complementarity: A Theology of Marriage," *Christian Century* 128, no. 10 (2011): 31.

21. Christos Yannaras, *The Freedom of Morality* (Crestwood: St Vladimir's Seminary Press, 1984), 23.

22. Ibid.

23. Ibid., 162.

24. Ibid., 164. Emphasis in the original.

25. Ibid.

26. Ibid., 165, n.27.

27. Here it must be strongly emphasized that I am categorically against the perverted vision of self-emptying and sacrifice that suggests that either spouse should suffer physical abuse or psychological torture. There is a huge difference between self-sacrificial love that keeps no record of wrongs (1 Cor 13:5) and a lack of the love of self that Christ commanded (Mk 12:31; Mt 22:39, quoted from Lv 19:18) that is necessary to the love of the other, whether neighbor or spouse. The blanket suggestion that a spouse should remain with their abuser at the risk of self-annihilation misses the point of the sacramental character of marriage.

28. Yannaras, *The Freedom of Morality*, 167.

29. Ibid.

30. Ibid., 101–02.

31. Ibid., 167–68, n.30.

32. Ibid., 167.

33. Hopko, *Christian Faith and Same-Sex Attraction*, 45.

34. Yannaras links this claim to the Hebrew use of *yāda'* (ידע—"to know") as an idiomatic expression for sexual intercourse. See Gn 4:1, 4:17, 4:25. Translated as a calque into Greek in Mt 1:25, Lk 1:34.

35. Yannaras, *The Freedom of Morality*, 161. Emphasis in the original.

36. Ibid., 163.

37. Ibid.

38. 1 Cor 7:8–9.

39. See chapter 7 of Zion, *Eros and Transformation*.

40. Elizabeth R. Moberly, *Homosexuality: A New Christian Ethic*, (Cambridge [Cambridgeshire]: James Clarke, 1983): 27.

41. Hopko, *Christian Faith and Same-Sex Attraction*, 56.

42. Moberly, *Homosexuality: A New Christian Ethic*, 27.

43. Hopko, *Christian Faith and Same-Sex Attraction*, 55.

44. For an in-depth study from an Orthodox perspective of the various figures and passages to be explored in this section, see my essay, Bryce E. Rich, "Something New under the Sun: Sexualities, Same-Sex Relationships, and Orthodoxy," in *Orthodox Tradition and Human Sexuality*, ed. Thomas Arentzen, Ashley Purpura, and Aristotle Papanikolaou (New York: Fordham University Press, 2022), 46–65.

45. See Derrick Sherwin Bailey, *Homosexuality and the Western Christian Tradition* (London: Longmans, Green and Company, Ltd., 1955), 9–28.

46. Cf. 1 Sm 31:4 (1 Kingdoms 31:4); 1 Chr 10:4 (1 Paraleipomenon 10:4), and Jgs 19:25. The word *abuse* (Greek ἐμπαίξωσί and ἐνέπαιζον, respectively, both from ἐμπαίζω) appears in both passages. LSJ notes that the occurrence in Jgs is euphemistic. See Henry George Liddell et al., *A Greek-English Lexicon*, 9th ed. (Oxford: Oxford University Press, 1996), 543.

47. 2 Sm 10:1–5 (2 Kingdoms 10:1–5).

48. See Harper, *From Shame to Sin: The Christian Transformation of Sexual Morality in Late Antiquity* (Cambridge: Harvard University Press, 2013), 90.

49. John J. Winkler, *Constraints of Desire: The Anthropology of Sex and Gender in Ancient Greece* (New York: Routledge, 1990), 37, 38, 43; Craig A. Williams, *Roman Homosexuality,* 2nd ed. (Oxford: Oxford University Press, 2010), 179, 86.

50. This is especially true of the imperial period. See Harper, *From Shame to Sin: The Christian Transformation of Sexual Morality in Late Antiquity*, 150–53.

51. See Sarah Ruden, *Paul Among the People: The Apostle Reinterpreted and Reimagined in His Own Time* (New York: Pantheon Books, 2010), 45–71.

52. Ws 14:22 ff. The referenced phrase is in v. 26, rendered as "sexual perversion" in the NRSV. For commentary, see Bailey, *Homosexuality and the Western Christian Tradition*, 45–48; Martti Nissinen, *Homoeroticism in the Biblical World: A Historical Perspective* (Minneapolis: Fortress Press, 1998), 90–91.

53. For the argument that the diatribe of Romans 1 is not Paul's own words, but rather a rhetorical exercise of *prosopopoia*, see Douglas A. Campbell, *The Deliverance of God: An Apocalyptic Rereading of Justification in Paul* (Grand Rapids: William B. Eerdmans Publishing Company, 2009). For an argument concerning the rhetorical use of παρὰ φύσιν in Romans 1 and 11, see Thomas Hanks, "Romans," in *The Queer Bible Commentary*, ed. Deryn Guest (London: SCM, 2006).

54. See Dale B. Martin, "*Arsenokoitês* and *Malakos*: Meanings and Consequences," in *Biblical Ethics & Homosexuality: Listening to Scripture* (Louisville: Westminster John Knox Press, 1996); William Lawrence Petersen,

"Can *Arsenokoitai* Be Translated by 'Homosexuals' (1 Cor 6:9, 1 Tim 1:10)," *Vigiliae christianae* 40, no. 2 (1986).

55. Gn 19; Jgs 19:22. Three contemporary scholars who deal with Lv 18:22, 20:13 are Saul M. Olyan, "'And with a Male You Shall Not Lie the Lying down of a Woman': On the Meaning and Significance of Leviticus 18:22 and 20:13," *Journal of the History of Sexuality* 5, no. 2 (1994); Nissinen, *Homoeroticism in the Biblical World: A Historical Perspective*, 37–44; Phyllis Bird, "The Bible in Christian Ethical Deliberation concerning Homosexuality: Old Testament Contributions," in *Homosexuality, Science, and the "Plain Sense" of Scripture*, ed. David L. Balch (Grand Rapids: William B. Eerdmans Publishing Company, 2000), 149–54.

56. Cf. Ez 16:49–50, Mk 6:11, Mt 10:15, 11:24, Lk 10:12. Also Bailey, *Homosexuality and the Western Christian Tradition*, 21–23, 26, 153; Nissinen, *Homoeroticism in the Biblical World: A Historical Perspective*, 93–97.

57. *Didache* 2.2, οὐ παιδοφθορήσεις. Found also in *Epist. Barn.* 19.4. See Bailey, *Homosexuality and the Western Christian Tradition*, 82–83. Cf. *Apocalypse of Peter* 31.

58. For a discussion of the condemnation of female same-sex acts in Tertullian and Clement, see Bernadette J. Brooten, *Love between Women: Early Christian Responses to Female Homoeroticism* (Chicago: University of Chicago Press, 1996), 314–36. Chrysostom inveighs against pederasty in *Ad. op.* and *Hom. in Rom.* IV. Gregory of Nyssa addresses the corruption of boys in his *Ep. Leo.* For commentary see Harper, *From Shame to Sin: The Christian Transformation of Sexual Morality in Late Antiquity*, 144–45.

59. For a study of canon laws and penitential handbooks that address same-sex genital acts, see chapter 3 of Stephen Morris, *"When Brothers Dwell in Unity": Byzantine Christianity and Homosexuality* (Jefferson: McFarland & Company, Inc., Publishers, 2016), 65–98.

60. Within Orthodox canon law, the term ἀρσενοκοιτία comes to denote a series of illicit sexual practices analogous to medieval Latin understandings of sodomy. While mutual masturbation is not considered full ἀρσενοκοιτία, the category includes both interfemoral and anal intercourse between males and anal intercourse between husband and wife.

61. Hopko, "On the Male Character of the Christian Priesthood: A Reply to Criticism," *St Vladimir's Theological Quarterly* 21, no. 3 (1977): 168, n.25; *The Orthodox Faith*, ed. Constance J. Tarasar, 2nd ed., 4 vols. (Yonkers: Orthodox Church in America and St Vladimir's Seminary Press, 1981), I:34–36.

62. Timothy Ware, *The Orthodox Church*, New ed. (New York: Penguin Books, 1993), 206.

63. Examples would include canons from the Quinisext Council that forbid clergy to eat with non-Orthodox, or to be present when music is performed.

They also include frankly embarrassing prohibitions such as forbidding Christians to consult with Jewish doctors.

64. Nikolay Berdyaev, *O naznachenii cheloveka: Opyt paradksal'noi etiki* [*The Destiny of Man: An Experiment in Paradoxical Ethics*] (Paris: Izdatel'stvo "Svoremenye Zapiski," 1931), 260n; *The Destiny of Man* trans. Natalie Duddington (New York: Charles Scribner's Sons, 1937), 242n.

8. Some Final Thoughts on Pastoral Care

1. Lawrence R. Farley, "Advice to the Confused," Orthodox Church in America, https://www.oca.org/reflections/fr.-lawrence-farley/advice-to-the -confused.

2. Orthodox Church in America Holy Synod of Bishops, "Synodal Affirmations on Marriage, Family, Sexuality, and the Sanctity of Life," News release, July 1992, https://oca.org/holy-synod/statements/holy-synod/synodal -affirmations-on-marriage-family-sexuality-and-the-sanctity-of-life.

3. Ibid.

4. John Breck, *The Sacred Gift of Life: Orthodox Christianity and Bioethics* (Crestwood: St Vladimir's Seminary Press, 1998), 89, 117. Here Breck does not appear to have all single-parent families in mind. Rather, his emphasis appears to be on those who seek to have or adopt children without entering marriage.

5. Thomas Hopko, *Christian Faith and Same-Sex Attraction: Eastern Orthodox Reflections* (Ben Lomond: Conciliar Press, 2006), 83–84.

6. See Robert M. Arida, "Response to Myself," in *Articles & Talks* (Boston: Holy Trinity Cathedral, 2011). The essay was subsequently republished as "Response to Myself. A Pastor's Thoughts on Same-Sex Marriage," in *"For I Am Wonderfully Made": Texts on Eastern Orthodoxy and LGBT Inclusion*, ed. Misha Cherniak, Olga Gerassimenko, and Michael Brinkschröder ([n.p.]: European Forum of LGBT Christian Groups, 2017).

7. Elizabeth R. Moberly, *Psychogenesis: The Early Development of Gender Identity* (London: Routledge & Kegan Paul, 1983), 78.

8. Breck, *The Sacred Gift of Life*, 89.

9. Paul Gassios, "To All Clergy, Monastics, and Faithful of the Diocese of the Midwest," news release, 2015, http://domoca.org/files/news/2015/2015-0626 -same-sex-marriage.pdf.

10. Lazar Puhalo, *On the Neurobiology of Sin* (Dewdney: Synaxis Press, 2010), 49.

11. See chapter 4.

12. Katherine Wu to Science in the News, October 25, 2016, http://sitn .hms.harvard.edu/flash/2016/gender-lines-science-transgender-identity/. Also Bianca D. M. Wilson and Ilan H. Meyer, "Nonbinary Adults in the United States," (Los Angeles: UCLA School of Law Williams Institute, 2021).

13. Russian Orthodox Church Holy Bishops' Council, "The Basis of the Social Concept. XII. Problems of Bioethics," The Russian Orthodox Church Department of External Church Relations, https://mospat.ru/en/documents /social-concepts/xii/.

14. Timotheos Matthaiakēs, "Euchē eis onomatothesian nean epi allagē phylou [A Prayer at the Giving of a New Name upon Change of Sex]," in Egkolpion euchologion (Athēnai: n.p., 1985).

15. Gregory Pappas to The Pappas Post, October 18, 2017, http://www .pappaspost.com/greek-orthodox-church-prayer-name-changes-following -gender-reassignment-surgery/.

16. Timotheos Matthaiakēs, A Prayer at the Giving of a New Name upon Modification of Gender (Chicago, 2015), https://www.pappaspost.com/wp -content/uploads/2017/10/sex-assignment-prayer-translation.pdf.

17. A highly informative resource for exploring the issues is Julia Serano, Whipping Girl: A Transsexual Woman on Sexism and the Scapegoating of Femininity, second ed. (Berkeley: Seal Press, 2016).

18. This schema briefly summarizes the four positions taken in James K. Beilby and Paul Rhodes Eddy, eds., Understanding Transgender Identities: Four Views (Grand Rapids: Baker Academic, 2019).

19. Moberly, Psychogenesis, 80–81, 82–83.

20. Robert Hart, "Surgical Fantasy," Touchstone: A Journal of Mere Christianity, May/June 2016. Touchstone is a culturally conservative publication, uniting Orthodox, Catholic, Protestant, and Evangelical authors to address social issues. Hart is not Orthodox, but his essay typifies the rhetoric associated gender essentialist theologies.

21. Paul McHugh, "Transgender Surgery Isn't the Solution," Wall Street Journal, June 13, 2014.

22. Cecilia Dhejne et al., "Long-Term Follow-Up of Transsexual Persons Undergoing Sex Reassignment Surgery: Cohort Study in Sweden," PLOS ONE 6, no. 2 (2011): 7.

23. See Puhalo, On the Neurobiology of Sin, 48–53.

24. "Reality of Transgender 1/1" (YouTube video, March 2011); "Another Response Re: Transgender," (YouTube video, August 2012).

25. Article XII.9 of The Basis of the Social Concept. See Russian Orthodox Church Holy Bishops' Council, "The Basis of the Social Concept. XII. Problems of Bioethics".

26. Ibid.

27. While some opponents of gender transitioning imagine that hormone replacement therapy and sex reassignment surgeries are being provided indiscriminately to trans children, this simply is not the case. Many trans advocates would argue that the bar for access to both treatments within the

medical establishment is too high and medical gatekeeping is a common problem.

28. Because medical gatekeeping is still common, some trans people will seek out the assistance of other trans people in their community to advise on matters of hormone replacement therapy. This is separate from the red flag raised by impulsive self-administered hormone replacement therapy I refer to above.

29. See Crystal Lynn Lubinsky, *Removing Masculine Layers to Reveal a Holy Womanhood: The Female Transvestite Monks of Late Antique Eastern Christianity* (Turnhout: Brepols, 2013).

BIBLIOGRAPHY

Aghiorgoussis, Maximos. *Women Priests?* Brookline: Holy Cross Orthodox
   Press, 1976.
Alfeev, Hilarion. "Orthodox Theology on the Threshold of the 21st Century:
   Will There Be a Renaissance of Russian Theological Scholarship?"
   Ecumenical Review 52, no. 3 (2000): 309–25
Ambrose of Milan. *Hexameron, Paradise, and Cain and Abel.* Translated by
   John J. Savage. New York: Catholic University of America Press, 1961.
Anastasius of Sinai. *Hexaemeron.* Translated by Clement A. Kuehn and John D.
   Baggarly. Orientalia Christiana analecta, 1590–7449. Vol. 278, Roma:
   Pontificio istituto orientale, 2007.
Anglican-Orthodox Dialogue: The Dublin Agreed Statement 1984. Crestwood:
   St Vladimir's Seminary Press, 1985.
Anthony, Paul A. "Sex, Sin and the Soul: How Galen's Philosophical
   Speculation Became Augustine's Theological Assumptions." *Conversations:
   A Graduate Journal of the Humanities, Social Sciences, and Theology* 1, no. 1
   (2013): 1–19. http://ojs.acu.edu/ojs/index.php/conversations/article/view/5.
Arida, Robert M. "Response to Myself." In *Articles & Talks*. Boston: Holy
   Trinity Cathedral, 2011.
———. "Response to Myself. A Pastor's Thoughts on Same-Sex Marriage." In
   "For I Am Wonderfully Made": Texts on Eastern Orthodoxy and LGBT Inclusion,
   edited by Misha Cherniak, Olga Gerassimenko and Michael Brinkschröder,
   126–31. [n.p.]: European Forum of LGBT Christian Groups, 2017.
Assembly of Canonical Orthodox Bishops of the United States of America.
   "2013 Assembly Statement on Marriage and Sexuality." News release, 2013,
   http://assemblyofbishops.org/about/documents/2013-assembly-statement-on
   -marriage-and-sexuality.

Augustine of Hippo. *The Works of Saint Augustine: A Translation for the 21st Century*. Edited by Edmund Hill, John E. Rotelle, and Boniface Ramsey. Brooklyn: New City Press, 1990.

Bailey, Derrick Sherwin. *Homosexuality and the Western Christian Tradition*. London: Longmans, Green and Company, Ltd., 1955.

Basil of Caesarea, and Umberto Neri. *Il Battesimo*. Brescia: Paideia, 1976.

Batto, Bernard Frank. *Slaying the Dragon: Mythmaking in the Biblical Tradition*. Louisville: Westminster John Knox Press, 1992.

Behr-Sigel, Elisabeth. Review of Women and the Priesthood. *Contacts: Revue française de l'orthodoxie* 36 (1984): 207–14.

———. "L'église orthodoxe: Est-elle patriarcaliste!" *Contacts: Revue française de l'orthodoxie* 38, no. 3 (1986): 235–37.

———. "L'ordination des femmes: Un problème œcuménique." *Contacts: Revue française de l'orthodoxie* 42, no. 2 (1990): 101–27.

———. "La consultation interorthodoxe de Rhodes: La femme dans l'église." *Contacts: Revue française de l'orthodoxie* 41, no. 2 (1989): 81–93.

———. "La femme aussi est à l'image de Dieu." *Supplément au Service Orthodoxe de Presse*, no. 64 (1982): 15–23.

———. "La femme dans l'église orthodoxe. Vision céleste et histoire." *Contacts: Revue française de l'orthodoxie* 29, no. 4 (1977): 285–326.

———. "La place de la femme dans l'église." *Irénikon* 58, no. 1, 2 (1983): 46–53, 58, 194–214.

———. "The Meaning of the Participation of Women in the Life of the Church." In *Orthodox Women: Their Role and Participation in the Orthodox Church. Report on the Consultation of Orthodox Women, September 11–17, 1976, Agapia, Roumania*, edited by Constance J. Tarasar and Irina Kirillova, 17–29. Geneva: WCC Publications, 1977.

———. "The Ordination of Women: A Point of Contention in Ecumenical Dialogue." *St Vladimir's Theological Quarterly* 48, no. 1 (2004): 49–66.

———. "The Ordination of Women: An Ecumenical Problem." *Sobornost* 13, no. 1 (1991): 25–40.

———. "'The Ordination of Women: An Ecumenical Problem': A Reply to a Reply." *Sobornost* 15, no. 1 (1993): 20–26.

———. "The Otherness of Men and Women in the Context of a Christian Civilization." Translated by Steven Bigham. Chap. 1 In *The Ministry of Women in the Church*, 25–79. Redondo Beach: Oakwood Publications, 1987.

———. "The Participation of Women in the Life of the Church." *Sobornost* 7, no. 6 (1978): 480–93.

———. "The Place of Women in the Church." Translated by Steven Bigham. Chap. 5 In *The Ministry of Women in the Church*, 149–80. Redondo Beach: Oakwood Publications, 1991.

———. "Woman Is Also Made in the Image of God." Translated by Steven Bigham. Chap. 2 In *The Ministry of Women*, 81–92. Redondo Beach: Oakwood Publications, 1991.

———. "Women in the Orthodox Church: Heavenly Vision and Historical Realities." Translated by Steven Bigham. Chap. 4 In *The Ministry of Women in the Church*, 103–47. Redondo Beach: Oakwood Publications, 1991.

Behr-Sigel, Elisabeth, and Kallistos Ware. *The Ordination of Women in the Orthodox Church*. Risk Book Series. Geneva: WCC Publications, 2000.

Behr, John. "The Rational Animal: A Rereading of Gregory of Nyssa's De hominis opificio." *Journal of Early Christian Studies* 7, no. 2 (1999): 219–47.

Beilby, James K., and Paul Rhodes Eddy, eds. *Understanding Transgender Identities: Four Views*. Grand Rapids: Baker Academic, 2019.

Belonick, Deborah. "Father, Son, and Spirit—So What's in a Name?". In *The Politics of Prayer: Feminist Language and the Worship of God*, edited by Helen Hull Hitchcock, 297–306. San Francisco: Ignatius Press, 1992.

———. *Feminism in Christianity: An Orthodox Christian Response*. Contemporary Life Series. 2nd ed. Yonkers: St Vladimir's Seminary Press, 2012.

———. "The Spirit of the Female Priesthood." M.Div. thesis, St Vladimir's Orthodox Theological Seminary, 1979.

———. "The Spirit of the Female Priesthood." In *Women and the Priesthood*, edited by Thomas Hopko, 135–68. Crestwood: St Vladimir's Seminary Press, 1983.

———. "Women in the Church." In *Orthodox Perspectives on Pastoral Praxis: Papers of the Intra-Orthodox Conference on Pastoral Praxis (24–25 September 1986) Celebrating the 50th Anniversary of Holy Cross Greek Orthodox School of Theology (1937–1987)*, edited by Theodore Stylianopoulos, 81–99. Brookline: Holy Cross Orthodox Press, 1988.

Berdyaev, Nikolay. *The Destiny of Man*. Translated by Natalie Duddington. New York: Charles Scribner's Sons, 1937.

———. *The End of Our Time: Together with an Essay on the General Line of Soviet Philosophy*. Translated by Donald Atwater. New York: Sheed & Ward, 1933.

———. "Etude II. The Teaching about Sophia and the Androgyne." frsj Publications, http://berdyaev.com/berdiaev/berd_lib/1930_351.html.

———. "Iz etyudov o Ya. Beme. Etyud II. Uchenie o Sofii i androgine. Ya. Beme i russkiy sofiologicheskiy techeniya." *Put'*, no. 21 (April 1930): 34–62.

———. *The Meaning of the Creative Act*. Translated by Donald A. Lowrie. New York: Harper, 1954.

———. *O naznachenii cheloveka: Opyt paradoksal'noi etiki* [The Destiny of Man: An Experiment in Paradoxical Ethics]. Paris: Izdatel'stvo "Sovremenye zapiski", 1931.

————. *Smysl tvorchestva: Opyt opravdaniya cheloveka* [Meaning of the Creative Act: An Attempt of Justification of the Human Being]. Moscow: Izdanie G A Lemana i S I Sakharova, 1916.

Betz, Hans Dieter. *Galatians: A Commentary on Paul's Letter to the Churches in Galatia*. Hermeneia. Philadelphia: Fortress Press, 1979.

Bird, Phyllis. "The Bible in Christian Ethical Deliberation concerning Homosexuality: Old Testament Contributions." Chap. 5 In *Homosexuality, Science, and the "Plain Sense" of Scripture*, edited by David L. Balch, 142–76. Grand Rapids: William B. Eerdmans Publishing Company, 2000.

Blackless, Melanie, Anthony Charuvastra, Amanda Drryck, Anne Fausto-Sterling, Karl Lauzanne, and Ellen Lee. "How Sexually Dimorphic Are We? Review and Synthesis." *American Journal of Human Biology* 12, no. 2 (2000): 151–66.

Blane, Andrew, Mark Raeff, and George H. Williams. *Georges Florovsky: Russian Intellectual and Orthodox Churchman*. Crestwood: St Vladimir's Seminary Press, 1993.

Bolotov, Vasily. "Thesen über das "Filioque" von einem Russischen Theologen." *Revue internationale de théologie* 6, no. 24 (1898): 681–712.

Boswell, John. *Same-Sex Unions in Premodern Europe*. New York: Villiard Books, 1994.

Boylan, Michael. "The Galenic and Hippocratic Challenges to Aristotle's Conception Theory." *Journal of the History of Biology* 17, no. 1 (1984): 83–112.

Breck, John. *The Sacred Gift of Life: Orthodox Christianity and Bioethics*. Crestwood: St Vladimir's Seminary Press, 1998.

Brock, Sebastian P. *The Luminous Eye: The Spiritual World Vision of Saint Ephrem*. Cistercian Studies Series. Kalamazoo: Cistercian Publications, 1992.

Brooten, Bernadette J. *Love between Women: Early Christian Responses to Female Homoeroticism*. Chicago: University of Chicago Press, 1996.

Brown, Peter. *Augustine of Hippo: A Biography*. Berkeley: University of California Press, 2000.

Brownson, James V. *Bible, Gender, Sexuality: Reframing the Church's Debate on Same-Sex Relationships*. Grand Rapids: William B. Eerdmans Publishing Company, 2013.

Bulgakov, Sergey Nikolayevich. *Agnets Bozhiy—O bogochelovechestve—Chast' I* [The Lamb of God: On God-Manhood, Part I]. Paris: YMCA Press, 1933.

————. *The Bride of the Lamb*. Translated by Boris Jakim. Grand Rapids: William B. Eerdmans Publishing Company, 2002.

————. *The Burning Bush: On the Orthodox Veneration of the Mother of God*. Translated by Thomas Allan Smith. Grand Rapids: William B. Eerdmans Publishing Company, 2009.

————. *The Comforter*. Translated by Boris Jakim. Grand Rapids: William B. Eerdmans Publishing Company, 2004.

————. *Drug zhenika: O pravoslavnom pochitaniy Predtechi* [*Friend of the Bridegroom: On the Orthodox Veneration of the Forerunner*]. Paris: Imprimerie de Navarre, 1927.

————. *The Friend of the Bridegroom: On the Orthodox Veneration of the Forerunner*. Translated by Boris Jakim. Grand Rapids: William B. Eerdmans Publishing Company, 2003.

————. "Ipostas' i ipostasnost' (*Scholia k Svetu neverchernemu*)." In *Sbornik statey posvyashchennyx Petru Berngardovichu Struve ko dnyu tridtsatipyatiletiya ego nauchno-publitsisticheskoy deyatel'nosti, 1890 30 yanvarya 1925*, 353–71. Prague: Legiografie, 1925.

————. "Ipostas' i ipostasnost' (*Scholia k Svetu neverchernemu*)." In *Trudy o Troichnosti*, edited by Anna Reznichenko. Issledovaniya po istorii russkoy mysli, 19–53. Moscow: OGI, 2001.

————. *Jacob's Ladder: On Angels*. Translated by Thomas Allan Smith. Grand Rapids: William B. Eerdmans Publishing Company, 2010.

————. *Kupina neopalimaya: Opyt dogmaticheskago istolkovaniya nekotorykh chert v pravoslavnom pochitanii Bogomateri* [*The Burning Bush: On the Orthodox Veneration of the Mother of God*]. Paris: YMCA Press, 1927.

————. *The Lamb of God*. Translated by Boris Jakim. Grand Rapids: William B. Eerdmans Publishing Company, 2008.

————. *Lestvitsa Iakovlya: Ob angelakh* [*Jacob's Ladder: On Angels*]. Paris: [Imp. de Navarre], 1929.

————. "Muzhskoe i zhenskoe v bozhestve." In *S. N. Bulgakov: Religiozno-filosofskiy put'*, edited by A. P. Kozyrev, 343–65. Moscow: Russkiy Put', 2003.

————. *Nevesta Agntsa—O bogochelovechestve—Chast' III* [*Bride of the Lamb: On God-Manhood, Part III*]. Paris: [YMCA Press], 1945.

————. "Pol v cheloveke: (Fragment iz antropologii)." In *Trudy po sotsiologii i teologii: stat'i i raboty raznykh let 1902–1942*, 175–90. Moscow: Nauka, 1997.

————. "Pol v cheloveke (Fragment iz antropologii)." *Khristiyanskaya mysl' ezhemesyachniy zhurnal*, no. 11 (1916): 87–104.

————. *Svet nevecherniy: Sozertsaniya i umozreniya* [*Unfading Light: Contemplations and Speculations*]. Moscow: n.p., 1917.

————. *Unfading Light: Contemplations and Speculations*. Translated by Thomas Allan Smith. Grand Rapids: William B. Eerdmans Publishing Company, 2012.

————. *Uteshitel'—O bogochelovechestve—Chast' II* [*The Comforter: On God-Manhood, Part II*]. [Tallinn]: YMCA Press, 1936.

Bundy, David. "Language and the Knowledge of God in Ephrem Syrus." *The Patristic and Byzantine Review* 5, no. 2 (1986): 91–103.

Burgos, Juan Manuel. *An Introduction to Personalism*. Translated by R. T. Allen. Washington, D.C.: The Catholic University of America Press, 2018.

Burmistrov, Konstantin. "Christian Orthodoxy and Jewish Kabbalah: Russian Mystics in the Search for Perennial Wisdom." In *Polemical Encounters: Esoteric Discourse and Its Others*, edited by Olav Hammer and Kocku von Stuckrad, 25–54. Leiden: Brill, 2007.

Burrow, Rufus, Jr. *Personalism: A Critical Introduction*. St. Louis: Chalice Press, 1999.

Burrus, Virginia. *Begotten, Not Made: Conceiving Manhood in Late Antiquity*. Stanford: Stanford University Press, 2000.

Butler, Judith. *Gender Trouble: Feminism and the Subversion of Identity*. New York: Routledge, 1990.

Cameron, Ron. *The Other Gospels: Non-Canonical Gospel Texts*. Philadelphia: Westminster Press, 1982.

Campbell, Douglas A. *The Deliverance of God: An Apocalyptic Rereading of Justification in Paul*. Grand Rapids: William B. Eerdmans Publishing Company, 2009.

Canguilhem, Georges. *On the Normal and the Pathological*. Translated by Carolyn R. Fawcett. Boston: D. Reidel Publishing Company, 1978.

Carlton, Clark. "Sexual Reorientation Therapy: An Orthodox Perspective." *Christian Bioethics: Non-Ecumenical Studies in Medical Morality* 10, no. 2–3 (2004): 137–53.

Christology of the Later Fathers. Library of Christian Classics. Edited by John Baillie, John T. McNeill, and Henry P. Van Dusen. London: SCM Press, 1954.

Clark, Elizabeth A. "Heresy, Asceticism, Adam, and Eve: Interpretations of Genesis 1–3 in the Later Latin Fathers." In *Ascetic Piety and Women's Faith: Essays on Late Ancient Christianity*, 353–85. Lewiston: Edwin Mellen Press, 1986.

———. *Jerome, Chrysostom, and Friends: Essays and Translations*. Studies in Women and Religion. 2nd ed. Vol. 2, New York: E. Mellen Press, 1982.

———. *Reading Renunciation: Asceticism and Scripture in Early Christianity*. Princeton: Princeton University Press, 1999.

Clement of Alexandria, Alain Le Boulluec, Patrick Descourtieux, and Annewies van den Hoek. *Les Stromates*. Sources chrétiennes. 7 vols. Paris: Les Éditions du Cerf, 1981.

Connell, Sophia M. "Aristotle and Galen on Sex Difference and Reproduction: A New Approach to an Ancient Rivalry." *Studies in History and Philosophy of Science* 31, no. 2 (2000): 405–27.

d'Onofrio, Giulio. "The *Concordia* of Augustine and Dionysius: Toward a Hermeneutic of the Disagreement of Patristic Sources in John the Scot's *Periphyseon*." Translated by Bernard McGinn. In *Eriugena: East and West,* edited by Bernard McGinn and Willemien Otten, 115–40. Notre Dame: University of Notre Dame Press, 1994.

Dahulich, Michael. "Archpastoral Letter of His Grace, Bishop Michael, Re-Affirming the Sanctity of Marriage." News release, June 24, 2011, http://www.nynjoca.org/files/2011/Release-2011.27.1.pdf.

Daub, Adrian. *Uncivil Unions: The Metaphysics of Marriage in German Idealism and Romanticism*. Chicago: University of Chicago Press, 2012.

David, Zdenek V. "The Influence of Jacob Boehme on Russian Religious Thought." *Slavic Review* 21, no. 1 (1962): 43–64.

Decrees of the Ecumenical Councils. Edited by Norman P. Tanner. London: Sheed & Ward, 1990.

Dhejne, Cecilia, Paul Lichtenstein, Marcus Boman, Anna L. V. Johansson, Niklas Långström, and Mikael Landén. "Long-Term Follow-Up of Transsexual Persons Undergoing Sex Reassignment Surgery: Cohort Study in Sweden." *PLOS ONE* 6, no. 2 (2011): e16885.

Diamond, Lisa M. *Sexual Fluidity: Understanding Women's Love and Desire*. Cambridge: Harvard University Press, 2008.

Drescher, Jack. "I'm Your Handyman: A History of Reparative Therapies." *Journal of Homosexuality* 36, no. 1 (1998): 19–42.

Drever, Matthew. *Image, Identity, and the Forming of the Augustinian Soul*. New York: Oxford University Press, 2013.

Dronke, Peter. "Eriugena's Earthly Paradise." In *Begriff und Metapher: Sprachform des Denkens bei Eriugena: Vorträge des VII. Internationalen Eriugena-Colloquiums, Werner-Reimers-Stiftung Bad Homburg, 26.–29. Juli 1989*, edited by Werner Beierwaltes, 213–29. Heidelberg: Winter, 1990.

Duclow, Donald. "The Sleep of Adam, the Making of Eve: Sin and Creation in Eriugena." 2011.

Dunn, David J. "Civil Unions by Another Name: An Eastern Orthodox Defense of Gay Marriage." In *The Huffington Post*: TheHuffingtonPost .com, 2011.

Elliston, Deborah A. "Erotic Anthropology: 'Ritualized Homosexuality' in Melanesia and Beyond." *American Ethnologist* 22, no. 4 (1995): 848–67.

Ephrem the Syrian. *Hymnen de ecclesia*. Corpus scriptorum Christianorum Orientalium. Edited by Edmund Beck Vol. 198, Louvain: Secrétariat du CorpusSCO, 1960.

———. *Selected Prose Works*. Translated by Edward G. Matthews, Jr. and Joseph P. Amar. Fathers of the Church. Washington: Catholic University of America Press, 1994.

Eriugena, Johannes Scottus. *Periphyseon: The Division of Nature*. Translated by I. P. Sheldon-Williams and John J. O'Meara. Washington, D.C.: Dumbarton Oaks, 1987.

Evdokimov, Paul. "The Charisms of Woman." Chap. 10 in *In the World, of the Church*, edited by Michael Plekon and Alexis Vinogradov, 231–42. Crestwood: St Vladimir's Seminary Press, 2001.

———. "La femme et la parole." *Catéchèse*, no. 16 (1964): 265–76.

———. *La femme et le salut du monde. Étude d'anthropologie chrétienne sur les charismes de la femme*. Tournai: Casterman, 1958.

———. *Le mariage. Sacrement de l'amour*. Paris: Éditions du livre français, 1945.

———. "Le Saint Esprit et la Mère de Dieu." Chap. 6 in *La nouveauté de l'Esprit. Études de spiritualité*, 253–78. Bégrolles: Abbaye de Bellefontaine, 1977.

———. "Les charismes de la femme." Chap. 10 in *La nouveauté de l'Esprit. Études de spiritualité*, 237–52. Bégrolles: Abbaye de Bellefontaine, 1977.

———. "Panagion and Panagia." *Bulletin de la Société français d'études mariales* 29 (1970): 59–71.

———. "Panagion and Panagia: The Holy Spirit and the Mother of God." Translated by Michael Plekon and Alexis Vinogradov. Chap. 6 in *In the Word, of the Church*, edited by Michael Plekon and Alexis Vinogradov, 155–73. Crestwood: St Vladimir's Seminary Press, 2001.

———. *The Sacrament of Love: The Nuptial Mystery in the Light of the Orthodox Tradition*. Crestwood: St Vladimir's Seminary Press, 1985.

———. *Sacrement de l'amour: Le mystère conjugal à la lumière de la tradition orthodoxe*. Paris: Éditions de l'ÉPI, 1962.

———. *Woman and the Salvation of the World: A Christian Anthropology on the Charisms of Women*. Crestwood: St Vladimir's Seminary Press, 1994.

Farley, Lawrence R. "Advice to the Confused." Orthodox Church in America, https://www.oca.org/reflections/fr.-lawrence-farley/advice-to-the-confused.

———. *Feminism and Tradition: Quiet Reflections on Ordination and Communion*. Yonkers: St Vladimir's Seminary Press, 2012.

Fausto-Sterling, Anne. *Sexing the Body: Gender Politics and the Construction of Sexuality*. New York: Basic Books, 2000.

Florovsky, Georges. "'As the Truth is in Jesus' (Ephes. 4:21)." *Christian Century* 68, no. 51 (1951): 1457–59.

———. "Bogoslovskie Otryvki." *Put'*, no. 31 (December 1931): 3–29.

———. "Eastern Orthodox Church and the Ecumenical Movement." *Theology Today* 7, no. 1 (1950): 68–79.

Ford, David. Review of "Eros and Transformation: Sexuality and Marriage: An Eastern Orthodox Perspective." *Sobornost* 16, no. 1 (1994): 82–84.

Ford, Josephine Massingberd. *The Spirit and the Human Person*. Dayton: Pflaum Press, 1969.

Foucault, Michel. *The History of Sexuality*. Translated by Robert Hurley. Social theory. 1st American ed. New York: Pantheon Books, 1978.

———. "Nietzsche, Genealogy, History." Translated by Donald F. Bouchard and Sherry Simon. In *Language, Counter-Memory, Practice*, edited by Donald F. Bouchard, 139–64. Ithaca: Cornell University Press, 1977.

Freud, Sigmund. "Leonardo da Vinci and a Memory of His Childhood." Translated by Alan Tyson. In *The Standard Edition of the Complete Works of Sigmund Freud*, edited by James Strachey, XI:59–137. London: The Hogarth Press and the Institute of Psycho-Analysis, 1957.

———. "On Narcissism: An Introduction." Translated by C.M. Baines. In *The Standard Edition of the Complete Psychological Works of Sigmund Freud*, edited by James Strachey, XIV:69–102. London: The Hogarth Press and the Institute of Psycho-Analysis, 1957.

———. "Three Essays on the Theory of Sexuality." Translated by James Strachey. In *The Standard Edition of the Complete Psychological Works of Sigmund Freud*, VII:125–245. London: The Hogarth Press and the Institute of Psycho-Analysis, 1953.

Friedman, Richard Elliott. *Commentary on the Torah: With a New English Translation*. New York: HarperSanFrancisco, 2001.

Furness, Raymond. "The Androgynous Ideal: Its Significance in German Literature." *The Modern Language Review* 60, no. 1 (1965): 58–64.

Gallaher, Anastassy Brandon. "Georges Florovsky on Reading the Life of St Seraphim." *Sobornost* 27, no. 1 (2005): 63–70.

Gallaher, Anastassy Brandon, and Irina Kukota. "Protopresbyter Sergii Bulgakov: Hypostasis and Hypostaticity: Scholia to *The Unfading Light*." *St Vladimir's Theological Quarterly* 49, no. 1–2 (2005): 5–46.

Gassios, Paul. "To All Clergy, Monastics, and Faithful of the Diocese of the Midwest." News release, 2015, http://domoca.org/files/news/2015/2015-0626 -same-sex-marriage.pdf.

Gavrilyuk, Paul L. *Georges Florovsky and the Russian Religious Renaissance.* Changing Paradigms in Historical and Systematic Theology. Oxford: Oxford University Press, 2013.

Gleason, Maud W. *Making Men: Sophists and Self-Presentation in Ancient Rome.* Princeton: Princeton University Press, 1995.

Green, Michael, David Holloway, and David Watson. *The Church and Homosexuality: A Positive Answer to Current Questions.* London: Hodder and Stoughton, 1980.

Gregory of Nazianzus. *Gregory of Nazianzus: Autobiographical Poems.* Translated by Carolinne White. Cambridge Medieval Classics. Cambridge: Cambridge University Press, 1996.

Gregory of Nyssa. *The Life of Moses.* Translated by Abraham J. Malherbe and Everett Ferguson. Classics of Western Spirituality. New York: Paulist Press, 1978.

———. *On the Soul and the Resurrection.* Translated by Catharine P. Roth. Crestwood: St Vladimir's Seminary Press, 1993.

Grillmeier, Aloys. *Christ in Christian Tradition.* Atlanta: John Knox Press, 1975.

Grishaeva, Ekaterina Ivanovna. "Uchenie o lichnosti v filosofii V. N. Losskogo: Istoriko-filosofskiy analiz [Study on Personhood in the Philosophy of V. N. Lossky: A Historico-Philosophical Analysis]." PhD diss., Ural Federal University, 2011.

Haig, David. "The Inexorable Rise of Gender and the Decline of Sex: Social Change in Academic Titles, 1945–2001." *Archives of Sexual Behavior* 33, no. 2 (2004): 87–96.

Halperin, David M. *How to Do the History of Homosexuality.* Chicago: University of Chicago Press, 2002.

———. *One Hundred Years of Homosexuality: And Other Essays on Greek Love.* The New Ancient World. New York: Routledge, 1990.

Hanks, Thomas. "Romans." In *The Queer Bible Commentary*, edited by Deryn Guest, 582–605. London: SCM, 2006.

Harper, Kyle. *From Shame to Sin: The Christian Transformation of Sexual Morality in Late Antiquity.* Cambridge: Harvard University Press, 2013.

Harrison, Verna E. F. "Male and Female in Cappadocian Theology." *Journal of Theological Studies* 41, no. 2 (1990): 441–71.

———. "Orthodox Arguments against the Ordination of Women as Priests." *Sobornost (incorporating Eastern Churches Review)* 14, no. 1 (1992): 6–24.

Hart, Robert. "Surgical Fantasy." *Touchstone: A Journal of Mere Christianity,* May/June 2016, 25–27.

Heffernan, Thomas J. *The Passion of Perpetua and Felicity.* New York: Oxford University Press, 2012.

Heidl, György. "Did the Young Augustine Read Origen's 'Homily on Paradise'?" In *Origeniana Septima: Origenes in den Auseinandersetzungen des 4. Jahrhunderts*, 597–604, 1999.

Heine, Ronald E., Origen, and Jerome. *The Commentaries of Origen and Jerome on St. Paul's Epistle to the Ephesians.* Oxford Early Christian Studies. New York: Oxford University Press, 2002.

Herdt, Gilbert H. *Guardians of the Flutes: Idioms of Masculinity.* New York: McGraw-Hill, 1981.

hooks, bell. *Feminist Theory: From Margin to Center.* 2nd ed. Cambridge: South End Press, 2000.

Hopko, Thomas. "Apophatic Theology and the Naming of God in Eastern Orthodox Theology." In *Speaking the Christian God: The Holy Trinity and the Challenge of Feminism*, edited by Alvin F. Kimel, Jr., 144–61. Grand Rapids: William B. Eerdmans Publishing Company, 1992.

———. *Christian Faith and Same-Sex Attraction: Eastern Orthodox Reflections.* Ben Lomond: Conciliar Press, 2006.

———. *Christian Faith and Same-Sex Attraction: Eastern Orthodox Reflections.* Chesterton: Ancient Faith Publishing, 2015.

———. "Galatians 3:28: An Orthodox Interpretation." *St Vladimir's Theological Quarterly* 35, no. 2–3 (1991): 169–86.

———. "God and Gender: Articulating the Orthodox View." *St Vladimir's Theological Quarterly* 37, no. 2–3 (1993): 141–83.

———. "On the Male Character of Christian Priesthood." *St Vladimir's Theological Quarterly* 19, no. 3 (1975): 147–73.

———. "On the Male Character of the Christian Priesthood: A Reply to Criticism." *St Vladimir's Theological Quarterly* 21, no. 3 (1977): 161–67.

———. *The Orthodox Faith.* Edited by Constance J. Tarasar. 2nd ed. 4 vols. Yonkers: Orthodox Church in America and St Vladimir's Seminary Press, 1981.

———. "Presbyter/Priest: A Masculine Ministry." In *Women and the Priesthood,* edited by Thomas Hopko, 139–64. Crestwood: St Vladimir's Seminary Press, 1999.

———. *The Spirit of God.* Wilton: Morehouse-Barlow Company, Inc., 1976.

———. "Women and the Priesthood: Reflections on the Debate." In *Women and the Priesthood,* 169–90. Crestwood: St Vladimir's Seminary Press, 1983.

Hull, Carrie L. "Letter to the Editor." *American Journal of Human Biology* 15, no. 1 (2003): 112–16.

Ivarsson, Fredrik. "Vice Lists and Deviant Masculinity: The Rhetorical Function of 1 Corinthians 5:10–11 and 6:9–10." In *Mapping Gender in Ancient Religious Discourses,* edited by Todd Penner and Caroline Vander Stichele. Biblical Interpretation Series, 163–84. Leiden: Brill, 2007.

Jeauneau, Édouard. "La division des sexes chez Grégoire de Nysse et chez Jean Scot Érigène." In *Études érigéniennes,* 343–64. Paris: Études augustiniennes, 1987.

———. "Pseudo-Dionysius, Gregory of Nyssa, and Maximus the Confessor in the Works of John Scottus Eriugena." In *Carolingian Essays: Andrew W. Mellon Lectures in Early Christian Studies,* edited by Uta-Renate Blumenthal, 137–49. Washington, D.C.: Catholic University of America, 1983.

Jewett, Paul King. *Man as Male and Female: A Study in Sexual Relationships from a Theological Point of View.* Grand Rapids: William B. Eerdmans Publishing Company, 1975.

John Chrysostom. *On Virginity, Against Remarriage.* Translated by Sally Rieger Shore. Studies in Women and Religion. Lewiston: The Edwin Mellen Press, 1983.

John of Damascus. *Writings.* Translated by Frederic Hathaway Chase, Jr. The Fathers of the Church: A New Translation. Washington: Catholic University of America Press, 1958.

Jordan, Mark D. *Convulsing Bodies: Religion and Resistance in Foucault.* Stanford: Stanford University Press, 2015.

———. *The Invention of Sodomy in Christian Theology.* Chicago: University of Chicago Press, 1997.

Karras, Valerie A. "Patristic Views on the Ontology of Gender." In *Personhood: Orthodox Christianity and the Connection between Body, Mind, and Soul,* edited by John T. Chirban, 113–19. Westport: Bergin & Garvey, 1996.

Kelly, John Norman Davidson. *Early Christian Doctrines.* 5th ed. San Francisco: HarperSanFrancisco, 1978.

Kinsey, Alfred Charles, Wardell Baxter Pomeroy, and Clyde Eugene Martin. *Sexual Behavior in the Human Male.* Philadelphia: W. B. Saunders Company, 1948.

King, Helen. "The Mathematics of Sex: One to Two, or Two to One?" *Studies in Medieval and Renaissance History* 17, no. 2 (2005): 47–58.

———. *The One-Sex Body on Trial: The Classical and Early Modern Evidence.* Farnham: Ashgate Publishing Limited, 2013.

Konstantinidis, Chrysostomos. "Priesthood and Women in Ecclesiological Perspective." In *The Place of the Woman in the Orthodox Church and the Question of the Ordination of Women,* edited by Gennadios Limouris, 117–32. Katerini: Tertios Publications, 1992.

Kozyrev, Anton Pavlovich. "Androgin "na piru bogov": Publikatsiya rabot o. Sergeya Bulgakova "Muzhskoe i zhenskoe," "Muzhskoe i zhenskoe v Bozhestve" (1921)." In *S. N. Bulgakov: Religiozno-filosofskiy put'. Mezhdunarodnaya nauchnaya konferentsiya, posvyashchennaya 130-letiyu so dnya rozhdeniya, 5–7 marta 2001 g.,* edited by Anton Pavlovich Kozyrev, 333–95. Moscow: Russkiy put', 2003.

Kronholm, Tryggve. *Motifs from Genesis 1–11 in the Genuine Hymns of Ephrem the Syrian with Particular Reference to the Influence of Jewish Exegetical Tradition.* Lund: CWK Gleerup, 1978.

Kuefler, Mathew. *The Manly Eunuch: Masculinity, Gender Ambiguity, and Christian Ideology in Late Antiquity.* Chicago: University of Chicago Press, 2001.

Laqueur, Thomas Walter. *Making Sex: Body and Gender from the Greeks to Freud.* Cambridge: Harvard University Press, 1990.

———. "Sex in the Flesh." *Isis* 94, no. 2 (2003): 300–06.

Leontius of Byzantium, and Brian E. Daley. *Complete Works* [in Parallel Greek and English texts translated from the Greek]. Oxford Early Christian Texts. Oxford: Oxford University Press, 2017.

Lester, CN. *Trans Like Me: Conversations for All of Us.* New York: Seal Press, 2017.

Lewis, C. S. "Priestesses in the Church?" In *God in the Dock: Essays on Theology and Ethics,* edited by Walter Hooper, 234–39. Grand Rapids: William B. Eerdmans Publishing Company, 1970.

Liddell, Henry George, Robert Scott, Henry Stuart Jones, and Roderick McKenzie. *A Greek-English Lexicon*. 9th ed. Oxford: Oxford University Press, 1996.

Liveris, Leonie B. *Ancient Taboos and Gender Prejudice: Challenges for Orthodox Women and the Church*. Ashgate New Critical Thinking in Religion, Theology, and Biblical Studies. Burlington: Ashgate Publishing, 2005.

Lossky, Olga. *Toward the Endless Day: The Life of Elisabeth Behr-Sigel*. Translated by Jerry Ryan. Notre Dame: University of Notre Dame Press, 2010.

———. *Vers le jour sans déclin. Une vie d'Élisabeth Behr-Sigel (1907–2005)*. Paris: Les Éditions du Cerf, 2007.

Lossky, Vladimir. "Catholic Consciousness: Anthropological Implications of the Dogma of the Church." Translated by Thomas E. Bird. Chap. 10 in *In the Image and Likeness of God*, edited by John H. Erickson and Thomas E. Bird, 183–94. Crestwood: St Vladimir's Seminary Press, 1974.

———. *Essai sur la théologie mystique de l'Eglise d'Orient*. Aubier: Éditions Montaigne, 1944.

———. "La procession du Saint-Esprit dans la doctrine trinitaire orthodoxe." Chap. 4 in *À l'image et à la ressemblance de Dieu*, 67–93. Paris: Aubier-Montaigne, 1967.

———. "La Tradition et les traditions." *Messager de l'Exarchat du patriarche russe en Europe occidentale*, no. 30–31 (1959): 101–21.

———. *The Mystical Theology of the Eastern Church*. London: J. Clarke, 1957.

———. *Orthodox Theology: An Introduction*. Crestwood: St Vladimir's Seminary Press, 1978.

———. "The Procession of the Holy Spirit in Orthodox Trinitarian Doctrine." Chap. 4 in *In the Image and Likeness of God*, edited by John H. Erickson and Thomas E. Bird, 71–96. Crestwood: St Vladimir's Seminary Press, 1974.

———. "Spor o Sofii [Controversy about Sophia]." In *Bogovidenie [Vision of God]*, 11–107. Moscow: ACT, 2006.

———. *Spor" o Sofii* [Controversy concerning Sophia]. Paris: E.I.R.P., 1936.

———. "The Theological Notion of the Human Person." Translated by Thomas E. Bird. Chap. 6 in *In the Image and Likeness of God*, edited by John H. Erickson and Thomas E. Bird, 111–23. Crestwood: St Vladimir's Seminary Press, 1974.

———. "The Theology of the Image." Translated by Joan Ford. Chap. 7 in *In the Image and Likeness of God*, edited by John H. Erickson and Thomas E. Bird, 125–39. Crestwood: St Vladimir's Seminary Press, 1974.

———. "Tradition and Traditions." Chap. 8 in *In the Image and Likeness*, edited by John H. Erickson and Thomas E. Bird, 141–68. Crestwood: St Vladimir's Seminary Press, 1974.

———. *The Vision of God*. London: Faith Press Ltd., 1964.

Louth, Andrew. *Maximus the Confessor*. The Early Church Fathers. New York: Routledge, 1996.

Lubinsky, Crystal. *Removing Masculine Layers to Reveal a Holy Womanhood: The Female Transvestite Monks of Late Antique Eastern Christianity*. Studia Traditionis Theologiae. Turnhout: Brepols, 2013.

Macarius the Egyptian. *Fifty Spiritual Homilies of St. Macarius the Egyptian*. Translated by Arthur James Mason. London: Society for Promoting Christian Knowledge, 1921.

Martin, Dale B. "*Arsenokoitês* and *Malakos*: Meanings and Consequences." In *Biblical Ethics & Homosexuality: Listening to Scripture*, 117–36. Louisville: Westminster John Knox Press, 1996.

Martin, Jennifer Newsome. *Hans Urs von Balthasar and the Critical Appropriation of Russian Religious Thought*. Notre Dame: University of Notre Dame Press, 2015.

Martyn, J. Louis. *Galatians: A New Translation with Introduction and Commentary*. The Anchor Bible. New York: Doubleday, 1998.

Matthaiakēs, Timotheos. "Euchē eis onomatothesian nean epi allagē phylou [A Prayer at the Giving of a New Name upon Change of Sex]." In *Egkolpion euchologion*. Athēnai: n.p., 1985.

———. *A Prayer at the Giving of a New Name upon Modification of Gender*. Chicago: The Pappas Post, 2015. https://www.pappaspost.com/wp-content/uploads/2017/10/sex-assignment-prayer-translation.pdf.

Matthews, Gareth B. *The Augustinian Tradition*. Berkeley: University of California Press, 1999.

Matusiak, John. "Divorce and Ordination." Orthodox Church in America, https://oca.org/questions/priesthoodmonasticism/divorce-and-ordination.

Maximus Confessor. *On Difficulties in the Church Fathers: The Ambigua*. Translated by Nicholas Constas. Dumbarton Oaks Medieval Library. Cambridge: Harvard University Press, 2014.

McDowell, Maria Gwyn. "The Iconicity of Priesthood: Male Bodies or Embodied Virtue?" *Studies in Christian Ethics* 26, no. 3 (2013): 364–77.

McGuckin, John Anthony. "Recent Biblical Hermeneutics in Patristic Perspective: The Tradition of Orthodoxy." *Greek Orthodox Theological Review* 47, no. 1–4 (2002): 295–326.

McHugh, Paul. "Transgender Surgery Isn't the Solution." *Wall Street Journal*, June 13, 2014, A13.

Meeks, Wayne A. "The Image of the Androgyne: Some Uses of a Symbol in Earliest Christianity." *History of Religions* 13, no. 3 (1974): 165–208.

Meyendorff, John. *Living Tradition: Orthodox Witness in the Contemporary World*. Crestwood: St Vladimir's Seminary Press, 1975.

Mitchell, Patrick. *The Scandal of Gender: Early Christian Teaching on the Man and the Woman*. Salisbury: Regina Orthodox Press, 1998.

Moberly, Elizabeth R. "Can Homosexuals *Really* Change?" *Journal of Christian Nursing* 9, no. 4 (1992): 14–17.

———. "Homosexuality and Truth." *First Things* 71 (1997): 30–33.

———. *Homosexuality: A New Christian Ethic*. Cambridge [Cambridgeshire]: James Clarke, 1983.

———. "Homosexuality: Restating the Conservative Case." *Salmagundi*, no. 58–59 (1982): 281–99.

———. "New Perspectives on Homosexuality." *Journal of the Royal Society of Health* 105, no. 6 (1985): 206–10.

———. *Psychogenesis: The Early Development of Gender Identity*. London: Routledge & Kegan Paul, 1983.

Money, John, Joan G. Hampson, and John L. Hampson. "An Examination of Some Basic Sexual Concepts: The Evidence of Human Hermaphroditism." *Bulletin of The Johns Hopkins Hospital* 97, no. 4 (1955): 301–19.

———. "Hermaphroditism: Recommendations Concerning Assignment of Sex, Change of Sex and Psychologic Management." *Bulletin of The Johns Hopkins Hospital* 97, no. 4 (1955): 284–300.

———. "Imprinting and the Establishment of Gender Role." *Archives of Neurology and Psychiatry* 77 (1957): 333–36.

———. "Sexual Incongruities and Psychopathology: The Evidence of Human Hermaphroditism." *Bulletin of The Johns Hopkins Hospital* 98, no. 1 (1956): 43–57.

Moore, Lazarus. *Sacred Tradition in the Orthodox Church*. Minneapolis: Light and Life Publishing Company, 1984.

Moriak, Matthias. "Archpastoral Letter of His Grace, Bishop Matthias." News release, August 2, 2011, http://www.domoca.org/news_110802_1.html.

Morris, Stephen. *"When Brothers Dwell in Unity": Byzantine Christianity and Homosexuality*. Jefferson: McFarland & Company, Inc., Publishers, 2016.

Nemesius of Emesa. "On the Nature of Man." In *Cyril of Jerusalem and Nemesius of Emesa*, edited by William Tefler, 224–453. Philadelphia: Westminster Press, 1955.

Nesteruk, Alexei V. "Patristic Theology and the Natural Sciences (Part I)." *Sourozh*, no. 84 (2001): 14–35.

———. "Patristic Theology and the Natural Sciences (Part II)." *Sourozh*, no. 85 (2001): 22–38.

Neumann, Erich. *The Great Mother: An Analysis of the Archetype*. London: Routledge & K. Paul, 1955.

Nicolosi, Joseph. *Reparative Therapy of Male Homosexuality: A New Clinical Approach*. Northvale: Jason Aronson Inc., 1997.

Nicolosi, Joseph, and Linda Ames Nicolosi. *A Parent's Guide to Preventing Homosexuality*. Downers Grove: InterVarsity Press, 2002.

Nissinen, Martti. *Homoeroticism in the Biblical World: A Historical Perspective*. Minneapolis: Fortress Press, 1998.

O'Connor, William Patrick. "The Concept of the Human Soul according to Saint Augustine." Ph.D. diss. Washington, D.C.: Catholic University of America, 1921.

O'Daly, Gerard J. P. *Augustine's Philosophy of Mind*. Berkeley: University of California Press, 1987.

Olyan, Saul M. "'And with a Male You Shall Not Lie the Lying Down of a Woman': On the Meaning and Significance of Leviticus 18:22 and 20:13." *Journal of the History of Sexuality* 5, no. 2 (1994): 179–206.

Origen. *Homilies on Genesis and Exodus*. Translated by Ronald E. Heine. Fathers of the Church. Washington, D.C.: Catholic University of America Press, 1982.

Orthodox Church in America Holy Synod of Bishops. "Synodal Affirmations on Marriage, Family, Sexuality, and the Sanctity of Life." News release, July 1992, https://oca.org/holy-synod/statements/holy-synod/synodal -affirmations-on-marriage-family-sexuality-and-the-sanctity-of-life.

Orthodox Church in America. Ecumenical Task Force. *Women and Men in the Church: A Study of the Community of Women and Men in the Church*. Syosset: Department of Religious Education, Orthodox Church in America, 1980.

Osiek, Carolyn. "Galatians." In *Women's Bible Commentary*, edited by Carol A. Newsom and Sharon H. Ringe, 333–37. Louisville: Westminster John Knox, 1992.

Ostrogorsky, G. A. "Gnoseologicheskiya osnovy vizantiyskago spora o sv. ikonakh." In *Seminarium Kondakovianum II*, 47–52. Prague: Seminarium Kondakovianum, 1928.

Otten, Willemien. "The Long Shadow of Human Sin: Augustine on Adam, Eve, and the Fall." In *Out of Paradise: Eve and Adam and Their Interpreters*, edited by Bob Becking and Susan Hennecke, 29–49. Sheffield: Sheffield Phoenix Press, 2010.

Paffhausen, Jonah. "Archpastoral Letter Regarding Marriage to the Faithful of the Archdiocese of Washington." News release, July 28, 2011, http://wdcoca .org/files/met_jonah/To-Faithful-re-marriage.pdf.

Papanikolaou, Aristotle. "Divine Energies or Divine Personhood: Vladimir Lossky and John Zizioulas on Conceiving the Transcendent and Immanent God." *Modern Theology* 19, no. 3 (2003): 357–85.

———. *The Mystical as Political: Democracy and Non-Radical Orthodoxy*. Notre Dame: University of Notre Dame Press, 2012.

———. "Personhood and Its Exponents." Chap. 15 in *The Cambridge Companion to Orthodox Christian Theology*, edited by Mary B. Cunningham and Elizabeth Theokritoff, 232–45. Cambridge: Cambridge University Press, 2008.

Papathomas, Grigorios D. "Homosexualité, *nature contre-nature?*" *Academia* (2000). https://www.academia.edu/19580826/43._The_existential_centrifugal _situation_between_endo-hypostatic_narcissism_Rm_1_23_and_intra -creationnal_orientation_Rm_1_25_in_French_.

Pappas, Gregory. "The Greek Orthodox Church Has a Prayer for Name Changes Following Gender Reassignment Surgery." In *The Pappas Post*. New York, 2017.

Park, Katharine, and Robert A. Nye. "Destiny Is Anatomy." *New Republic* 204, no. 7 (1991): 53.

Parker, John Edgar III. "The Sanctity of Chastity: An Orthodox Approach to Homosexuality." Crestwood: St Vladimir's Orthodox Theological Seminary, 2004.

Payne Smith, R. *A Compendious Syriac Dictionary: Founded upon the Thesaurus Syriacus of R. Payne Smith*. Oxford: Clarendon Press, 1979.

Petersen, William Lawrence. "Can *Arsenokoitai* Be Translated by 'Homosexuals' (1 Cor 6:9, 1 Tim 1:10)." *Vigiliae christianae* 40, no. 2 (1986): 187–91.

Phan, Peter C. "Gender Roles in the History of Salvation: Man and Woman in the Thought of Paul Evdokimov." *Heythrop Journal* 31 (1990): 53–70.

Philo of Alexandria, Albert C. Geljon, and David T. Runia. *Philo of Alexandria, On Cultivation*. Philo of Alexandria Commentary Series. Leiden: Brill, 2013.

Philo of Alexandria, and David T. Runia. *On the Creation of the Cosmos according to Moses: Introduction, Translation and Commentary*. Translated by David T. Runia. Philo of Alexandria Commentary Series. Vol. 1. Leiden: Brill, 2001.

Plato. *Platonis opera*. Oxford Classical Texts. 5 vols. New York: Oxford University Press, 1902–1906.

Plato, M. C. Howatson, and Frisbee C. C. Sheffield. *The Symposium*. Translated by M. C. Howatson. Cambridge Texts in the History of Philosophy. New York: Cambridge University Press, 2008.

Plato, and Stephen Scully. *Plato's Phaedrus*. Newburyport: Focus Publishing, 2003.

Plato, and Donald J. Zeyl. *Timaeus*. Indianapolis: Hackett Publishing Company, 2000.

Pokorný, Petr. *A Commentary on the Gospel of Thomas: From Interpretations to the Interpreted*. Jewish and Christian Texts in Contexts and Related Studies. New York: T & T Clark, 2009.

Pomazansky, Michael. *Orthodox Dogmatic Theology: A Concise Exposition*. Edited by Seraphim Rose Platina: St. Herman of Alaska Brotherhood, 2005.

Pontus, Evagrius of, and Robert E. Sinkewicz. *Evagrius of Pontus: The Greek Ascetic Corpus*. Oxford Early Christian Studies. Oxford: Oxford University Press, 2006.

Pseudo-Dionysius, and Paul Rorem. *Pseudo-Dionysius: The Complete Works*. Translated by Colm Luibhéid. Classics of Western Spirituality. New York: Paulist Press, 1987.

Puhalo, Lazar. "Another Response Re: Transgender." YouTube video, August 2012.

———. *On the Neurobiology of Sin*. Dewdney: Synaxis Press, 2010.

———. "Reality of Transgender 1/1." YouTube video, March 2011.

Ramelli, Ilaria L. E. "Origen in Augustine: A Paradoxical Reception." *Numen: International Review for the History of Religions* 60 (2013): 280–307.

Reuther, Rosemary Radford. "Augustine: Sexuality, Gender, and Women." Chap. 1 in *Feminist Interpretations of Augustine*, edited by Judith Chelius Stark, 47–67. University Park: The Pennsylvania State University Press, 2007.

Rich, Bryce E. "Something New under the Sun: Sexualities, Same-Sex Relationships, and Orthodoxy." Chapter 2 in *Orthodox Tradition and Human Sexuality*, edited by Thomas Arentzen, Ashley Purpura, and Aristotle Papanikolaou, 46–65. New York: Fordham University Press, 2022.

Roberts, Alexander, James Sir Donaldson, A. Cleveland Coxe, and Allan Menzies. *The Ante-Nicene Fathers: Translations of the Writings of the Fathers Down to A.D. 325*. 10 vols. Grand Rapids: William B. Eerdmans Publishing Company, 1980.

Rogers, Eugene F. Jr. "Same-Sex Complementarity: A Theology of Marriage." *Christian Century* 128, no. 10 (2011): 26–29, 31.

Rosenthal, Bernice Glatzer, ed. *The Occult in Russian and Soviet Culture*. Ithaca: Cornell University Press, 1997.

Rubin, Dominic. *The Life and Thought of Lev Karsavin: "Strength Made Perfect in Weakness. . . ."* On the Boundary of Two Worlds: Identity, Freedom, and Moral Imagination in the Baltics. New York: Rodopi, 2013.

Ruden, Sarah. *Paul Among the People: The Apostle Reinterpreted and Reimagined in His Own Time*. New York: Pantheon Books, 2010.

Runia, David T. *Philo in Early Christian Literature: A Survey*. Compendia Rerum Iudaicarum ad Novum Testamentum Section 3, Jewish Traditions in Early Christian Literature. Minneapolis: Fortress Press, 1993.

———. *Philo of Alexandria and the Timaeus of Plato*. Philosophia Antiqua. Edited by W. J. Verdenius and J. C. M. Van Winden. Leiden: Brill, 1986.

Russian Orthodox Church Holy Bishops' Council. "The Basis of the Social Concept. XII. Problems of Bioethics." The Russian Orthodox Church Department of External Church Relations. https://mospat.ru/en/documents/social-concepts/xii/.

Sax, Leonard. "How Common Is Intersex? A Response to Anne Fausto-Sterling." *Journal of Sex Research* 39, no. 3 (2002): 174–78.

Schaff, Philip, and Henry Wace. *A Select Library of Nicene and Post-Nicene Fathers of the Christian Church: Second Series.* 14 vols. New York: The Christian Literature Company, 1890.

Schaupp, Joan P. *Woman: Image of the Holy Spirit.* Bethesda: International Scholars Publications, 1996.

Scheeben, Matthias Joseph. *The Mysteries of Christianity.* Translated by Cyril O. Vollert. St. Louis: B. Herder Book Company, 1946.

Schmemann, Alexander. "Concerning Women's Ordination: A Letter to an Episcopal Friend." *St Vladimir's Theological Quarterly* 17, no. 3 (1973): 239–43.

———. "On Mariology in Orthodoxy." *Marian Library Studies* 2, no. 1 (1971): 25–32.

———. "Our Lady and the Holy Spirit." *Marian Studies* 23, no. 1 (1972): 69–78.

Scholem, Gershom. *Kabbalah.* New York: Quadrangle/The New York Times Book Company, 1974.

Sedgwick, Eve Kosofsky. *Epistemology of the Closet.* 2nd ed. Berkeley: University of California Press, 2008.

Sepher ha-Zohar (Le livre de la splendeur): Doctrine ésotérique des Israélites. Translated by Jean de Pauly. Paris: Leroux, 1906.

Serano, Julia. *Whipping Girl: A Transsexual Woman on Sexism and the Scapegoating of Femininity.* Second ed. Berkeley: Seal Press, 2016.

Shaw, Teresa M. "Creation, Virginity and Diet in Fourth-Century Christianity: Basil of Ancyra's *on the True Purity of Virginity.*" *Gender & History* 9, no. 3 (1997): 579–96.

Silva, Tony. "Bud-Sex: Constructing Normative Masculinity among Rural Straight Men That Have Sex with Men." *Gender & Society* 0 (2016): 1–23. Published electronically November 24, 2016. doi:10.1177/0891243216679934.

Singer, Isodore. *Jewish Encyclopedia.* 12 vols. New York: Funk and Wagnalls, 1901.

Solovyov, Vladimir Sergeyevich. "The Meaning of Love." Translated by Vladimir Wozniuk. Chap. 4 in *The Heart of Reality: Essays on Beauty, Love, and Ethics by V. S. Soloviev,* edited by Vladimir Wozniuk, 83–133. Notre Dame: University of Notre Dame Press, 2003.

———. "Plato's Life-Drama." Translated by Vladimir Wozniuk. Chap. 9 in *Politics, Law, and Morality: Essays by V. S. Soloviev,* edited by Vladimir Wozniuk, 213–54, 316–19. New Haven: Yale University Press, 2000.

———. "Smysl' lyubvi." In *Sobranie sochineniy Vladimira Sergeevicha Solov'eva,* edited by M.S. Solovyov and E. L. Radlov, 3–60. St. Petersburg: Knigoizdatel'skoe Tovarishchestvo "Prosveshchenie", 1913.

———. "Zhiznennaya drama Platona." In *Sobranie sochineniy Vladimira Sergeevicha Solov'eva,* edited by M.S. Solovyov and E. L. Radlov, 194–241. St. Petersburg: Knigoizdatel'skoe Tovarishchestvo "Prosveshchenie," 1913.

Solovyov, Vladimir Sergeyevich, and Judith Deutsch Kornblatt. *Divine Sophia: The Wisdom Writings of Vladimir Solovyov*. Ithaca: Cornell University Press, 2009.

Stein, Edith. "Problems of Women's Education." Translated by Hilda Graef. Chap. III.B in *Writings of Edith Stein*, 126–60. Westminster: The Newman Press, 1956.

———. "The Vocation of Man and Woman according to Nature and Grace." Translated by Hilda Graef. Chap. III.A in *Writings of Edith Stein*, 101–25. Westminster: The Newman Press, 1956.

Stein, Kathleen. "Interview [with] John Money." *Omni* 8, no. 7 (1986): 79–80, 82, 84, 86, 126, 28, 30, 31.

Stone, Alison. "Sexual Polarity in Schelling and Hegel." Chap. 11 in *Reproduction, Race, and Gender in Philosophy and the Early Life Sciences*, edited by Susanne Lettow, 259–82. Albany: State University of New York Press, 2014.

Swete, Henry Barclay. *The Holy Spirit in the Ancient Church: A Study of Christian Teaching in the Age of the Fathers*. London: Macmillan and Company, Limited, 1912.

Tavard, George H. *Woman in Christian Tradition*. Notre Dame: University of Notre Dame Press, 1973.

Tertullian. *De anima*. Edited by J. H. Waszink Amsterdam: J. M. Meulenhoff, 1947.

Teske, Roland J. "Origen and St Augustine's First Commentary on Genesis." In *Origeniana Quinta: Historica, Text and Method, Biblica, Philosophica, Theologica, Origenism and Later Developments: Papers of the 5th International Origen Congress, Boston College, 14–18 August 1989*, 179–85. Leuven: Peeters, 1992.

Theodore the Studite. *St. Theodore the Studite on the Holy Icons*. Translated by Catharine P. Roth. Crestwood: St Vladimir's Seminary Press, 1981.

Thomas, Stephen. "Anthropology." In *The Westminster Handbook to Origen*, edited by John Anthony McGuckin, 53–58. Louisville: Westminster John Knox Press, 2004.

Thunberg, Lars. *Man and the Cosmos: The Vision of St. Maximus the Confessor*. Crestwood: St. Vladimir's Seminary Press, 1985.

Thunberg, Lars, and A. M. Allchin. *Microcosm and Mediator: The Theological Anthropology of Maximus the Confessor*. 2nd ed. Chicago: Open Court, 1995.

Trible, Phyllis. "Eve and Adam: Genesis 2–3 Reread." *Andover Newton Quarterly* 13, no. 4 (1973): 251–58.

Van den Gehn, I., ed. "Passio antiquior SS. Sergii et Bacchi graece nunc primum edita." *Analecta bollandiana* 14 (1895): 373–95.

VanderWal-Gritter, Wendy. *Generous Spaciousness: Responding to Gay Christians in the Church*. Grand Rapids: Baker Publishing Group, 2014.

Verkhovskoy, Serge S. "Creation of Man and the Establishment of the Family in the Light of the Book of Genesis." *St Vladimir's Seminary Quarterly* 8, no. 1 (1964): 5–30.

———. "Procession of the Holy Spirit According to Orthodox Doctrine of the Trinity." *St Vladimir's Seminary Quarterly* 2, no. 1 (1953): 12–26.

Vogt, Kari. "'Becoming Male': One Aspect of an Early Christian Anthropology." In *Women: Invisible in Theology and Church*, 72–83. Edinburgh: T & T Clark, 1985.

Ward, Elizabeth Jane. *Not Gay: Sex between Straight White Men*. Sexual Cultures. New York: New York University Press, 2015.

Ware, Kallistos. "'In the Image and Likeness': The Uniqueness of the Human Person." Chap. 1 in *Personhood: Orthodox Christianity and the Connection between Body, Mind, and Soul*, edited by John T. Chirban, 1–13. Westport: Bergin & Garvey, 1996.

———. "La théologie orthodoxe au vingt-et-unième siècle." *Irénikon* 77, no. 2–3 (2004): 219–38.

———. "Man, Woman and the Priesthood of Christ." In *Women and the Priesthood*, edited by Thomas Hopko, 5–53. Crestwood: St Vladimir's Seminary Press, 1999.

———. "Man, Woman and the Priesthood of Christ." Chap. 6 in *Man, Woman, Priesthood*, edited by Peter Moore, 68–90. London: Fletcher and Son, 1978.

———. *Orthodox Theology in the Twenty-First Century*. Doxa & Praxis. Edited by Pantelis Kalaitzidis Geneva: Word Council of Churches, 2012.

———. "The Witness of the Orthodox Church." *Ecumenical Review* 52, no. 1 (2000): 46–56.

Ware, Timothy. *The Orthodox Church*. New ed. New York: Penguin Books, 1993.

Wesche, Kenneth Paul. "God: Beyond Gender—Reflections on the Patristic Doctrine of God and Feminist Theology." *St Vladimir's Theological Quarterly* 30, no. 4 (1986): 291–308.

Wessel, Susan. "The Reception of Greek Science in Gregory of Nyssa's 'de Hominis Opificio.'" *Vigiliae Christianae: A Review of Early Christian Life and Language* 63, no. 1 (2009): 24–46.

West, Candace, and H. Zimmerman Don. "Doing Gender." *Gender and Society* 1, no. 2 (1987): 125–51.

Whitman, Jon. *Interpretation and Allegory: Antiquity to the Modern Period*. Leiden: Brill, 2000.

Williams, Craig A. *Roman Homosexuality*. 2nd ed. Oxford: Oxford University Press, 2010.

Williams, Don. *The Bond That Breaks: Will Homosexuality Split the Church?* The New Ancient World. Los Angeles: BIM, 1978.

Williams, Rowan. "The Theology of Vladimir Nikolaievich Lossky: An
    Exposition and Critique." Oxford University, 1975.
Wilson, Bianca D. M., and Ilan H. Meyer. "Nonbinary Adults in the United
    States." Los Angeles: UCLA School of Law Williams Institute, 2021.
Wilson, Sarah Hinlicky. "Tradition, Priesthood, and Personhood in the
    Trinitarian Theology of Elisabeth Behr-Sigel." *Pro Ecclesia* 19, no. 2 (2010):
    129–50.
Winkler, John J. *The Constraints of Desire: The Anthropology of Sex and Gender
    in Ancient Greece.* New York: Routledge, 1990.
Women and the Priesthood. Edited by Thomas Hopko. Crestwood: St Vladimir's
    Seminary Press, 1983.
Wu, Katherine. "Between the (Gender) Lines: the Science of Transgender
    Identity." In *Science in the News.* Cambridge: Harvard University, 2016.
Yannaras, Christos. *The Freedom of Morality.* Crestwood: St Vladimir's
    Seminary Press, 1984.
Zion, William Basil. "Elizabeth Moberly: Orthodox Theologian." *St Vladimir's
    Theological Quarterly* 32, no. 1 (1988): 43–60.
———. *Eros and Transformation: Sexuality and Marriage: An Eastern Orthodox
    Perspective.* Lanham: University Press of America, 1992.
Zizioulas, John D. *Being as Communion: Studies in Personhood and the Church.*
    Contemporary Greek theologians no. 4. Crestwood: St Vladimir's Seminary
    Press, 1985.
———. *Communion and Otherness: Further Studies in Personhood and the
    Church.* London: T & T Clark, 2006.

INDEX

1 Cor 6:9, 157. *See also arsenokoitēs, malakos*
1 Cor 11 (headship argument), 34, 35, 67, 87
1 Tm 1:9–11, 157. *See also malakos*
1 Tm 3:2 (qualifications of bishops/presbyters), 125, 220n10

Adam, fallen, 66, 68, 82, 124
agender, 109
Aghiorgoussis, Maximos, 129, 130, 131
aisthēsis (perception, sensation, senses), 21, 25, 30, 31, 33, 35, 86, 107
allegory, 24, 26, 33, 35, 186n26; in Orthodox theological reflection, 197n182; recovery of, 53–54
Ambrose of Milan, 31, 35, 46
Anastasius of Sinai, 49, 200n35
androgyne, 187n41; in *Gospel of the Egyptians*, 189n64; in Jacob Böhme, 80; in Nikolay Berdyaev, 82; in Plato, 20, 184n5; in rabbinic midrashim, 45; in Sergius Bulgakov, 83; in Vladimir Solovyov, 79
Arida, Robert, 165, 166
Aristotle, 15, 183n29, 215n50
arsenokoitēs, 160
arsenokoitia, 229n60
Athanasius of Alexandria, 9, 11, 37, 192n97
Augustine of Hippo, 53, 74, 83, 149, 157, 190nn77, 79, 190nn80,81,83, 191n89, 194n144, 205n109; on masculinity and virtue, 30; and sexed allegory, 33–35; on sexed bodies, 46–48; on traducianism, 50

baptism, 27, 30, 35, 129–30, 189n62; and children of same-sex couples, 166; and intersex children, 168, 169; and taking a new name, 175; transgender individuals, 173
Bachofen, Johann, 8, 78, 82, 127, 206n110
Bailey, D. Sherwin, 206n112
Barth, Karl, 75, 139, 223n13
Basil of Ancyra, 15
Basil of Caesarea, 29, 36, 37, 38, 49, 89, 128, 129, 130, 182n17, 221nn27,33
Behr, John, 40
Behr-Sigel, Elisabeth, 88–90, 91, 92, 103, 104, 116, 117, 118, 123, 128, 134, 199n24, 220n169, 211nn176,190
Belonick, Deborah, 212*n*2
Berdyaev, Nikolay, 5, 8, 81–82, 83, 86, 89, 97, 109, 206n112
Bloom, Anthony, 123
Boethius, 99–100, 101
boēthos (helper, also strength, help, rock), 23, 24, 186n23
Böhme, Jacob, 58, 79, 80, 82, 83, 91, 126, 139, 206n118, 207n120, 208n132
Bride (Church)/ Bridegroom (Christ), 30, 66, 67, 70, 71, 72, 77, 131, 133, 150–51, 154, 222n46
brides of Christ, 38, 73, 150, 227n19
Bulgakov, Sergius, 5, 58, 73, 79, 82, 83–88, 94, 109, 205n109, 206n112; on the *Deisis* icon, 85; male/female image and the Trinity, 126–27; on the Mother and Christ Child icon, 87, 204n99, 209n154; and the sophiology conflict, 95–96
Burrus, Virginia, 37–38, 192n97
Butler, Judith, 107, 217n66

Bryce E. Rich holds a PhD in Theology from the University of Chicago. He has participated in six conferences on Orthodoxy and sexuality in Finland, Norway, and England.

ORTHODOX CHRISTIANITY AND
CONTEMPORARY THOUGHT

SERIES EDITORS
Ashley M. Purpura and Aristotle Papanikolaou

Christina M. Gschwandtner, *Welcoming Finitude: Toward a Phenomenology of Orthodox Liturgy*

Pia Sophia Chaudhari, *Dynamis of Healing: Patristic Theology and the Psyche*

Brian A. Butcher, *Liturgical Theology after Schmemann: An Orthodox Reading of Paul Ricoeur.* Foreword by Andrew Louth.

Ashley M. Purpura, *God, Hierarchy, and Power: Orthodox Theologies of Authority from Byzantium.*

George E. Demacopoulos, *Colonizing Christianity: Greek and Latin Religious Identity in the Era of the Fourth Crusade.*

George E. Demacopoulos and Aristotle Papanikolaou (eds.), *Orthodox Constructions of the West.*

John Chryssavgis and Bruce V. Foltz (eds.), *Toward an Ecology of Transfiguration: Orthodox Christian Perspectives on Environment, Nature, and Creation.* Foreword by Bill McKibben. Prefatory Letter by Ecumenical Patriarch Bartholomew.

Aristotle Papanikolaou and George E. Demacopoulos (eds.), *Orthodox Readings of Augustine* [available 2020]

Lucian N. Leustean (ed.), *Orthodox Christianity and Nationalism in Nineteenth-Century Southeastern Europe.*

John Chryssavgis (ed.), *Dialogue of Love: Breaking the Silence of Centuries.* Contributions by Brian E. Daley, S.J., and Georges Florovsky.

George E. Demacopoulos and Aristotle Papanikolaou (eds.), *Christianity, Democracy, and the Shadow of Constantine.*

Aristotle Papanikolaou and George E. Demacopoulos (eds.), *Fundamentalism or Tradition: Christianity after Secularism*

Georgia Frank, Susan R. Holman, and Andrew S. Jacobs (eds.), *The Garb of Being: Embodiment and the Pursuit of Holiness in Late Ancient Christianity*

Sarah Riccardi-Swartz, *Between Heaven and Russia: Religious Conversion and Political Apostasy in Appalachia*

Thomas Arentzen, Ashley M. Purpura, and Aristotle Papanikolaou (eds.), *Orthodox Tradition and Human Sexuality*

Bryce E. Rich, *Gender Essentialism and Orthodoxy: Beyond Male and Female*

Ecumenical Patriarch Bartholomew, *In the World, Yet Not of the World: Social and Global Initiatives of Ecumenical Patriarch Bartholomew.* Edited by John Chryssavgis. Foreword by Jose Manuel Barroso

Ecumenical Patriarch Bartholomew, *Speaking the Truth in Love: Theological and Spiritual Exhortations of Ecumenical Patriarch Bartholomew.* Edited by John Chryssavgis. Foreword by Dr. Rowan Williams, Archbishop of Canterbury.

Ecumenical Patriarch Bartholomew, *On Earth as in Heaven: Ecological Vision and Initiatives of Ecumenical Patriarch Bartholomew.* Edited by John Chryssavgis. Foreword by His Royal Highness, the Duke of Edinburgh.